CONSTANTINE THE GREAT

HARPER & ROW / HR 1567

Constantine The Great

HERMANN DOERRIES

Constantine The Great

Translated by

Roland H. Bainton

HARPER TORCHBOOKS
Harper & Row, Publishers
New York, Evanston, San Francisco, London

To my friend and understanding translator
Roland H. Bainton

First TORCHBOOK edition published 1972.

LIBRARY OF CONGRESS CATALOG CARD NUMBER: 72–179281

STANDARD BOOK NUMBER: 06–1384957

2-17-75

Contents

Introduction

Hermann Doerries' *Constantine the Great* is theological. This description may repel those who revel in the gorgeousness of imperial pageantry, the excitement of chariot races in the hippodrome and the splendor of sunsets over the Bosporus. But Constantine did not significantly alter sunsets over the Bosporus. He was the first Christian emperor who set a pattern for the relations of Church and state which persist in some lands to this day and have conditioned the development of the whole civilization of the West.

A life of Constantine is trivial which does not ask why he allied his own fortunes and those of the empire with the Christian religion. Was he himself genuinely converted or did he align himself with the Christians with an eye to political power? In what sense was he converted? To what degree did he understand Christianity? What was his role as emperor in relation to the new religion? What was his philosophy of history? What was the impact of the Church on the empire and of the empire on the Church? How far was Constantine understood and followed by his successors?

These are the proper questions to ask. Of course a great deal else will come into the picture. The question of the effect of the Christian alliance on the empire calls for a description of the state of the empire. The reorganization of the army brings in the problem of the Christian ethic of war. The failure to abolish slavery leads to a discussion of the Christian doctrine of the dignity of man. The social legislation of Constantine brings in the Christian ideals of love and charity.

No man is better in a position to answer these and many other questions than Hermann Doerries because he is thoroughly grounded in the sources and in the history of the whole period. Prior to this work he published a volume called *Constantine's Witness to Himself* (in German), printing all of the documents in Greek and Latin which may be attributed to the emperor himself. In addition all of the numismatic evidence is taken into account.

What are the answers to some of the above questions? Was Constantine converted? The traditional accounts of the vision or dream of the cross and the words "By this sign conquer" may be legendary, at least in part, but not altogether because Constantine, addressing an assembly of bishops at Arles in 314, told them that he had experienced a conversion. We have his own word for it. The date of this address confirms the traditional assignment of the conversion to the year 312. One historian has called this into question on the assumption that Constantine was actuated only by the drive for political advantage and in 312 no political advantage was to have been foreseen by adherence to Christianity, seeing that the conflict then was for the control of the west and in the west the Christians were too few to render their support worthy of being sought. Hence the adherence of Constantine to the standard of the cross must be deferred till twelve years later when the struggle was for control of the entire empire in which the Christians had come to be numerous. The emperor's own statement disposes of this revisionism. There is also the witness of a coin minted in 315 on which appears the monogram of Christ. Direct testimony and numismatics settle the question.

But there is still the question of the sense in which Constantine was converted. There was a certain political angle to his stance, and Doerries insists that we cannot dissociate politics and religion

anywhere along the line. Constantine did hope for the favor of
the Christian God rather than to curry support from the Christian
populace. He believed in providence. The Christian God is the
only god and he presides over the destinies of states and individuals. He had chosen Constantine to be his instrument to lead
men into the "lighted house of truth" and to guide them in the
"way of deathlessness." But what had Christ to do with all this?
His cross had routed the demonic forces which incite the nations
to mutual carnage. The cross was a symbol of victory—victory
over the demons, victory over death. That is why Christianity is
the "way of deathlessness." The martyrs had served God's cause
by their sufferings. Constantine would now serve him by his
victories. He was the man of God, the servant of God, the instrument of God.

Very serious problems were raised by the emperor's adherence
to the Christian faith and his collaboration with the Christian
Church. The men of the classical age believed that the welfare
of the state depended on the favor of the gods. Constantine
shared that view, though he believed the divine to be but one.
Reverence for deity, he assumed with the pagans, to be necessary
for the tranquility of the commonwealth. That reverence should
be expressed through a cultus image. It should be of such a
character as to command the allegiance of all the citizens of
the empire. The rulers from Augustus on had found the answer
in the cult of the deified emperor. But two religions had refused
to worship the emperor, Judaism and Christianity. The Jews
had tacitly been granted exemption because they were truculent
and because they could be contained. The Christians were gaining adherents increasingly in the gentile world. Either, then, they
must be exterminated or else the empire must be desacralized
in the sense that the emperor could no longer be regarded as
divine. He must give up being a god and the religion of the
intransigeant dissidents would become the religion of the state.
Diocletian tried extermination and failed. Constantine abdicated
as god.

But if the empire must have only one religion and the pagans would not accept Christianity, the logic would call for the extermination of the pagans. But on such a program Constantine would not embark. "The battle for deathlessness requires willing recruits. Coercion is of no avail." The emperor himself had been a pagan. He had been converted voluntarily. He hoped that all of the pagans would in like manner be converted, but he would not compel. Temporarily, at least, he was driven to religious pluralism and throughout to religious liberty. He was not followed by his successors.

As for the relation of Church and state Constantine, as already remarked, gave up being a god. He was not even a bishop, though he was in a sense a lay overseer. There was still that 'divinity which doth hedge a king' and an etiquette of reverence in the imperial presence, but the ruler was not divine. He was only God's lieutenant. Such a view opened the door for resistance to the emperor in case he encroached on the sphere of the Church and Constantine met with some stout opposition from the Donatists in the west and the Athanasians in the east. These controversies are well described as to both their religious and social aspects.

If the empire had to retrench in order to be allied with the Church, the Church no less had to forfeit liberties when the imperial arm enforced the decisions of Church councils. Constantine dealt gently with pagans, but harshly with Christian dissidents because he regarded them as obstinate violators of Christian concord when they refused to abide by the decisions of Christian majorities. The unbeliever was entitled to more consideration than the schismatic or heretic.

Did all of these changes constitute an advance or a retrogression from the Christian point of view? The subject has been much debated. Some have looked upon Constantine as the great corrupter. The Church was deemed to have been closer to its Master when small, persecuted and powerless. Others have said that the alliance with the empire gave the Church an opportunity to collaborate in the building of a Christian society. Doerries inclines to the latter view, though he recognizes that in a measure power did corrupt. Nor would he try to rehabilitate Constantine's solution for our day. The point is that Constantine sought to implement his Christian convictions within the framework set for him by the institutions and ideas of his age. He perceived the significance of the hour and grasped the opportunities as wisely and as well as circumstance and conviction allowed.

The translator wishes to thank his colleague Professor Hans Frei for checking his work.

Roland H. Bainton
Yale University

Constantine The Great

I. Diocletian

No figure in history stands apart from his time, for the interconnectedness of history is unbroken and inescapable; and even though he may oppose the past and its traditions, he is nevertheless a product of them and indebted to them. This is true for both individuals and nations, though the manner of the relationship can vary greatly.

When we come to consider the age of Constantine in relation to the previous era,[1] there is no point in concentrating on inconsequential details. Rather, we must examine the entire structure of Diocletian's empire, which for the succeeding age constituted both the pattern and the contrast, for we cannot otherwise understand the achievements of Constantine.

Diocletian himself had inherited from the Emperors Aurelian and Probus the task of preserving the unity of the empire. Essential to this unity was the imperial office itself, the dignity of

1. On Diocletian consult W. Seston, *Dioclétien et la Tétrarchie*, vol. I (Paris, 1946) and also his article in the *Reallexikon für Antike und Christentum* (III, 1036–1053). Seston takes the position that the Byzantine Empire was founded by the two emperors Diocletian and Constantine, who were, however, opposed to each other in their religious policy. His view contains a tension on which it goes aground. Seston finds himself driven to push Diocletian's persecution of the Christians to the periphery of the administration. Only if one confines attention to the external operations of the state can one lay stress on what the two emperors had in common. To do that is to fail to understand what each conceived to be his role and to perceive that each emperor must have misunderstood the other.

which, fed from heaven, transmitted its power to the holder who in turn, by embodying the spirit of the empire, both preserved its original character and invested it with new life. The office, therefore, had to be guarded against the constant threat of usurpation. The legions had elevated the emperors—Diocletian himself had been raised to power by his troops and regarded his eventual retirement as a farewell to his soldiers. Yet he took great care to keep the imperial purple out of their hands by investing it with an aura far above human choice and ambition. The monarch sat in his palace enthroned as if in a temple, preserved from any unhallowed touch by a stately ceremonial,[2] akin to if not borrowed from the Oriental. What a contrast to the democratic simplicity of the first Augustus was this ritual prostration before the imperial presence, from which not even the highest officials nor even relatives were excused![3]

Although the services of the emperor were sorely needed at every threatened area on the frontier, obviously he could not take personal charge at every point. Hence Diocletian had devised the tetrarchy, the scheme of four rulers. Two Augusti exercised the supreme authority, one in the east and one in the west. Each was assisted by a Caesar, the second in command. The problem of succession was solved by having the Augusti retire at discretion, but coincidentally, being succeeded by the Caesars, who would then appoint new Caesars. The dynastic principle entered only to the extent that the Caesars were adopted by the families of the Augusti and usually married their daughters. The entire system was not instituted at one time, but developed by stages. When the peasants rebelled in France and the Germans pressed upon the Rhine, Diocletian appointed Maximian as his assistant in the

2. A. Alföldi, "Die Ausgestaltung des monarchischen Zeremoniells am römischen Kaiserhofe," (1934), and by the same author, "Insignien und Tracht der Römischen Kaiser" (1935).

3. On the concept of the ruler in the late imperial period consult F. Taeger, *Saeculum*, VII (1956), 182–195, and his subsequent and fuller treatment entitled "Charisma," *Studien zur Geschichte des antiken Herrscherkultes*, I (1958), II (1960).

west with the title of Caesar, which was soon changed to that of the Augustus of the West (286). When a general commissioned to rid Gaul's west coast of pirates became their leader instead and proceeded to establish his rule over Britain, Diocletian sent against him the trusted commander Constantius with the rank of Caesar. The same year the Persian threat required an independent general in the east, and Galerius was appointed to this post with the title of Caesar (293). The imperial families thus established considered themselves to be the successors of the old Roman gods—Diocletian's of Jupiter, the chief deity, Maximian's and the others' of Hercules, the assisting god. These alignments did not preclude the worship of other gods.

Safeguarding the empire's center depended on first securing the frontiers, and the decentralization of power to achieve this goal was eminently successful. The barbarians pressing on the Rhine and the Danube were contained, while in the east the Persians were so far repulsed that the frontier was advanced to the Tigris. (Nisibis remained a Roman city until the Emperor Julian was killed in battle on an eastern campaign.) Because the defense of the empire required a considerable increase in the military forces, extensive reforms of the army system were also necessary. These in turn led to other reforms. Diocletian increased the number of provinces to approximately a hundred and equalized the territory allotted to each. The tax reform distributed the oppressive burden on the basis of units of cultivated land and the number of their occupants. The monetary reform staved off the depreciation of gold and established a uniform ratio between coins. Revenues for the support of the army had to be largely in kind and the much-discussed maximum tax of A.D. 300 was designed to protect both troops and officials from exploitation by regulating the maximum prices allowed for essential foodstuffs. However, not even draconian penalties could ensure permanent enforcement of these prices. The weakness of the system consisted in its undue attention to the needs of the military and an unwarranted optimism as to what could be achieved by state regulation. All too little care was expended on the popular welfare which, had it been adequate, would have rendered the other reforms superfluous. The entire system, ostensibly prompted by immediate necessities, was anachronistic in that by seeking to revive the glories of the past it did not recognize the true state of affairs, and in consequence not only failed to utilize the resources available but further aggravated the problems of the present.

The empire of Diocletian had a religious base. His first coins indicate that the empire was founded not upon the authority of the Senate or of the army but on a special relationship to Jupiter; the *religiosissimus* emperor in his official pronouncements showed himself to be zealous in the service of the ancient gods, especially Mithras, that great benefactor of the empire.

In two edicts the emperor set forth with perfect clarity his basic convictions and the main themes of his religious policy. The March, 295 Decree on marriage declared that what the Roman laws determined to be pure and holy must be devoutly observed. And again, "We may not doubt that the immortal gods are gracious and well disposed to the Roman name when we observe that under our rule all pursue a godly, quiet and peaceful life."[4]

Of vastly greater import was an edict dealing with what was deemed anything but pure and holy. Issued in Alexandria in 296, it was directed against the Manichees, a Persian sect infiltrating the empire, whose creed was based on a profound and absolute dualism between spirit and matter. To the Manichees, the bearing of children was considered a sin because thereby more souls were imprisoned in bodies. Diocletian's edict against them began by referring to the divine origin of the old order and declared that "the old religion is not to be criticized by a new religion. . . . It is the greatest crime to repeal that which was determined and established by the ancients and continues on a sure course. . . . Therefore we are very much concerned to punish the

---

4. *Mosaicarum et Romanorum Legum Collatio*, VI, 4, p. 1, ed. T. Mommsen, *Collectio Librorum Juris Anteiustiniani*, III (1890).

malicious obstinacy of base men who displace the old worship of the gods by unprecedented sects in order thus through noxious caprice to make an end of that which was once delivered to us from the gods." Then came specific reference to the Manichees: "There is reason to fear that in the course of time the unbridled practices and perverted laws of these Persians will poison innocent persons, the sober and peaceable Roman people and indeed the entire globe."

This unequivocal edict and the emperor's personal confession explain the severity of the penalties decreed. The Manichaean leaders were to be burned, together with their writings; their adherents also were to be executed and their goods confiscated. "The plague of this evil is to be pulled up by the roots and extinguished in our happy age."[5]

The fundamental assumptions underlying this edict could lead to no other conclusion and were bound to apply equally to any other non-Roman religion, including the Christian; and in fact only a brief time elapsed before the outbreak of a clash with the Christian Church. The beginning was made in the army. To be sure, the outbreak of 299 was provoked by particular circumstances, but behind the effort at suppression undoubtedly lay the will of the emperor. Certainly it was his intention to make the eternally valid Roman order secure at its core, and therefore the army and the court alike were pressed to seek the powerful favor of the gods by universal veneration. First Christian officers and officials, then many common soldiers, were confronted with the choice of sacrifice or dismissal; many chose dismissal. This requirement for universal worship very quickly began to be regarded as the logical extension of Diocletian's basic convictions, and the great Christian persecution then started. No doubt there were many accessory causes and personal influences, not least that of the Caesar Galerius, who was credited with having instigated the persecution. But the decision was that of the emperor himself and was all the more significant because it

5. *Ibid.*, XV, 3, p. 187.

matured only through long deliberation. The first edict, issued on February 23, 303, the day of the god Terminus, called for the destruction of the churches and the confiscation of Church properties (such as cemeteries), and forbade assemblies and any sort of worship. The second and third edicts affected the clergy, who were first to be imprisoned, then induced to offer sacrifices by every device, including severe torture. Those who refused to comply were condemned to the most extreme penalties, including death. This was done in the expectation that the congregations, deprived of their leaders, would the more readily be dispersed.

The fourth edict early in 304 abandoned every reservation. Sacrifices, together with the consumption of meat and wine offered to the gods, were demanded of everyone. Those who complied were rewarded, those who refused were threatened with imprisonment, torture, and death. Thereby the door was opened to the terror which stalked town and country. At the outset the emperor had sought to prevent the shedding of blood, but how could that be avoided now? As a stream fed by brooks grows into a river, so the persecution, once started, was swollen by various factors and interests until it raged beyond control. Religious zeal, personal animosities, or ambition swept many beyond the terms of the edict. Even representatives of the highest spiritual interests were not above swelling the flood, and many scholars and philosophers were to be found in the ranks of the persecutors.

The persecution was begun by Galerius, in whom contemporaries saw the prime instigator. On a designated day the two emperors, Galerius and Diocletian, watched from the roof of the imperial palace while army officers searched the nearby church for images of the Christian God, burned any Scriptures that came to light, and thoroughly plundered and levelled the church. The older emperor would not allow the edifice to be fired for fear of igniting the adjoining buildings. But he was enraged when a blaze broke out in the palace, kindled, according to Constantine, by lightning, but according to the Christian author Lactantius by Galerius himself, who then cast the blame on the Christians. The outraged Diocletian conducted an investigation in person, himself passed the first sentences of death, and compelled his wife and daughter, who entertained Christian sympathies, to make sacrifice. The persecution then took its course in earnest in both east and west, except in those areas where the Caesar Constantius withheld his assistance. The persecution has received so infamous a reputation not only because of the great number of its victims but because this great empire, the self-proclaimed guardian of righteousness, was now itself guilty of violating the most basic claims of conscience.

It is not surprising, then, that members of the body politic were disturbed, not simply because groups of varying sizes were excluded from economic pursuits, but because the informing on and hunting down of suspected Christians engendered fear and distrust among citizens everywhere.

The purpose of the edict was given by Galerius when he found himself constrained to rescind it in 311:

Among the measures which we undertook for the common weal we desired especially to revive the laws and ordinances of the Romans and we sought to bring to their right minds the Christians who had forsaken the religion of their ancestors. But, for various reasons, the Christians were possessed by such obstinacy and folly that no longer did they follow the practices of the ancients, which perhaps their own forefathers had established, but according to their fancy made laws of their own and everywhere gathered a following. Since our decree required that they adhere to the ancient ways, many were subjected to punishment.[6]

Thus Galerius justified the persecution in the very decree that abolished it.

Diocletian was not at hand to set his name to this reversal. On the first day of May in the year 305, on the hill of Jupiter in Nicomedia, before the assembled army, he surrendered the im-

6. *DMP*, XXXIV. For an English translation of the main documents consult vol. I of P. R. Coleman-Norton, *Roman State and Christian Church* (London, 1966), 3 vols.

perial purple to that god from whom his power was derived. A coach stood ready to transport him to his Dalmatian home near Spalato. It was on this very hill that he had first assumed the office of emperor and it was here too that he had invested Galerius with the authority of Caesar and designated him as his successor. Diocletian's retirement at this time might have been motivated by several factors—sickness, pressure from the ambitious Galerius, forebodings about the persecutions—but the withdrawal itself was part of a pre-arranged plan to which the emperor adhered and to which he had obligated his co-Augustus, Maximian. Although his resignation might have occurred at this time in any case, there is no doubt that Diocletian did lay down his office with a sense of failure. Still, he was in no sense disillusioned with the rightness of the cause which he now committed to younger hands.

In his high-walled retreat, the emperor spent his last years disappointedly witnessing the collapse of the administrative system he had so carefully constructed. And Galerius' Edict of Toleration in 311 was a public admission that the policy of religious renewal failed. His age had rejected Diocletian and his work.

The beginning and the end of a course of action must answer for each other. Naturally, a man and his era cannot be judged by the standards of another age. But when an age itself reaps the harvest of its own planting, it is not unfair to judge it by the fruits of its endeavors.

This principle can be applied to Diocletian. We cannot sever from his career, as if they were not properly his, those last years which have branded his name with infamy, for they were the fruits of his own persuasion, only gradually matured to be sure, but growing nevertheless by an inner necessity from the soil of his basic assumptions.

How far was this perceived at the time? The Christians near the court, who felt the first shock, were not unmoved by the greatness of Diocletian and by his contributions to the welfare of the empire. Their spokesman, Lactantius, who had himself survived the outbreak of the persecution in Nicomedia, did not fail to make excuses for the deserving emperor, although the tone of most of Lactantius' work is far different. The aging emperor, he suggested, was unable to withstand the constant pressure from his Caesar and yielded when the palace fire and other disturbances were attributed to the Christians. Diocletian became, in fact, the victim of pagan hate-mongering.

However, Lactantius did not regard these excuses as adequate. They might explain the sudden outbreak of persecution, but the emperor was not relieved of responsibility by feebleness and poor judgment. Diocletian remains for Lactantius "the inventor of the crime and the instigator of the evil who, after he had corrupted everything, did not hold back his hand even from God."[7] The darkness which settled on the last years of this reign overshadows all else. Everything which constitutes the historic contribution of Diocletian—the scheme of administration and succession, the redistribution of the provinces, the increase and reorganization of the army, the imposition of the maximum price tax, the enrichment and enlargement of Nicomedia—all of this for Lactantius signified only the misery of the empire, with its populace groaning under the burden of taxation necessary to maintain these reforms.

It was not hate that guided the stylus of Lactantius. He gave expression to the widespread dismay occasioned by the frightful scenes of the persecution. For Lactantius, as for his contemporaries, these occurrences betokened nothing other than the judgment of God, whose terrible punishment he chronicled as a warning for posterity. Little wonder then that his work became an indictment. While this all too hasty interpretation of history must be subjected to critical scrutiny, Lactantius' attitude was

7. *Ibid.*, VII, 1. A. Momigliano's verdict on Lactantius, "a voice shrill with implacable hatred," does not take into account the genuine concern of Lactantius in *De mortibus persecutorum*. "Pagan and Christian Historiography in the fourth Century A.D." in: A. Momigliano (Ed.), *Conflict* (1963), p. 79.

not considered unwarranted then and indeed merely put into words what many felt to be the true state of affairs.

Lactantius wrote of the persecution under Diocletian as an eyewitness. We have another account from the pen of Eusebius, bishop of Caesarea in Syria, who by contrast placed his experiences in the context of his whole interpretation of Church history, incorporating his account of the persecution in his *Ecclesiastical History,* the first of its kind.* Withstanding the temptation to lose himself in diatribes against the persecutors and in laments over the injustice endured, he placed the blame on the Church because, during the years when the government had tolerated their presence, the bishops and the congregations had forgotten their first concern and "blew neither hot nor cold." To Eusebius, as to Lactantius, the main cause of the persecution was not the enmity of emperors or the rage of demons, but the wrath of God, who had at last unleashed His long-deserved judgment on the Church. As soon as God withdrew His protecting hand and allowed "the princes of this world" their will, the awful punishment began, ceasing only when the time of penitence was fulfilled. After giving this opinion, Eusebius simply chronicled the main events: the posting of the edicts, the outbreak of the storm and, after that, not so much the horror as the examples of endurance. He wrote the history not of the executioners but of the martyrs.

However, the unwitting tools in this punishment were not thereby relieved of responsibility for their deeds, and their final ends were cited as fitting punishments.[8] The debilitating and

---

* Lactantius, who came from North Africa, where anti-Roman feeling always smoldered, wrote in Latin and has been called the Christian Cicero. He had been brought to the East by Diocletian to serve as a teacher. There he had lived through the persecution and afterwards wrote *De Mortibus Persecutorum* (*On the Deaths of the Persecutors*) in the manner of the Book of Acts, which relates how King Herod Antipas, having had himself proclaimed as God, was at once struck dead and eaten by worms (Acts 12:21–23).

Eusebius (called Eusebius of Caesarea to distinguish him from Eusebius of Nicomedia, a contemporary whom we shall encounter in the Arian controversy) wrote in Greek, presenting the Christian attitude of the East—R.H.B.

8. *HE,* VIII, 13, 15.

pitiable illness of Diocletian and his inglorious exit appeared as judgment. Maximian's shameful end and the subsequent smashing of his statues and inscriptions were looked back upon as the final verdict on a "criminal and godless person."[9] Galerius was driven by a frightful illness to repeal the edicts and died shortly thereafter. Plainly Eusebius, for all his studied detachment, viewed "the end of the persecutors" no differently than did Lactantius.

But should the victims be the ones to judge? Even when they make the effort to report accurately and to avoid all self-justification, one can hardly expect a truly objective appraisal, let alone an understanding of the enemy's motives and the part that the problems of the state played in the unfolding of events. All the more significant, therefore, is the judgment of the man destined to follow Diocletian, namely, Constantine, who resided at the court and, unlike Lactantius, had direct access to the emperor. He witnessed the beginnings of the persecution at the imperial level, but took no part in it, astutely forming his own opinion. In this regard, he was not alone at the court. In later years he would voice the sentiments which had circulated among "reasonable people" at that time. They had expressed without reserve their indignation at the outrage perpetrated against the reverent worship of God by blameless men in an era officially dedicated to peace. It was the general opinion that divine wrath for so much unjustly shed blood would not be long deferred and that then the innocent might well suffer along with the guilty, for the deity would spare no one. Evidently this son of a Caesar moved in a circle of vehement, though uninfluential, opposition to government policy. The proverbial sarcasm against the ruler most aptly fitted this case: "What marvelous concern for the laws! What protection of the army for the citizens!" The eventual outcome fulfilled their expectations. "Divine Providence inflicted punishment for the crimes not without great public loss." The

9. *VC*, II, 49, 51ff., and 54.

very disturbances which followed the abdication of the old emperor were laid at his door.

Constantine, when emperor, retained the convictions of his youth. His great proclamations recall the circumstances and repeat the judgment:

When I was still young I heard how the wretched one, who was chief among the emperors of Rome—he really was wretched and misled by error—inquired of one of his bodyguards what was meant by the complaint in the oracle of Apollo of "those just ones." Then one of the Emperor's own priests answered, "No doubt, the Christians!" The Emperor lapped up the answer as easily as honey and turned the sword ordained to be used against evildoers against those of blameless holiness. With a stylus dipped in blood, he wrote the edict of death and commanded judges to use their wits to devise new tortures. At that time the world, stained by bloodshed, cried out and the very day hid its face for sadness.

To the shame of the Romans, the fugitives were granted asylum by the barbarians. But judgment was not long delayed. "The instigators of this crime are all gone, cast down to suffer eternal punishment in Acheron. Hewn down in wars among themselves, they have left neither name nor progeny."[10]

In Constantine's repudiation of the religious and political policies of his predecessors, Diocletian was not spared. The judgment of God was considered to fall upon him as upon the others. After these many years, the anger of Constantine, the statesman, still smoldered at the remembrance that instead of safeguarding the empire from outward attack, his predecessors had followed that unwise, inhuman, and godless policy which had shattered its powers through internal dissension.

Though Constantine's major concern was with affairs of state and with the political consequences of Diocletian's religious policy, he concurred with the Christians that religion was inextricably bound up with the future of the empire. While Diocletian had correctly assessed the importance of religion to the res-

10. *VC*, II, 49–54. *Oratio ad Sanctorum Coetum*, XXV, 4.

toration of the empire, he had chosen the wrong religion. The Neoplatonic philosophers, who aided in the suppression of the Christians, were also convinced that the fate of the empire depended on the upholding of that faith for which Diocletian sought to ensure total and exclusive recognition.

The internal impact of the persecutions extended far beyond the circle of the Christian congregations, raising questions about the very basis of the empire. The Christians were accused not merely of dismantling its outward structure but of undermining its foundations, which in order to shore up Diocletian had entered into a life-and-death struggle. The collapse of his endeavors revealed the brittleness of these foundations, on which his entire work was plainly unable to stand. Thus the persecuting emperor was himself precisely the one to bring to the fore the religious question as never before.

The contrast between the two fundamentals becomes the more discernible since the protagonists were worthy of respect. When the motives were not those of cruelty, recklessness, frivolity, or ambition, but rather the deep concern of a mature wisdom for the welfare of the state; when the initiator of the whole policy made his decision only after overcoming severe reservations; then no one can fail to see how deep was the cleavage. What the brutality of a Galerius and the irresponsibility of a Maximinus Daza could not bring to light was rendered unmistakable by the immense prestige of Diocletian, for this disclosed to all beholders the magnitude of the decision he was called upon to make.[11] Egypt

11. The primary point is the requirement and the refusal of sacrifice. What the persecutions proved in their own day they may also prove in ours—that there was an irreconcilable rift between the pagans and the Christians. The tendency among many today is to tone it down. But if the Christians in that day were like the pagans not only in dress and speech but in their whole manner of thought and life, why the persecution? We do better to assume that both the persecutors and the martyrs knew what they were doing. We must try to pin down the nub of their difference. The old saying holds that what differentiates is the kernel. (When I read the sympathetic feeling for the persecutors on the part of modern historians I blush to confess that my own sympathies gravitate to those who were sacrificed!) Consult J. Moreau, *La persécution du christianisme;* J. Vogt and H. Last, article "Christenverfolgung" in *RAC,* II.

gave expression to this realization by beginning a new chronology with the age of Diocletian, not in relation to his contributions to the empire but in reference to his persecutions. This was to be known as the "age of the martyrs."

II. The Rise of Constantine

The question of the place of religion in the fate of the Roman Empire, posed by Diocletian, was taken up by Constantine, who condemned his predecessor for following a course which brought the empire to the brink of collapse. But Diocletian had acted in good faith and indeed felt himself in a position to assert that no one could have done better. That this best possible course had failed so disastrously simply proved that no solution existed. Certainly the answer was not to point out particular mistakes and call for ever new reforms, none of them proving sufficiently drastic. There must be an entirely new approach.

Diocletian and his circle had taken their norms from the ancient Romans. Lactantius, the Christian tutor of Constantine's sons, took pains to remind them that the ancient Romans were fallible men who had not intended to relieve their descendants from solving their own problems. Said Lactantius: "If asked to give a reason for their persuasion, the pagans have recourse to the judgments of ancestors on the ground that they were wise and experienced and knew what was best. Thus these pagans lose their senses, abdicate reason, and are addicted to alien errors."[1] Loyalty to ancestors was a laudable virtue, but it could serve as an excuse for indolence, evasion of responsibility, and selfishness. In making a cult out of its own greatness the Roman Empire had

1. Lactantius, *Institutiones*, V, 19, 3.

undergone a demonic corruption in which the state came to be regarded as an end in itself. The attempt to build the empire on a universal religious foundation had constructed about the person of the emperor an artificial heaven, and the very effort to arrest the decay of the empire through the role of the emperor became a primary source of corruption. The Roman imperium's attempts to eradicate the Christian Church—whose tenets alone threatened to disrupt its magic circle—were entirely consistent with its religious policy. The Church was condemned to silence and oppression, and in consequence its noblest spirits abandoned the world and fled to the desert, renouncing all political service.

The future depended on the emergence of a figure who understood the exact nature of the crisis the empire faced and could lay hold of viable forces to revitalize it. The man who would assume this role had to be thoroughly versed in statecraft and its manifold duties; had to understand the empire's needs and the various attempts to meet them; had to be a military man, able to guard the frontiers; and, above all, he had to have the courage to attempt something new—not in blindly demolishing (as a doctrinaire iconoclast), but in building. Only in the school of Diocletian could such a man learn how to replace Diocletian.

We encounter Constantine for the first time in 296, a prince in the flower of his youth, standing on the right of the old Augustus in the imperial chariot. Diocletian was crossing Palestine to Alexandria to quell the great Egyptian insurrection in person. The spectators (among them Eusebius, Constantine's future biographer) were sufficiently impressed to sense in Constantine the future ruler, and they scanned his face hopefully to divine his nature and thereby their own destiny.[2] Constantine's biographer relates this as an eyewitness, though doubtless his reminiscence was colored by subsequent impressions.

Constantine's early years lie for us in shadow. He came from Illyrian stock, which in the third century contributed so many stalwart soldiers and emperors. His father, Constantius, was

2. *VC*, I, 19.

already of high rank in the army when around the year A.D. 285 a son was born to him by Helena at Naissus (Nish).[3] The father passed on to his first born, as he would to his entire family, a share in the soldierly "constancy" of his own name—Constantine. He was not able to keep the son with him very long because, in 289, he put away Helena and her child in order to marry the step-daughter of the Emperor Maximian. There were many such political marriages in the system of Diocletian. Constantine remained with his mother, in whom he placed implicit trust throughout his life. Her portrait reveals the self-discipline and nobility of an exceptional woman. Her humble origin did not prevent her from fulfilling with dignity the imperial honor which her son later bestowed upon her.

We cannot conclude from his biographer whether Constantine was already destined for a high post when he was brought to the court of Diocletian, though we do know that his father had not disowned him and that the emperor regarded him as his father's son. The many chains linking the four rulers of the empire may have included the proviso that the son of Constantius be reared at the court of the chief Augustus. In any case the son could serve as a hostage for the loyalty of the father. Since the system of Diocletian excluded hereditary succession, it was all the more important that the sons be imbued with the principles and the spirit of the empire which they were to support, though not actually rule.

From the time of his youth Constantine's exceptional status impelled him to choose an independent course. Though for more

3. The data for determining Constantine's age rest on the descriptions of him as a young man standing beside Diocletian in his chariot in 296 (VC, I, 19); Constantine's own statement about his age at the outbreak of the persecution in 303 (VC, II, 51) and the description of Constantine as a young man by the panegyrist of the year 310 (Paneg., VII (6), 21, 6). Consequently the year of his birth can scarcely be pushed back beyond the year 285 (Vogt) or 282 (Palanque). The earlier reckoning of 272–74 rests on the testimony of Eutropius (X, 4) and Eusebius (VC, I, 5 and IV, 53), but their summary accounts cannot be allowed to invalidate the other evidence.

than a decade he had to stay at the court of Diocletian, not all
of his time was spent at Nicomedia, for the court followed the
emperor from place to place according to the needs of the empire.
During this period Constantine visited Trèves, the imperial capital
in the west. There an orator related having seen in the palace at
Aquileia a painting in which Fausta, the daughter of Maximian,
then only three years old (she was later to be Constantine's wife)
handed him a decorated helmet—"a dowry," commented the
speaker in retrospect.

To have grown up under the eyes of the old ruler was of the
greatest significance to Constantine, for he acquired an intimate
knowledge of the empire's self-image and some practice in the
difficult art of presenting this imperial image. In this period too,
Constantine acquired the foundations of a knowledge of the administration's various branches and a keen awareness of the
intricacies of the juridical system. The influx of men from all
parts of the empire gave him experience in handling people and
the opportunity to learn at first hand the wishes and needs of the
provinces. As a commander he was trained on the field, winning
the confidence of his troops by his combination of boldness and
prudence. And he was initiated into the sharp exclusiveness of
the concept of *Romanitas*—he was ashamed and appalled when
the Christian Romans were lost to Rome by being accepted as
refugees by the barbarians. While he deplored the shedding of
Roman blood, he considered an occasional letting of barbarian
blood a simple necessity: it tended to ensure the empire's frontiers.

On Diocletian's abdication, it was generally expected that
Constantine would be accorded the purple,[4] but here we must
remember that despite his qualifications Constantine did not
easily fit into Diocletian's scheme of things. Even if the founder
of the system were inclined to break his rule and give the succession to the son of an emperor, certainly he would never have
chosen Constantine. There was no mistaking Constantine's lack of
enthusiasm for a policy of religious unification. He would be

4. *DMP*, XIX.

as negligent as his father in enforcing the edict against the Christians. One can imagine with what misgivings the eastern emperors regarded this aspiring and independent young prince, toward whom so many eyes were directed and whose enigmatic future defied control!

The importance of these years lies, on the one hand, in the initiation of Constantine into the system of Diocletian and, on the other, in his increasing divergence from its driving impulses. Both by acceptance and rejection Constantine prepared himself for the role which awaited him.

A legend often captures the significance of an event. There is a story that after Diocletian's abdication, Constantine so distinguished himself in the Sarmatian campaign that the jealous Galerius attempted to goad him into a fight with a lion in the arena. But Constantine, turning the plot to his advantage, then obtained permission to leave the court and staged the dramatic flight which set him on the course so different from that of his career hitherto.

"The gods have called you."[5] So said a court orator looking back on Constantine's arrival at Boulogne just in time to voyage with his father to Britain, where he took part in Constantius' last campaign against the Picts and the Scots. Sensing that he had not long to live, the father had summoned his son to designate him as his successor. On July 25, 306, the troops at York clad him in the purple of his deceased father. As Alexander succeeded to the work of Philip of Macedon, so did Constantine to that of Constantius.

Constantine had inherited more than a piece of territory. The manner in which he assumed the duties of the imperial office indicated that he was carrying forward his father's policies. Everywhere—in the rebuilding of cities, in the reclamation of abandoned lands through settlement of captured Franks, in advancing the school at Bordeaux and in developing Trèves as his residence—Constantine proved himself his father's son. His first

5. *Paneg.*, VII (6), 7, 5.

duty, however, was to secure the Rhine frontier against the incessant inroads of the Germanic tribes, especially the Franks and the Alemanni. His practice was to seek them out in their own territories and inflict heavy losses. At the same time he continued the old policy of accepting Germans into the army, and in so doing he forged a mighty broadsword to be used not only in the constant border skirmishes but in his subsequent conquest of Rome.

In internal administration Constantine also felt himself to be following his father who, of course, shared the views of his age. As a scion of Hercules, Constantius had not hesitated to speak of aid from his divine forebears. He had erected a temple to Apollo, and the full-toned vocabulary of the imperial cult resounded in the speech when in his presence the orator used the phrases "heavenly words," "eternal meaning," "foresight of the present *Numen* of the Emperor." At the same time Christian tendencies existed. A daughter was given the Christian name Anastasia, meaning "the one who has risen from the dead." Constantius evidently found reconcilable what Diocletian had considered incompatible. The subordination of all the gods to the sun god enabled him to include Christianity, a syncretism which, in this period of mingling of gods, was not restricted to the philosophers alone. Because of this, Constantius did not approve of the persecution of the Christians, although he did not directly oppose it. His obedience to the first edict of persecution was perfunctory—if the one isolated report that he destroyed some houses of prayer and forbade worship to the congregation at the court can be so interpreted. On his accession, Constantine hastened to repeal this order, thereby fulfilling his father's basic intent.[6]

While Constantine was quietly building up Gaul and strengthening his own position, in Italy a catastrophe was under way which would bring about the downfall of Diocletian's system. Severus, the new Augustus in the West, extended the imperial tax to Rome and disbanded the Praetorian guard. The popular resentment was capitalized by Maxentius, the ambitious son of the former emperor Maximian, who had abdicated along with

6. *Donatismusurkunden,* no. 11 (April 15, 313).

Diocletian. On October 28, 306, Maxentius was hailed as emperor by the people of Rome; the long-emptied imperial palace again had a master. When Severus marched against him with an army recruited from the old soldiers of Maximian, Maxentius appealed to his retired father for help. The old emperor responded willingly, making his son, the Senate, and the people of Rome request him to resume the purple. An orator represented Jupiter as saying to him, "I did not simply lend you the imperial office, I intended you to have it permanently. I will not take it back, but will support you in its exercise."[7]

The troops of Severus were not willing to fight against their old general and went over to him. Severus retreated to Ravenna, where he surrendered to Maximian on condition that his life be spared. Maximian then proceeded over the Alps to win Constantine as an ally. At Trèves he gave his young daughter Fausta to this Caesar of the West and adopted him into the family of Hercules, at the same time conferring upon him the title of Augustus, a further deviation from the system of Diocletian.

With the collapse of Severus, Galerius, the Augustus of the East, himself led an army into Italy but soon recognized that he could not take the heavily fortified city of Rome. When the loyalty of his troops began to waver he managed by various concessions to stage a hasty retreat, leaving behind scorched earth and an embittered population. Maximian suggested that Constantine cut off Galerius' retreat and annihilate him, but Constantine refused in that spirit of moderation which had already been evident while he was Caesar. On his return to Rome, Maximian found the situation totally changed. Maxentius had violated his father's promise to spare Severus' life. A joint administration of father and son was out of the question, for Maxentius demanded priority over his father on the grounds that he had resumed the purple only after it had been bestowed upon the son. The infuriated Maximian, in the presence of the

7. *Paneg.*, VI (7), 12, 6. The Christian Middle Ages in contrast looked upon rulership as a "loan" (fief) and not as a permanent possession.

soldiers, tore the purple from his son's shoulders. But the troops stood by the younger man and the old emperor had to flee the city.

Galerius and Maximian, united in defeat and not knowing where to turn, begged Diocletian to take a hand, for only his prestige, they said, could restore things to the proper *status quo*. But the old monarch was willing to agree only to a conference. At Carnuntum, near Vienna, he induced his old colleague to re-sign once more. To replace the murdered Severus he appointed, not Constantine, who was left with the rank of Caesar, but Licinius, an old comrade-in-arms of Galerius. Maxentius was of course denied recognition of any sort. The Caesar in the East, Maximinus Daza, had to be satisfied, as did the Caesar of the West, with the title Son of an Augustus. But both quickly gave themselves the full title of Augustus. There were then four emperors: Galerius, Licinius, Constantine, and Maximinus Daza.

But the restless Maximian was not satisfied merely to receive respectful treatment at Constantine's court. While his son-in-law was occupied in fighting the Alemanni, Maximian, seizing his treasure and taking command of a part of the resident troops, betook himself to Arles where, for the third time, he assumed the purple. When Constantine swooped down on him, he entrenched himself in Massilia but was deserted by his own people and came to an inglorious end.

Alongside these outward events, the inner spirit of Constantine was evolving. Something of this can be garnered from the ora-tions delivered at public celebrations, and there is a collection of such speeches which throw considerable light on this decade. In late antiquity these celebrations were focused on some occur-rence connected with the emperor. The speeches embodied the temper of the age and gave expression to national sentiment. The orator, who thanked the emperor for his victories and his good administration, was chosen by the emperor himself, and the sub-ject of the address was always the emperor and the régime which he had inaugurated. Under such circumstances the speaker might

deal a little cavalierly with the truth—seldom did he retain anything like the inner freedom of a Pliny delivering his famous
address to the emperor Trajan. The object was to depict the emperor as he wished to be seen and to make clear the designs
of his administration. Despite all this coloring, however, the
speeches do in fact express the major forces of the age.

The earliest addresses in honor of Constantine are especially
valuable because for this period of his life we have nothing from
his own pen. They recount and praise his deeds, justify his authority, define his position, and they let us see how his religious
views matured. They very nearly make us forget that the words
sometimes expressed the speaker's views rather than Constantine's. The first of these speeches, given on the occasion of Constantine's marriage to Fausta, the daughter of Maximian,
celebrates the elevation of Constantine to the rank of Augustus,
stressing the legitimacy of his claim to the honor—a theme which
would recur in other speeches. Constantine was actually hailed as
Augustus only by the troops of his father. Galerius had assigned
to him only the rank of Caesar. The orator goes on to say that
Constantine was entitled to the succession not by reason of
heredity alone, but by virtue of his abilities and by the appointment of his father-in-law. The speech also mentions that at the
same time he was taken into his father-in-law's family, and
thereby into the clan of Hercules, which divine ancestor he
emulated by his mighty deeds.

This recounting of the descent from Hercules is omitted after
the treachery and shameful demise of Maximian. The next orator
takes up the dynastic approach, claiming Constantine as the de-
scendant of two emperors—the first, his father Constantius; the
second, Claudius Gothicus, a somewhat earlier emperor (this
is the first we hear of him in this connection). Consequently,
Constantine was bestowed with the imperial dignity at birth,
and as a born emperor he naturally takes precedence over his
colleagues. At the same time reference is again made to his acclamation by the soldiers at York. Providence was seen to have

been at work in enabling the young prince to arrive just in time to catch his father's ship. Thus the principle of the tetrarchy is here set aside in favor of the hereditary claim. And for the first time there appears the introduction of the theme, later on to be very prominent, of Constantine's feeling that he had been called from on high. This call was always linked with Britain.

The oration goes on to the war with the Franks, the end of Maximian, and then to the relation of a prophetic experience of Constantine. On his return from southern Gaul to the Rhine frontier, he who was so manifestly under the care of Providence had made a detour in order to offer the promised sacrifice in the most beautiful temple of Apollo in all Gaul. "There you saw [the orator addresses Constantine directly] your Apollo, accompanied by Victory, and this god crowned you with two laurel wreaths, each marked with the number 30 [thus promising him a reign of long duration]. You have recognized yourself in the figure prophesied as destined to rule over the entire world."[8] With this reference to Virgil's Fourth Eclogue, which foresaw a new age about to be ushered in by a hero yet to come, Constantine was hailed as the one who would fulfill all the aspirations of that present age.

Constantine's break with Maximian also resulted in the repudiation of his god Hercules and the adoption instead of the cult of the sun god, who had been worshipped by the emperor Claudius and, in a measure also, by Constantius. But the cult of the sun god also contained a claim to universal monarchy. Again, religious and political motifs were inextricably combined.

Another witness to the changes taking place in the religious outlook of Constantine appeared for the first time in the images and inscriptions on his coins. (Their testimony will have to be heard later in a still more significant context.) The four emperors of Diocletian's tetrarchy had corresponded to the four divinities honored on their coins. Jupiter the Sustainer was on those minted by Diocletian, himself called Jovius; Hercules on those of the Herculean, Maximian. Galerius chose the "unconquerable sun";

8. *Ibid.*, VII (6), 21, 4.

Constantius the god of battles, Mars. After the shift of emperors, Jupiter appeared on the coins of the new Jovius—Augustus Galerius. On the coins minted in the east Galerius placed Hercules on the coins of Constantius, the new western Augustus, though Constantius himself, in the mints under his jurisdiction, retained the image of Mars which he had used while a Caesar. Constantine at first followed his father's practice, but after the break with the family of Hercules, he dropped the corresponding symbol and after the year 310 the sun god appeared on the coins as his companion. Sometimes the intimate association of the emperor and the god was emphasized by portraying them in profile, alongside each other, with such similarity that they appeared to be twins. One recalls the orator saying that Constantine recognized himself as represented in his Apollo. The emblem of the *sol invictus*—that is, "the unconquerable sun"—was retained by Constantine well into his Christian period.

While in Gaul the memory of Maximian the western persecutor was expunged, his images overturned, and his name chiseled from the inscriptions, in the east the Augustus Galerius himself put an end to the bloody work which he had pursued with such vigor. The famous Edict of Toleration proclaimed the end of the era of Christian persecution. On his deathbed in Sardica in 311, Galerius repealed the anti-Christian edicts, though more as a confession of failure than as an admission of fault. The Christians were still regarded as obstinate fools who repulsed the emperor's well-intentioned efforts to restore them to the religion of their ancestors. The result of their stubbornness was that many subjects of the empire practiced no religion at all, for they would not honor the old gods and were not permitted to honor their own. Since the welfare of the state was considered to depend on religious practice, it was thought that the Christians should be permitted to resume their own worship and urged to pray for the emperor and the empire, thus enlisting for the commonwealth the favor of their own god. This was the edict that emptied the prisons and the mines and allowed the thousands released to wander throughout the land. With the recounting of this event Eusebius concluded the first edition of his great history of the Church. This was in truth the last word on the age of Diocletian.

Galerius had tried to maintain Diocletian's system, but after his death the forces of dissolution grew too strong. In the west, relations between Constantine and Maxentius became ever more strained. Whereas the one "damned the memory of his father-in-law," the other, who thought better of his father dead than alive, elevated him to the rank of divinity. On whose part the hostilities began is not clear—whether Constantine in taking Spain without a war, or Maxentius in causing Constantine's statue to be overthrown in Rome. But in the fall of 312 began the struggle on the outcome of which hinged the future of the Roman Empire.

III. The Milvian Bridge

Orators and historians vie in describing Constantine's march on Rome. Together they give us a vivid picture, not correct in every particular, but essentially clear. We cannot go into detail as to the military aspects: how small the army was which Constantine led in swift march over the Cottian Alps, how the fortified Susa was taken at a stroke, how in the open field near Turin the heavy cavalry of the Cataphracts was overcome by new military methods, how in a stiff fight near Verona, Ruricius, the hardy general of Maxentius, was subdued, how Milan and Aquileia opened their gates—and how despite all of these successes the outcome of the autumn march against the well-walled city of Rome was fraught with danger and Constantine was no better equipped to subject the city to a siege than Galerius before him.

The narrators, with bated breath, describe the march. Was it expedient, seeing that the strategic experts (with good reason) as well as the augurers advised against it? Dubious and amazed men watched as the young commander, disregarding all warnings, embarked upon an enterprise which, to say the least, was of uncertain outcome. On the other hand, though, Rome was not impregnable. There was dissension within her walls. The disaffection of the Senate and the people was not without influence on the course of Maxentius and prompted the indiscretions which led to his downfall. The discontent had been gathering for some time. After the elevation of Maxentius southern Italy,

Africa, and Spain accepted him with surprising speed, but he very soon encountered difficulties to which he was not equal. These were related not the least to the dubious legitimacy of his position. A countermovement arose in Africa, where another emperor was raised up and the grain ships which supplied Rome were held back. To be sure, after a long period an able general managed to quell this revolt and take bloody reprisal. Nevertheless, the aftereffects on Rome and Italy were calamitous. The extra drain meant that the countryside could not continue to supply the needs of the Roman population indefinitely, and the increased taxation, especially on the senatorial families, did not serve to endear Maxentius. Street fighting between the Praetorian guard and the populace thoroughly alienated the ordinary citizen. People began to loathe Maxentius as a tyrant who was also reputedly addicted to licentious behavior. How far he deserved these reproaches we do not know. On the other hand, the Christian community had no ground for particular complaint. Admittedly, Maxentius banished two bishops, but that was because of disorders connected with the disputed elections. He not only did not hesitate to publish Galerius' Edict of Toleration but also went further and restored to a newly elected bishop the property of the Church. While Maxentius showed no Christian inclinations, the tension between him and Galerius served to keep him from the ranks of the persecutors—not to mention the fact that he had enough difficulties beyond his capacities without deliberately antagonizing the Christians.

When in the fall of 312 the war had begun, the northern cities had fallen to the foe, and Constantine was approaching the capital, there was every reason for the defender of Rome to barricade himself within the walls and avoid battle. Evidently this was his plan, since he dismantled the Milvian Bridge. Was it the success of a sortie that led him to abandon this strategy? On a quickly constructed pontoon bridge his army moved against the assailants. Apparently popular unrest and the charge that he was not doing his duty as an emperor drove Maxentius to abandon considerations of personal safety. A sacrifice was made to the gods, the oracle was favorable, the senators were requested to consult the sibylline oracles. The response was ambiguous. "On this day the enemy of the Romans will fall." Maxentius thereupon resolved to leave the protection of the walls and join his army. At that moment the fighting was intense. The Praetorians, true to their tradition, held to the last man. Then the line began to break. The fugitives pressed back on the bridge, which gave way and carried with it the "enemy of the Romans" into the waters of the Tiber. The gates opened to the conqueror. The city with jubilation received its liberator.

October 28, 312, was a fateful day for Rome as well as for Constantine. Although its importance cannot be overestimated, its meaning was and still is open to question. Constantine had marched on Rome against the tyrant, not against the persecutor of the Christians. But later, Constantine, viewing the two great periods of his life, assigned Maxentius to the ranks of persecutors, linking his fall with theirs.[1]

The first religious interpretation of the event comes from the pen of a pagan orator speaking at Trèves in 313.[2] He dealt with the taking of Rome but at the same time recognized a spiritual transition which had left its trace even upon those having no part in it. The orator celebrates the tremendous event with evident feeling for its greatness. Almost without so intending he becomes the first witness to the conqueror's point of view. The old world of the gods is no longer mentioned in the speech—there is not a word even of Sol Apollo. Appeal is made only to the highest divinity of many names who, according to the philosophers, either pervades the universe, living and moving with no

1. Libanius has Constantine lead his Gallic troops against Rome. "They went against the gods to whom formerly they had prayed." Thus the heathen orator also interpreted the fight for Rome in terms of the religious controversy of the time. *Oratio pro templis* (*Or.* 59), ch. 6. On this chapter compare E. Delaruelle, "La conversion de Constantin, état actuel de la question" (1953).

2. *Paneg.*, IX (12).

outward impetus, or looks down from the heavens, as from a fortress, upon his work below. Care for mankind is delegated to lesser divinities. But the way for Constantine is opened by that highest divinity with whom he stands in secret league. Hence he has no need of human council, is free to disregard the bad omen and the warnings of the soothsayers. Through this divine leading he knows that the time for the liberation of the city has come.

He may also have been swayed by the thought that the better cause could not be defeated. Over against military strength on the one side stands the might of righteousness on the other. More is involved here than a mere power struggle, though the issues cannot be comprised under a particular name. In contrast with the crimes of Maxentius—godlessness, cruelty, undisciplined behavior, superstitious rites, robbery of temples, and the like—stand the virtues of Constantine—filial piety, gentleness, discipline, regard for the divine commandments and the welfare of the state. This enlightened pagan orator is as ready as Constantine to condemn the superstitious rites of Maxentius and thereby carries the contrast into the realm of religion. As a matter of fact Maxentius had behaved like another Diocletian and in accordance with the old Roman faith. But now the oracle, which Constantine no longer believed and by which Maxentius had been deluded, was dissociated by the orator from the popular belief in the gods and set over against it. The speaker represents Maxentius as brought low by supernatural forces. Nightmares and furies drive him from the palace and the divinity itself, as well as the eternal majesty of Rome, impel him to give battle outside the walls, and a premonition of death leads him to involve as many as possible with him in disaster.

While the oration given at the time of the march on Rome in the summer of 312 spoke of the invincible Apollo, now after only a little more than a year, Apollo has disappeared. There is no mention of any god by name. Instead we have such expressions as "the divine spirit," the "godhead," "a supernatural power," but the religious interpretation is thereby strengthened.

The pagan point of view is not abandoned, but a tension has been introduced which can be explained only in terms of some pressure from without—namely, that of Constantine. The eulogist was supposed to voice the views of the person eulogized. If these views, however, did not accord with his own and if he were not willing to be simply a microphone, he had to discover some neutral expression which would cover both his and the emperor's views. And quite possibly this orator was so impressed by what had happened that he was willing to follow the ruler on a path which carried him beyond himself.[3]

In 315, ten years after the assumption of the purple by Constantine, the Senate and the Roman people erected in his honor the triumphal arch which is still standing today. In a few tightly packed words the inscription on the monument celebrates the victory. "Because under the impulse of divinity and by the might of his own spirit, using just weapons, he has vindicated the common weal against the tyrant and his faction."[4] The Senate thus ratifies the emperor's faith in the justice of his march, ascribes to him and to his army the execution of vengeance on the oppressor and his minions, and attributes the victory to the emperor's greatness of spirit, together with divine aid. He was impelled by the godhead, *instinctu divinitatis.* Significantly, this is the same expression as that used by the orator of Trèves in 313, with no mention here of the deity by name. On such a solemn occasion the pagan world would undoubtedly have spoken of Jupiter Optimus Maximus, or of Mars, of Apollo, or of the immortal gods. The indeterminate expression stems directly from the emperor,

3. The same picture with legendary accretions is found in the speech pronounced at Rome in 321 by the Gallic orator Nazarius. *Paneg.,* X (4).

4. *Dö.,* pp. 224ff. The orator at Trèves also had the emperor commence his march on Rome, *"divino monitus instinctu." Paneg.,* IX (12)c. XI, 4. Some see in this vague expression an influence of Neoplatonism. But this assumption is highly dubious. Neoplatonism became popular in the west only after the middle of the fourth century and its chief representatives earlier in the east, Porphyry and Hierocles, were leaders of the persecution against the Christians. The philosophers whom Constantine tolerated at his court in Constantinople did not influence his views.

or at any rate conforms as closely to his confession as was possible for the pagan inscribers. The words were susceptible of either a Christian or a pagan interpretation. Equally worthy of note is the ascription of the liberating victory to a divine hand. The pagan witnesses in their questing ambiguity thus point to something new and special of which they take account without being able to endorse it.

Let us see whether the Christian authors help us to understand this any better. Eusebius of Caesarea could do justice to the great event only by a biblical comparison. Like Pharaoh at the Red Sea, Maxentius was engulfed by the waves of the Tiber before the face of the new Moses, Constantine.[5] The fateful battle made so profound an impression that its delineation in Christian art became stereotyped. In order to deliver Rome, God himself drove the tyrant with a scourge out of the city, struck him down with his miraculous power, and caused him to drown in the Tiber.

The Christian authors not only describe the importance and significance of the event, but discover the beginning and cause of the upheaval in the experience of the emperor himself. Lactantius reports a heavenly directive given by night to Constantine on the eve of the battle at the Milvian Bridge:[6] "Constantine was admonished during the night to place the heavenly sign of God on the shields of his soldiers and thus to start the battle. He did as instructed, placing an X with the upper arm bent over, the sign of Christ, on the shields. Beneath this emblem the army took up the fight." What had happened during the night within the soul of the general was confirmed on the next day by the battle. With signs and wonders a higher power intervened and this power must be acknowledged. Such visions were not alien to the spirit of the times. Diocletian and Licinius had them as

5. *HE,* IX, 9, 5. The *Vita* (*VC,* I, 12) carries this comparison further. As Moses was reared in Pharaoh's house in order that later he might liberate his people, so Constantine was brought up at the court of the persecuting emperor.

6. *DMP,* XLIV, 5ff.

well as Constantine, who in claiming visions was a man of his age.

The sign has frequently been interpreted[7] in different ways. One thing is plain: it was not meant to be ambiguous. A secret rune which each might interpret as he liked would have divested the event of its significance. The soldiers could not be satisfied with any magical sign whatever. They must be persuaded that it was the sign of a divine power, able to ensure victory. Would the general merely make surmises about the superstitious beliefs of his soldiers? Three years later, on the anniversary of the victory, Constantine himself put the monogram of Christ on his helmet, and thus placed himself under Christ's image.

But what was its form? If, following Lactantius, one turns the X until one stroke is upright we have a cross. But if the intention had been only to represent a cross, a much more obvious form could have been chosen. There was the additional intent to represent a letter of the alphabet. For even if the capital X is turned on its side to make a cross, it is still the Greek Chi (X), the first letter in Christ's name. If the upright stroke is then bent over we get the Greek letter Rho (with the sound of the Latin R but the shape of the Latin P). This is the second letter in the name of Christ. With the two together we get the so-called cross monogram, of unquestionable Christian significance, ⳨.

But is there not a further complication? Because the same coin which showed the sign on the shield to have been the Christ monogram showed it also in another form (☧). The change from the unaccustomed form of the cross monogram to the familiar form of the Christ monogram is understandable. Since the sense is identical, the more common form could easily have supplanted the other with no one noticing the alteration. For us, the initial rarity of the form which only later became prevalent is the proof of its genuineness.

Alongside of the account of Lactantius stands Eusebius' well-

7. For a discussion of Lactantius consult P. Franchi de' Cavalieri, *Constantiniana* (Rome, 1953) and the comment by J. Vogt, *Gnomon,* XXVII (1955), 44–48.

known story of Constantine's vision of the cross.[8] He writes: "Toward sunset Constantine saw with his own eyes in heaven above the sun the conquering sign of a cross formed by the light. Alongside was the legend which read 'by this conquer.'" This, then, was a heavenly forecast of the sign of Christ as a token of victory. The words of the promise are preserved also on a coin from the middle of the century in what may have been the more original form, "by this sign you will conquer," *hoc signo victor eris.*

The account of Eusebius differs from that of Lactantius in that the sign is simply a cross and not a monogram and it appears during the day. The differences are greater when one observes that in Eusebius the vision is part of a longer sequence. He begins with the recognition by Constantine that the power of the sword without divine aid will not avail. Reflecting on the experiences of the earlier emperors, Constantine realizes that only his father, who worshipped but a single God, was successful.

The son then appeals to this God and receives as answer the heavenly sign. The dream the following night connects the sign with Christ, who tells Constantine to set the standard of the cross over against the enemy. On the following day the emperor obeys the command and thus the *labarum* originated. Some Christian priests, viewing the cross, see in it further "the symbol of immortality," "the sign of victory over death." Constantine promptly commences a cultus of the God who had appeared to him. Undergirded by faith in this champion he opens the war against Maxentius.

Eusebius thus places the vision of the cross, as distinct from the battle, into the sequence of Constantine's religious development. The vision is given its full theological significance, is connected with the institution of the imperial standard and with the introduction of religious worship into the army. Eusebius' account was written after the death of the emperor and at least a quarter of a

8. *VC,* I, 26ff. For the etymology of the word *"labarum"* consult H. Grégoire with whom, at this point, I agree.

century subsequent to the march on Rome. For the vision he
appealed to the testimony of the emperor. Likewise, the great
oration which Eusebius delivered before the emperor in the
year 335 refers to the vision of the cross and thus defines the
significance that Constantine attached to it. The daily reminder
of its meaning was the golden cross on the ceiling of the throne
room in Constantinople. But still, although the testimony of the
emperor does corroborate the appearance of the cross it does not
validate the historical picture given by Eusebius, who com-
presses separate events into the compass of a few days. His
review may well have a value of its own since it injects into the
beginning the understanding which evolved in the course of
subsequent events, but one cannot expect historical accuracy
as to details. The elements used to explain the cross of light
(which hardly needs an explanation) jostle each other; the inscription, the vision by night, the interpretation given by priests—
this confusion is most apparent in the case of the *labarum*.
Eusebius describes the military standard in the form in which
he knew it after 325. He pictures the *labarum* (really *laureatum*,
crowned with a laurel wreath) as a gold-overlaid lance with
crossbar, topped by a golden wreath framing the Christ monogram (☧). From the crossbar hung a bejeweled cloth of gold of
the same length and breadth, to which were attached three medallions representing Constantine and his two oldest sons, Crispus
and Constantine (the latter to become Constantine the Second).
If we have to choose between the accounts of Eusebius and
Lactantius we shall take the one closer to the event; the impro-
vised shield in preference to the artful goldwork; the hour of
danger rather than the time of initial preparation. If, in the
account of Eusebius, we see the legend already at work, we are
not necessarily to dissociate the appearance of the cross and the
institution of the *labarum*. It may have developed from the sign
on the shield mentioned by Lactantius. And if the cross and the
monogram of Christ are disjoined, a more impressive picture
emerges. Then the origin of the *labarum* is not to be found, as

with Eusebius, on the march to Rome, but in the very midst of the battle which sealed the victory. By an inner necessity the general, now become the emperor, must hereafter cause his legions to be led by that sign which determined the outcome of the first battle.

Finally we must listen to the most important voice of all, that of the emperor. His contemporary utterances do not begin until after the decisive day of October 28, 312. For the earlier period we are thrown back on his reminiscences and reviews. The rest is a matter for inference.

For Constantine the decision came directly before the battle. Under the sign he gave his soldiers stood Constantine himself. Like the attack on Rome, the decision to rely on Christ was a venture which engaged his whole person. He entrusted himself and his cause entirely to the Helper into whose service he now committed himself. This was an irreversible step. The loss of the battle would have shattered his faith. He could not look beyond this day and envision any other course. Given his assumptions, nothing else was possible.

These assumptions were a blending of the Roman understanding of religion, the Christian impact, and, not least, his own experiences in which, of course, both viewpoints had their part. The appeal to a heavenly champion was Roman. Thus Aurelian appealed to the sun god at Emesa before the battle which restored the unity of the empire at Palmyra. Roman, too, was the confidence in the power of magical signs. On the Christian side was the influence of the steadfastness of the martyrs, which pointed to a higher power. Above all was the Christian proclamation of the omnipotence of God. Constantine, the general, could not for a moment doubt that this Almighty God would disclose himself in the battle. Finally, Constantine's personal experience led him to view the fates of the persecuting emperors as a demonstration that behind the sequence of events stood a higher power, intervening in their course and subjecting even the greatest rulers to its will. Everything depended on being in league with this power. He who showed himself to be the Lord of history was also the director of battles. With these assumptions the conclusion easily followed that military prowess did not suffice to win the battle. That Constantine should thus have called upon the Christian God to give the victory to his army is something new and special. It was possible only on the basis of all these assumptions and became actual only in the moment of conflict at the Milvian Bridge.

This event recalls the parallel of another battle, decisive for the faith, that of the young Frankish king Clovis, who two hundred years later undertook to conquer Gaul. He had first to overcome the Alamanni. In the extremity of the battle, when his army began to give way, he called upon the heavenly power: "Jesus Christ, to those who hope in Thee Thou dost give victory. I beseech Thee for Thy help. If I experience Thy power I will believe in Thee and will be baptized in Thy name."[9] That was a good Germanic way of thinking. The proof of power settled the question of faith. The decision to be baptized was contingent upon victory.

Constantine stipulated no conditions and did not wait for results. His decision came before the actual battle. When his appeal was heard and confirmation given in a dream, he placed himself under the sign of the heavenly God in a venture of faith as well as of weapons. If Clovis' prayer had remained unanswered he would have remained what he was; he would simply have pursued his objective some other way. But we cannot think of Constantine as defeated, disillusioned, turning away from Rome like Galerius. Of course it is quite possible that his ambitions and his gifts might have enabled him, for a while, to stir up the waters like an unbelieving *condottiere*, but as such he would never have emerged as the historical figure he became, exerting an influence far beyond his time.

Is the battlefield a fitting place for a religious decision? Earthly aims, the clash of arms, the strife for renown and victory, all the

9. Gregory of Tours, *Historia Francorum*, II, 30ff.

passions and the very devils are let loose, but here also is a scene of inescapable seriousness; the proximity of death is the fiery test of all wonted ideas and the certainties of a lifetime. For what Constantine sought and wanted, this was certainly the proper place. Constantine's striving for mastery did not change. There is no suggestion of his withdrawing from the world, but by putting himself under a heavenly Lord he gained the certitude of a superior right and the aid of an unconquerable power. Although one recognizes the limits of his faith one cannot question its genuineness. The point here is to penetrate to the core of its peculiar quality. The nature of his faith is brought out in a trait to which he himself called attention. This was in the year 314, when the emperor directed a message to the assembled bishops of the Council of Arles. He portrayed himself as one who, by the divine goodness, had been called back to the way of salvation. Said he: "The eternal, holy, incomprehensible goodness of our God does not allow mankind to wander in the shadows but reveals the way of salvation and converts men to the standard of righteousness. I have experienced this in others and in myself, for I walked not in the way of righteousness and I did not suppose there was any higher power which could see what lay in my breast. What disastrous consequences must have flowed from this assumption! But the Almighty God who sits in the court of heaven granted what I did not deserve. I cannot relate what, in His heavenly goodness, He has vouchsafed to me His servant."[10]

These are weighty words. They contain such a sharp judgment on the emperor's past that they could have come from none other than himself. No one would have dared to place such words in his mouth. What Constantine records—he says so expressly—is a conversion. He counts himself among those whom God has called to the way of righteousness. He became aware that from the citadel of heaven an eye watches over the secrets

10. *Donatismusurkunden,* no. 18.

of the heart.[11] He became convinced of the moral order, evidenced by God's turning from the threat of chastisement to the flood of mercies upon His servant. Among these mercies were included his victories, especially that of the Milvian Bridge. The conversion included the experience of a higher leading, the sense of responsibility under the eye of God, the understanding of the fates of peoples as rewards and punishments. These points were determinative for the emperor's understanding of religion from this day forward.

Constantine at the peak of his career saw his successes as an undeserved gift. Victory was, then, not a reward for walking in the way of righteousness. He perceived now how his hand had been stayed and what then was the responsibility devolving upon him. Fate and righteousness were for him henceforth bound together. We may say that he was mindful of a gift which was also a guide for his future.

On the basis of this understanding Constantine felt himself to be of one mind with the Christian bishops. This was the place for him to make a Christian confession. He had taken the step which, from this time forward, characterized his position. The decisive battle that gave him the lordship of Rome had occasioned also his inner decision. From now on Constantine regarded himself as a Christian. Conversion and the venture of faith—the answer to the vision of the cross—these inner experiences which went before the battle of the Milvian Bridge were no less historically significant than the event itself. Only as a Christian could Constantine win the battle and only because the battle was won by a Christian emperor did it become decisive for the destiny of the Roman Empire.

11. The concept of the deity looking down from the castle of heaven and searching the hearts of men is to be found in both of the orations which celebrate the campaign against Rome. They confirm the emperor's testimony to his conversion.

IV. After The Battle

The first day of the new era began with the triumphal entry of the victor into Rome. Exuberant were the words of the orators,[1] exuberant the people. The very houses and hills seemed to join in the celebration as the emperor's chariot rumbled with heavy elegance into the city. The dense crowd and the pressing senators both shoved him forward and held him back. The bystander who could see counted himself lucky and he who could not bemoaned his location. The throng was so numerous that one wonders how so many people could have survived the six-year tyranny of Maxentius. But when the procession arrived at the forum and ought to have proceeded up to the capitol to offer the sacrifice in the temple of Jupiter, the chariot suddenly turned aside and the emperor disappeared into the palace. The sacrifice was not offered.[2]

Everything else—games, the visit to the Senate, largesses—all these followed the ancient usage. Constantine was no revolutionary. But at one point the line had been drawn between old and new. Constantine never again offered a sacrifice and suppressed those offered to himself as part of the imperial cult. On the frieze of the triumphal arch which the pagan Senate erected

1. *Paneg.*, IX (12), 19.
2. Compare J. Straub, "Konstantins Verzicht auf den Gang zum Kapitol" (1955).

in his honor the usual sacrificial animals do not appear. There was no longer any place for them in the ritual of the empire.

This is a significant turning point. Subsequent pagan historians reproached Constantine for neglecting "the ancestral shrines." From their point of view the responsibility for the decline of Rome devolved on him. Whether they (after their fashion) and the Christian writers understood what the battle meant for Constantine, only the sequel can determine; and likewise whether he gave substance to what he had experienced and how deeply it affected him.

Among the first acts of the new master was the presentation of the Lateran Palace and its adjacent lands to the Roman bishop. This area included the barracks of the Praetorians, whom Constantine had disbanded. In their place he erected a basilica to Christ the Savior. This became the church of the Roman bishops. (Its baptismal chapel, probably built earlier, was the scene of the Roman legend of the Donation of Constantine, which will occupy us later.) The Senate dedicated to the emperor a recently completed monumental building in the Roman forum, the basilica of Maxentius,[3] and, having decided to erect a statue of Constantine, placed it in that part of the west apse formerly used as a tribunal. The remains of the statue in the court of the Conservatory Palace disclose its colossal proportions. The head alone measures over eight feet. One can imagine how awesome the entire figure must have been. The eyes of someone entering from the east court into the tremendous nave would be drawn to the figure, elevated not simply for glory, but as it were for speech. As the observer became accustomed to the vast expanse he would notice a slight inclination of the emperor's marble head, which directed the attention to his right hand. The hand, discovered in another location, obviously grasped something like a staff. If the historian who described the erection of the statue had not told us that this was a long lance in the form of a cross,

3. Compare H. Kähler, "Konstantin 313" (1952).

we should know it from the inscription supplied by Constantine himself. "Under this one sign, the sign of true virtue, I have liberated Rome, the Senate and the people from the yoke of the tyrant and restored them to their ancient freedom and dignity."[4] This was the unmistakable sign connected with the hour of destiny. That it was not just a magical sign is plain from the accompanying explanation. When the true power is mentioned, a repudiation of the false power in which Constantine's enemies placed their trust is also made. Constantine testifies to having found the "true source of his power." This was what had renewed the ancient glory of Rome. The emperor speaks to the people of Rome out of his own experience—an experience in which, however, they have shared. The sign in the statue's hand recalls that other sign which the soldiers of Constantine were to carry ever after on their shoulders as the token of victory. The conclusion lies to hand that we have again to do with the basic form of the *labarum*.

Just as the statue recalls the Milvian Bridge, so also does the most eloquent coin of Constantine. The bust of Constantine on the face of the silver medallion minted on the tenth anniversary of his reign in 315 is depicted in warrior dress. The reverse shows him as a general addressing his troops. Thus both sides refer to the most important event of the last decade. Of the greatest significance is the emperor's helmet on the face side. Just as in later coins the diadem was reserved for the emperor, so in the earlier ones the helmet was the distinguishing mark of the Augustus. And the sign on the helmet conveyed the import of the anniversary coin. Here was concentrated the "impulse of the Godhead" mentioned by the orator at Trèves and in the inscription on the triumphal arch. Here, for the first time, we have the cross scepter which we encounter on all the later coins of Constantine. The staff with the cross above the circle of the earth was an impressive graphic symbol. Only three of these medallions

4. *VC*, I, 40. Compare J. Vogt, "Die Bedeutung des Jahres 312 für die Religionspolitik Konstantins des Grossen" (1942).

have come down to us. The Vienna one might be deciphered as having a star. The St. Petersburg example is clearer but still dubious. But the one most recently discovered, at Munich, has the unmistakable monogram of Christ. Under this sign on the anniversary coin is inscribed the name of the battle and the fact of Constantine's victory.[5]

The stand taken by Constantine, as disclosed by the coin and the statue, resulted in measures of which we learn through three letters sent to Africa at the turn of 312–13.[6] In them Constantine restored all their confiscated property to the Christian congregations, allowed relief to be distributed to the churches through the hand of the bishop of Carthage, and relieved the clergy from the duties of public services. The basis for these actions is stated in the third letter: the commonwealth had been in great danger through neglect of the worship of God. Constantine counted such worship a great good fortune for the Roman name if conducted under "sanction of the law." The clergy, he held, greatly benefited the state when they gave due reverence to God. The peril to and the renewal of the state were believed to stand in direct relation to the suppression and the restoration of Christian worship. The "good fortune" to which Constantine referred was undoubtedly the victory which con-

5. For the interpretation of the coin consult Andreas Alföldi, "The Initials of Christ on the Helmet of Constantine" (1951), and Konrad Kraft, *Das Silbermedaillon Constantins des Grossen mit dem Christusmonogramm auf dem Helm* (1954/55). Worthy of attention, though not invalidating the theses of Kraft, are the considerations adduced by Guido Bruck, "Die Verwendung christlicher Symbole auf Münzen von Constantin I bis Magnentius" (Vienna, 1955), pp. 26–32. Especially to be consulted is Maria R. Alföldi, *Die Constantinische Goldprägung* (1963), pp. 139–141, "Das Stirnjuwel des Kaisers." See also *The Roman Imperial Coinage*, vol. VII: Constantine and Licinius, by Patrick M. Bruun (1966), p. 364. Though an acknowledged numismatist, M. A. Alföldi's interpretation of the emperor's staff on the coin as the lower end of a lance the spearhead of which is placed on the ground, is hardly correct. Using the lance this way when alighting from his horse the emperor surely would have ruined the spearhead. Even more amusing is Delbrück's suggestion that the supposed lance might have been employed as a "break."

6. *Donatismusurkunden*, nos. 7–9 (312/13).

cluded the war on Rome. This tremendous event, which Christians and pagans alike regarded as a more than human struggle, was considered by Constantine to be part of God's judgment upon that age. Only this religious interpretation could be adequate. The Godhead had unleashed its wrath against the outrages perpetrated against Christian worship. The restoration was the mark of divine favor.

The assumption that the welfare of the state was so closely bound up with the cultus was a very Roman way of thinking, but now it was no longer the ancestral religion but the new Christian worship which would bring such far-reaching benefits. The favor thus shown to the African clergy was not only due to Constantine's inner convictions but partly also to considerations of state. The cultus thus fostered would benefit the empire. But even with the rescinding of the edicts of Maxentius there was still a need for a total reorganization of the religious situation. The right to enact laws pertaining to the chief Augustus had been expressly conceded to Constantine by the Senate when he was declared to be the chief emperor.[7] And the power relationships had become so altered that the other two Augusti acquiesced in subordinating their earlier rights. Thus the primary role in the regulation of religion had also passed to the ruler of the west.

The first to be made aware of the changed situation was the eastern emperor, Maximinus Daza, then in Asia Minor. Constantine, in both his and Licinius' name, reported the passage of events and informed him of a "perfect law."[8] Maximinus thereupon hastened to issue an indulgence in his own name so as to preserve at least the appearance of independence.

Licinius was less reluctant to comply and in response to an invitation from Constantine he traveled to Milan in February, 313. There, through the marriage of Licinius to Constantine's sister Constantia, an alliance was sealed and the main lines of future policy were drafted. The chief result was the famous and

7. *DMP*, XLIV, 11.
8. *HE*, IX, 9, 12.

highly controverted Edict of Milan. We have it in two versions. The first was promulgated by Licinius in Nicomedia and the second in Palestine a few months after the victory over Maximinus. We have the first in the Latin of Lactantius[9] and the second in the Greek of Eusebius.[10]

By this edict all persons, Christian and pagan alike, were free to practice their religion so that "whatever divinity there be in heaven may be gracious and favorable to us and all the citizens of the empire." No one would be forbidden the worship or other practices of the Christian religion, so that "the highest divinity whom we freely serve may continue in every way to show grace and favor." Restrictive laws of any sort were to be rescinded. All confiscated houses of worship or other property should be restored. This would serve the public peace, for in this way the divine favor "which in such great things we have experienced" would be won on behalf of the stability of the empire and the common weal.

In Eusebius' *Life of Constantine* a preamble stresses the emperor's concern for religious freedom. "Whereas in the past severe restrictions may have held many from Christian worship, let it now be known that this worship of God is free." More pointedly than in Lactantius' *Nicomedian,* in which reference was made merely to the example of the rulers who, of their own free will, served the Godhead, the Eusebian version declares that previous restrictions were perverse and alien to the benevolence of the emperors.

In a vein reminiscent of Constantine's letters to Africa we have an appeal to "the divine favor manifest in such great events," which must continue to be secured for the existence of the imperium and thereby of the public weal. Also Constantinian is the right of free decision which he had himself exercised and accorded others. Constantinian, likewise, is the proof of gratitude to the divinity by the extension of protection to the Christian re-

9. *DMP*, XLVIII.
10. *HE*, X, 5.

ligion. While the word "divinity" is ambiguous, no one could miss the Christian point of reference on being told that the Godhead was pleased by the restoration of the churches and the freedom accorded to the Christian cultus. The edict of general tolerance especially benefited the Christians. Freedom of decision permitted them to do openly what had hitherto been forbidden. Aid to those on whom plainly the divine favor rested would ensure the good fortune of the state. On the other hand, the expression in the edict, "whatever divinities there may be in heaven," is to be ascribed to the pagan Licinius, a convinced sun worshipper. The Edict of Milan represented for him the very limit of concession. Because of the compromise, the edict, while going beyond Galerius' by restoring the churches, fell short of the privileges granted to the churches in Constantine's letters to Africa. The religious assumptions of the edict include the belief that religion consists in the cultus, on whose proper observance rests the welfare of the state. Since Licinius conceded the rank of first Augustus to Constantine he could do no other than take the lead on the religious question, which was expressly declared to be of greatest importance.[11]

The Lateran Palace, the statue of Constantine, his coin, the

11. J. Moreau ascribes the edict essentially to Licinius on the following grounds: 1) If Licinius had had in his hands a complete document when he departed from Milan he would have issued it immediately on his arrival at Nicomedia instead of waiting four weeks; 2) Eusebius would not have omitted the mandate in the last edition of his work had it really been by Constantine; 3) there was need for an Edict of Toleration only in the territory of Maximinus Daza. For the rest of the empire the Edict of Galerius sufficed. Reply: 1) Licinius was dilatory precisely because the edict was not his work but that of Constantine; 2) Eusebius omitted the Edict of Milan in his last edition because he substituted for it the Edict of Restitution of 324 which went further than the other; 3) Maximinus had already restrained the persecution because of pressure from Constantine and the Edict of Milan went far beyond that of Galerius. Although admittedly the term "Edict of Milan" is not strictly correct as a title it does correctly describe what happened. Compare also Milton V. Anastos, "The Edict of Milan (313). A Defence of its traditional Authorship and Designation," *Revue des Études Byzantines* XXV (1967) pp. 13–41. Anastos rightly connects the "divinitas" of the edict with the inscription on the Roman arc "instinctu divinitatis."

letters to Africa, the letter to the eastern emperor, Maximinus Daza, the Edict of Milan—all these point back to the victory at the Milvian Bridge. They all testify that the emperor had made the inner decision to which he bore witness and had already commenced the work with which his name is linked in history, that as the founder of Christian Europe.

But what does that mean? To be called a Christian can mean everything and nothing. The most difficult questions are not answered but merely posed. What did this step mean for Constantine? How did he understand Christianity? How much did he carry over from paganism? How much did he reject? What bearing did his faith have upon his behavior? What did the decision mean for Constantine himself, for the empire, and for his work?

The difficulty in answering these questions appears at once in the case of the triumphal arch,[12] the one surviving monument of Constantine's time, lying in the depression between the Palatine and the Celian hills. It dominates the Via Triumphalis, the street of Constantine's triumph.

Of white marble, rising to a height of sixty-five feet, it once shone with bright festive colors in honor both of the greatness of the man and of his deeds. Adorned with pillars, statues, and reliefs, the monument depicted the imperial glory. Since the pressure of time and the deficiencies of craftsmanship did not allow for independent composition, reliefs were borrowed from earlier monuments of the second century. The inscription by the Senate over the high arch was framed by scenes taken from depictions of the campaign of Marcus Aurelius against the Marcomanni and by statues of the Dacian captives of Trajan. Also from Trajan's Dacian campaign is the beautiful stone frieze which fills out the spaces on both sides between the arch and the horizontal line above. The dedication is to "the liberator of the city" and "the founder of peace." Over the two side portals are medallions taken from scenes of hunting and sacrifice by Hadrian. In all these

12. Cf. H. P. L'Orange–A. v. Gerkan, "Der spätantike Bildschmuck des Konstantinsbogen," *Studien zur spätantiken Kunstgeschichte* (1939).

carvings, the heads of the emperors originally portrayed were replaced by those of Constantine and his colleagues. Beneath the
statue of Hadrian is a small frieze which runs around the entire
monument, portraying in six scenes Constantine's work of liberation. The series begins on the narrower west side with the
departure of Constantine and his army from Milan. The south
front has the siege of Verona and the battle of the Milvian
Bridge. The narrow east side has the entry into Rome. The
north side, which looks toward the city, depicts the victorious
ruler addressing his soldiers in the forum and, with rich largesses,
inaugurating the good fortune of his age. Old and new are combined and the entire composition brings together many aspects
which explicitly and implicitly betoken the form of the new
age. This is equally true of the details. The columns of the
tetrarchs behind the emperor, as he addresses his troops, show
not only that this is the forum but symbolize the legal validity
of the régime. The lion and the boar from Hadrian's monument
are not just animals of the chase but symbols of the dark forces
imperiling the empire and now mastered by the emperor. The
present rulers succeed to the piety of their predecessors. When
the bodies of the former emperors received the heads of the
new rulers, Constantine appeared making an offering to Diana
and Sylvanus, and Licinius was sacrificing to Apollo and Hercules. But above all, Constantine was again and again brought
into relation with the unconquerable sun. On the left portal
Licinius stands next to Jupiter, but on the right side Constantine
is next to the sun god. As the deity of soldiers, the sun god lays
claim to continued worship from the army and the ruler. The
large round portrayals of the sun and the moon place the entire
composition within the cosmic order.

Whereas the inscription speaks only vaguely of the divinity
which impelled the emperor, the images are clearly unambiguous
and declare their pagan origin. Constantine allowed this. Why?
Was it out of consideration for the religious persuasions of the
majority of his subjects? The Roman Senate, which erected this

arch to honor the incoming emperor, long remained the spokesman for the ancient faith. Did Constantine himself consider
the cult of the "unconquered sun" to be compatible with that of
Christ as "the sun of righteousness"? Perhaps a coin of Constantine showing the cross beside the sun god might provide an
affirmative answer to this question. At any rate, these are the
questions insistently posed by this representative monument.
They permit no hasty reply. They were to attend Constantine
throughout his entire career. For an answer we must look at his
deeds as well as at his words. Only after surveying his entire
work can we venture a judgment.

V. The Road to World Monarchy

Constantine stayed only a few months at Milan and then returned to the Rhine frontier to confront the Franks again. Little
time elapsed between the celebration of the victory over Maxentius at Rome and over the Germans at Trèves. Sometime earlier,
ominous reports had called Licinius to the east. The eastern
Augustus Maximinus Daza interpreted the alliance of the other
two emperors as directed against himself and resolved to act
before they did. With a hastily gathered army and at an unfavorable season of the year he invaded Asia Minor, advanced
into Europe, took Byzantium and Heraclea, and moved into
Thrace. There Licinius met him, also with hastily assembled
troops. The battle took place on April 30, 313. Just like Constantine, Licinius received directives in a dream. An angel dic-
tated to him a prayer, word for word, which he had recorded
on the morrow by a secretary and transmitted to his troops in
order that this supplication might ensure for his army that
heavenly aid which had given the victory at the Tiber.[1] In the
bloody encounter Maximinus was worsted and had to escape
disguised as a slave. His personal guard, deprived of their leader,
offered no resistance. In the course of his flight Maximinus issued
an edict at Nicomedia completely renouncing his religious policy.[2]

1. *DMP*, XLVI.
2. *HE*, IX, 10, 7–11. For the interpretation of the Edict of Maximinus
Daza see *Dö.*, pp. 232–239.

Unlike Galerius, who while terminating the persecution justified it nonetheless, the last of the persecutors threw the blame for the failure upon the others. Beyond the Taurus, sickness and then death (at Tarsus) overtook him late in the summer of the same year, thus completely terminating any possible conflict. Licinius was able to take revenge only on the family and the advisers of his rival. His savagery extended to the wife and daughter of Diocletian who, after the death of Galerius, had placed themselves under the protection of Maximinus. The plea of the aged Diocletian for their lives was unavailing. A few weeks after entering Nicomedia, Licinius, the new lord of the East, issued his proclamation of toleration, the so-called Edict of Milan. A few months later, when he came into control of the remainder of the territory of Maximinus, he promulgated another version in Palestine. These two versions we have already reviewed.

But the alliance between the two victors was not of long duration. In order to stabilize the administration, Constantine reverted to the system of appointing Caesars. This title was conferred upon Bassianus, who was given Constantine's half-sister, Anastasia, to wife. Africa and Italy were entrusted to him by Constantine, and Pannonia, of great military importance, by Licinius. But the new appointee permitted himself to be implicated by his brother, a confidant of Licinius, in a plot against Constantine and was, of course, executed. Licinius refused to allow the guilty brother's extradition and permitted the overthrow in his territory of some of the statues of Constantine. A rapid campaign by Constantine in the fall of 316, marked by one decisive and one indecisive battle, caused Licinius to withdraw from the Balkans except for the southeast. The ensuing peace established a balance of power for nearly a decade. Licinius was allowed to issue laws in the names of both emperors, and the division of the two halves of the empire was not meant to signify a separation. The religious policy established at Milan was still valid in both areas, although Licinius wished to restrict and Constantine to extend the measure of toleration.

Constantine visited Rome briefly for his tenth anniversary, then Gaul, and thereafter made his headquarters at Sirmium-Sardica, near the dangerous Danubian frontier. In the year 317 at Sardica he conferred the title of Caesar on his two oldest sons—Crispus, and Constantine his namesake, who at the time was only a year old. The son of Licinius, by name Licinius, the legitimized child of a slave girl, was also elevated. Thus the dynastic principle had definitely displaced Diocletian's bureaucratic system. The Caesar was now a prince with no territory to rule, though not without early responsibilities. In the next generation the Caesar was to become simply a representative of the emperor.

The "peace" was full of tension and differed little from an armistice except in its duration. The divided rule had not furthered the unity of the empire, as during the first days of the tetrarchy, but rather served to weaken it. This became quite evident when seven years later Constantine, in order to halt the Goths, entered the territory of Licinius, who viewed this as an act of belligerency. War, a long time brewing, then ensued. A sign rather than a cause of the estrangement was Constantine's failure to include Licinius when naming the consuls for the years 321 to 322. As the first Augustus he enjoyed the prerogative, but Licinius took umbrage and countered by naming others. Although such a quarrel over precedence fed suspicion, the growing divergence over religious policy was more serious. Whereas every year Constantine eliminated more pagan vestiges[3]—after 321 the *sol invictus* began to disappear from his coins—Licinius placed his

3. The coins which so directly accompanied the political changes disclose only imperfectly the religious policy of the pagan emperors and that of Constantine only gradually. Compare H. v. Schoenebeck, "Beiträge zür Religionspolitik des Maxentius und Constantin." The evidence from the coins is naturally limited and not to be compared with that of the laws and letters of Constantine, whose proclamations were real speeches. As Duchesne said, "He was always 'sermonizing' his subjects." Cf. *Dö.*, p. 163. Nevertheless, the coins are sometimes decisive, as in the case of the Christ monogram on the coin from Ticinium—the one with the *labarum*—and the coin of the consecration, on which see L. Koep, "Die Konsekrationsmünzen Kaiser Konstantins . . ." (1958). Compare in general K. Aland, "Die religiöse Haltung Kaiser Konstantins" (1957).

reliance all the more definitely on the abandoned gods. An inscription gives evidence that he obligated his soldiers to render the annual service to the Syrian sun god with incense, candles, and sacrificial wine. The last coin depicting an emperor in the act of sacrifice bears Licinius' name. Naturally, the status of the Christian Church in the east deteriorated correspondingly. The historian describes in detail[4] how complete tolerance became ever more restricted and how the scornful tone of the edicts became doubly galling: Is the air bad in the churches? Then, said the edict, the people may worship only out of doors. The emperor is the guardian of good morals; therefore the sexes should hold services separately. The emperor protects the innocent; on that account no priest should instruct female catechumens. Is visiting prisoners a Christian virtue? This is disturbing to civil justice. Synods of the bishops were indispensable for settling questions of common interest. Reason enough that they should be suppressed. Since at a later time the Church venerated martyrs who had suffered under Licinius, and reinstated penitents from his reign, we may infer that overzealous officials did persecute in compliance with the emperor's unspoken wishes. In any case, like Diocletian and his successors, Licinius weeded out the Christians from his court, his army, and his administration. He believed that their prayers would not benefit him because they were offered on behalf of his rival.

This is the place to inquire whether the religious proclamations of the period were intended as propaganda. Modern concepts of psychological warfare and of fifth columns make one wonder whether similar tactics were employed in Constantine's day. Some historians have assumed that the coins and edicts of the era were designed to induce the Christian or pagan subjects of a rival to change sides. The sign on the shield of Constantine is interpreted by them as a device to win the adherence of the Christian congregation in Rome.[5] Similarly, the prayer given to

4. *VC*, II, 1ff.
5. Pauly-Wissowa, *RE*, XIV, 2478 (Groag).

Licinius by the angel was meant to bring about the desertion of the Christian soldiers of Maximinus.[6] These historians assume that religion was then just potent enough to influence believers in the other camp, who themselves were so far emancipated as to use the same device! Can we suppose that the beliefs of the Christians would make them open to this sort of approach? Their faith forbade them to practice civil disobedience so long as they were not called upon to renounce their religion. There may, of course, have been those who did not live up to this ideal. There were apostates, but to continue as Christians they had to submit to penitential discipline. In the pre-Constantinian period we have no example of civil disobedience except for the faith. Later on there were instances, but those guilty were excluded from the fellowship of the Church.

In the wars at the turn of the fourth century we frequently find desertions of whole regiments to the other side. The legions of Severus refused to fight against their old general Maximian. He, in turn, attempted to win over Constantine's troops with money and promises. Maximinus thought in the same way to suborn the army of Licinius. But in all these instances only pagans were involved and religion had nothing to do with their attempts at subversion. Were there enough Christians in the armies of Maximinus and Licinius that it was worthwhile on their account to alienate the pagans by a Christian approach? In the churches misgivings about military service were not extinct. Christianity was not a religion of the camp and however many Christians there may have been in the armies of Diocletian, Galerius, Maximinus, and Licinius, these emperors had done

6. H. Grégoire, "About Licinius' Fiscal and Religious Policy," 551–560. Grégoire's thesis and insights, like bubbles in champagne, have excited and somewhat intoxicated the scholars, but his contentions are not tenable. For discussions of his thesis consult J. Vogt, *Römische Mitteilungen,* LVIII (1943), 190–203 and again *Historia,* II (1953), 463ff; P. Franchi de Cavalieri, *Studi e Testi,* CLXXI (1953), 51ff; F. Vittinghoff, *Rheinisches Museum,* Neue Folge, XCVI (1953), 352ff. F. Winkelmann, "Zur Geschichte des Authentizitätsproblems der Vita Constantini," *Klio,* XL (1962), pp. 187–243, 213; see note 4 for a list of Grégoire's many essays.

their best to root them out. At the very least, officers were demoted so that if there were some Christian soldiers disposed to desert to the enemy, they would have had no leaders. For all of these reasons the Christians did not constitute a military bloc ready to intervene in the political struggle for power.

The one thing which the suspicious Licinius feared on the part of the Christians in his circle was that they might pray for Constantine.[7] Eusebius states that this fear arose from Licinius' bad conscience. Had there been a Christian underground resistance, Eusebius, in relating Constantine's victory, would undoubtedly have emphasized it. But he said only that Licinius by banishing the Christians from his court had lost the benefit of their supplications.

Constantine, when he drew Christians from their passive loyalty into an active share in the political life of the state, was the first person to bring about an atmosphere in which such propaganda would have been feasible. To attribute the creation of such an atmosphere to anyone in earlier times is to succumb to sheer historical fantasy. By the time of Clovis, king of the Franks, such a tactic was quite practicable. When Clovis pledged adherence to the Catholic orthodox faith and then undertook to overcome the Arian Goths in Gaul, he could count on the sympathy of their Catholic subjects. Christians had become so politically minded that religion could be manipulated for political ends.

In the war between Constantine and Licinius the point was not to influence public opinion but to enlist the help of the gods. The contrast between the rivals drove each to an ever more conscious and pronounced effort to ensure divine assistance. Above the visible armies the hosts of heaven would assist in the strife. In that era, it was considered realistic to make sure of a mighty helper from above; but to attempt, by appeals to religious affiliation, to spread disaffection in the ranks of the enemy was undreamed of.

When we come to an account of the campaign we are de-

7. *VC*, I, 52, and II, 2.

pendent upon two sources which complement each other, one by Zosimus[8] and the other by Eusebius.[9] The first, from the pen of a pagan who disliked Constantine and indulged in nasty gossip, rests nevertheless on a superior contemporaneous tradition. Zosimus pictures the events with a sure hand and great vividness, so that we follow closely the extensive preparation which made possible this war, in comparison with which the campaign of 316 appears but a skirmish. Licinius had assembled a mighty fleet from all the maritime provinces and a formidable army from the landed areas. He was firmly entrenched in Adrianople. Constantine had likewise drained his territories to the limit. He had obtained ships from Greece, though by no means in numbers equal to Licinius, and placed Crispus in command.

On the third of July a battle took place at Adrianople. Constantine succeeded in encircling the enemy with his cavalry and on the night of the bitter encounter he took the camp. Zosimus tells us that the fallen numbered 34,000. Many of Licinius' men fled to the mountains but later surrendered to Constantine. Licinius, who had withdrawn with whatever troops remained, entrenched himself in fortified Byzantium. Constantine then laid siege to the city and word was sent Crispus to break into the Hellespont. In the entrance lay the fleet of Licinius, never suspecting an attack from an inferior force. The bold and adroit onslaught of Crispus caught the enemy vessels out of formation and produced such confusion that, with the fall of darkness, they lost all contact with each other. On the following day shifting storms cast many of the remaining ships onto the rocks, thus consummating the disaster. Without any more resistance, the fleet of Crispus sealed off Byzantium by sea.

Licinius escaped to the Asiatic shore with a small company and there hastily gathered new forces. But he was unable to halt Constantine. Near Chrysopolis, across from Byzantium, the decisive conflict occurred on September 18. From the murderous

8. Zosimus, *Historia Nova* (1887), II, 22ff.
9. *VC*, II, 3ff.

onslaught Licinius extricated only about a quarter of his troops and withdrew to Nicomedia. But since Byzantium and Chalcedon had opened their gates to Constantine, Licinius surrendered to the victor. Constantia interceded with her brother for the life of her husband and he was taken to Thessalonica. But there he began to conspire with the Goths and Constantine had no choice but to have him put to death. The struggle for universal monarchy was ended. The empire acknowledged a single lord.

While this outcome was the focus of interest for the pagan historian, the Christian Eusebius preferred to give primary attention to the inner rather than the outer events. The driving forces throughout the struggle had not been those of mortal men. On the one side were the evil demons whose envy could not brook the good fortune of the western half of the empire and who, therefore, drove Licinius to his godless policy. In contrast, God Himself impelled Constantine to deliver the oppressed eastern half of the empire. Licinius is pictured step by step as the exact opposite of Constantine, both before and during the war. Constantine realized that now, if ever, Christian prayers were necessary and strove mightily to merit heavenly protection. He took bishops into his circle and in his own prayer tent prepared himself by pious exercises for visions and leadings from above. Contrariwise, Licinius surrounded himself with soothsayers, sacrificial priests, and magicians, placing himself at the service of their assurances. In the holy grove, after sacrificing to the gods, he delivered an address to his confidants which highlighted the religious difference. He appealed to the ancestral gods whose worship had been handed down by the forefathers. Opposed to them was the "godless illusion," "the strange God . . . and his shameful sign." "Constantine," said Licinius, "is fighting not against us but against the gods. Now we shall see who is wrong. If the gods prove themselves in battle to be true helpers we shall march against all the godless. But if that stranger god wins we have sacrificed to our gods in vain. We shall know what to do, for one must follow the conquering god." Eusebius says that this speech was reported to him by one of the hearers. Here we have Licinius behaving like Maximinus, who, before the battle against Licinius, made vows to Jupiter for a renewal of the Christian persecution.

At the beginning of the battle Constantine proclaimed the name of the savior God as the watchword and instructed a select company of his guard to carry the "victory-giving sign," the *labarum*, at all endangered posts. Everywhere it proved its miraculous power. Licinius after his defeat, perceiving the powerlessness of his gods, reported to other more numerous helpers, that is, the gods of the Goths. Since he recognized the secret power of the Constantinian *labarum* he counseled avoiding it and would not even look at it. Instead he placed the old Roman standards with the images of the gods at the head of his troops and, relying on these, commenced the last battle. Again he lost and Constantine won the final victory, over both the enemy and the demons. Licinius, and those who counseled him to fight against the Christian God, had received their due recompense. They learned too late that Constantine's God was the true and only God. The reunited empire now had one head, and to the monarchy of God corresponded the monarchy of the Roman Empire. Such was the account of Eusebius.

In this last encounter the issue had been that of universal monarchy—he does not disguise it. Not only did the outcome of the war settle the question of what religion would dominate in the empire but religion throughout the war had determined its course. Both sides sought assistance from heaven. The *vexilla* (banner) of the gods stood over against the banner of Christ. For Licinius the struggle was a test of the power and therefore of the authority of the gods. But Constantine with the help of his God won on the Bosporus as he had at the Tiber; the sign of the Savior triumphed over his enemy and his enemy's gods. Such was his view, but this does not mean that he was fighting or seeking to extend the faith by violence. Even the crusades and the religious wars, which to our thinking so perversely combined religion and politics, nevertheless separated religion and politics more clearly than antique thinking could ever do. Constantine was able to fight only under the aegis of religion, but not on its behalf.

A coin expresses the significance of the great victory. On it the *labarum* is represented severing a serpent, the banner of the cross thus overcoming the demonic powers. The war did not simply involve two earthly rulers and two armies but reached beyond the human sphere. This same concept was graphically represented on the gable of the entry to the imperial palace at Constantinople. There stands the emperor with his sons, the cross above their heads, the dragon beneath their feet, who, pierced, falls away into the abyss.

The emperor himself voiced his own understanding of the events in two proclamations issued after the victory. In these addresses he presented himself and his program to his new subjects. The genuineness of the first edict[10] was for a long time a subject of bitter controversy, for modern historians simply would not believe that so many wrongs remained to be righted on behalf of the victims of earlier and later persecutions. However, a recent discovery has silenced all doubt. On the reverse of a receipt an Egyptian chancellery noted down the provisions of the edict for its own official use.[11] The edict was issued in two forms; one addressed to the Christians, the other to the pagans. Only the second is extant. It counsels listening to the voice of history, the instructor in righteousness, that admonishes the emperor to annul the injustice committed by others. Those who participated in this injustice are called upon to make such restitution as is possible. In particular the edict decrees that those

10. *Ibid.,* II, 24ff. Whereas previously this document was commonly regarded as spurious, its genuineness has been established through the discovery of a papyrus from the office of an imperial administrator. This example enforces the maxim that the resources of interpretation should first be exhausted before having recourse to surgery to obviate difficulties.

11. *Papyrus Londiniensis,* 878. Consult A. H. M. Jones, "Notes on the Genuineness of the Constantinian Documents in Eusebius' Life of Constantine" (1954) and J. Winkelmann, "Die Textbezeugung der vita Constantini" (1962) pp. 60–70, 121–131.

banished can return to their homes and property; those condemned to compulsory labor and slavery should be freed; demoted army officers might resume their rank unless they preferred an honorable discharge; the goods of the martyrs should go to the heirs, if any, otherwise to the Church; to the Church also belong the tombs of those who witnessed with their blood, as the monuments of their glorious departure; those who held Christian goods unjustly must make immediate restitution—this would be an act of penance, making amends to the emperor and to God in order that He might pardon the offense; a person who had purchased such unjustly seized property might be indemnified after restoration; what the *fiscus* had impounded must be returned to the Church. The second edict, however, which will later receive a more detailed analysis, proclaims tolerance no longer for the Christians, as in the Edict of Milan, but rather for the pagans.

VI. The Mission

Rector totius orbis, ruler of the whole world.[1] This inscription on a coin in honor of the victor at Rome now for the first time received full realization. The conquest of Licinius made Constantine a world ruler. This was a great hour. What was its significance?

We are not lacking in contemporary testimony, for in this period we have the most important documents from the pen of Constantine. In two proclamations he addressed himself to his new subjects.[2] The very form of these documents is striking. In other instances imperial edicts had brief preambles stating the principles, but here the entire compositions deal with fundamentals and no part can be singled out as conveying the genuine meaning. When Diocletian appealed to the laws given by God and called for a return to what was originally valid, he had no need to offer reasons and demanded no personal decision on the part of those addressed. But Constantine could not stop at hortatory reminiscences. He had to convey the significance of what had happened, elicit the lessons implied, and bring home their demands. For this the traditional form did not suffice.

The victory [so said the victor] speaks for itself. The fall of the persecutors and the vindication of the persecuted disclose the power as well as the justice of God. These events were simply the

1. Alföldi, "The Helmet of Constantine" (1932), p. 21, no. 16.
2. VC, II, 24ff., and II, 48ff.

culmination of what had been taking place before the eyes of all during the last two centuries. A criminal hatred of mankind had tried to stamp out justice and pious reverence—to the great harm of the empire. The attempt was bound to collapse. Here plainly, said Constantine, history seems to be ruled by divine Providence. If this insight was first apparent only to the perceptive, recent events must have opened the eyes of all. The emperor therefore demands that everyone observe what a turning point in the fortunes of the empire this power and grace have brought about. He attributes to his hearers the perception of this reality and leaves each for himself to deduce the demands entailed. Those who hitherto have walked in the darkness of corruption must now reverse their direction. By thus turning to righteousness of their own accord and by assisting it, they will make the proper expiation. But still, this appeal to embrace the hitherto-rejected truth is not the primary point of originality and peculiarity in this pronouncement of Constantine's in the year 324.

The emperor appeals to the experience of all, and not as if he were simply the first to have grasped the meaning of what has happened; nor does he speak simply as the herald of the truth enshrined in the event. To a very exceptional degree he was himself the prime factor in that hour of victory which he was interpreting. He had brought it to pass. Therefore men should know what he was, what he willed, and what he ought to do. Most emphatically the emperor insists that he is only the tool of a higher power. "Only through the power, summons and help of the Almighty God" had he been able to bring about the work called for by the empire's need. Constantine realizes that he has been sent to fulfill a higher will. But the commission is not ended here. That which thus far has been accomplished looks beyond. "By a higher power I have dispelled the terrors, that I might bring men back to the service of the holy law and that the All Highest should lead them to the faith."[3] The education of mankind—that looks to the future. Justice, the acknowledgment of

3. *Ibid.*, II, 28; cf. II, 65.

God, and true reverence should be combined; the hearts of all peoples must be united to achieve the renewal of the world already under way. The emperor thus sees himself confronted by a double task: to knit the shredded world together once more into a vital whole and to bring the minds of all into a complete unity.

The mission,[4] then, had two objectives: to restore the empire and to renew the world. Both were implicit in the titles bestowed upon Constantine as the seal of the past and the sign of the future. For Constantine was no revolutionary who, with only the might of his fist and the destiny of his star, overturned the established and rejected the valid. From the very beginning he had undertaken to legitimize his authority, and consequently his titles became more pretentious with the rise of his fortunes. He had been delegated by his father, called by the army, recognized by the emperor in the east, elevated by the "Herculean" Maximian, and dynastically legitimized by marriage to Maximian's daughter, and he had been named by the Senate as the first Augustus. Finally, above all else, the emperor could claim that God Himself had entrusted the earth to his sway. This assurance did not abrogate the earlier titles but went beyond them to an election transcending all human suffrage. God was the source of the highest authority. But by that very token Constantine could not claim to be God. The cult of the divine ruler was at an end. The emperor himself was only a "servant." The title of this chosen one was not "the God Emperor" but "the Servant."

As "Servant" Constantine took his place in that "hour" to which he referred: as one still in service he confronted the future. Only now did the title become fully significant for him. If the first duty assigned were a service, how much more the work which he had yet to complete! A goal beyond the power of man opened before him. In peculiar contrast to this exaltation stood the title of servant by which he should be known. There was here, however,

4. Constantine's sense of mission will have matured slowly. His later utterances indicate that the beginning was in Britain, that is to say, on July 25, 306, when the soldiers hailed him at York.

no idle self-deprecation, for Constantine never hesitated to lay claim to the attributes of imperial majesty. Enthroned at Constantinople, he wore a band of pearls above his head, the diadem, as a visible token of the highest dignity. But he stopped short of self-deification, as earlier emperors had not. Constantine had no objection to the enhancement of pretensions and titles when meaningful and necessary, but he observed the bounds. Where the task exceeds human capacity there is need for a power beyond that of man. The emperor becomes the servant of a power incapable of nothing. By virtue of this power he may essay the very greatest tasks. This is the sense in which the loftiness of the goal befitted the modesty of the title.

Constantine was fully aware of the distinctiveness of this assignment, which for him was "the best service"[5] and the "grace vouchsafed." This he joyfully confessed in a very personal tone. "I firmly believe that I owe utterly and completely my whole soul, every breath and that which nerves my innermost thoughts to the great God . . . therefore I have brought to Thee my soul in love and fear." The assignment, understood both as service and as a gift, demanded not only obedience but complete commitment.

The man to whom a mission has been entrusted is determined by his view of history; the meaning of this mission is defined for him by what he regards as the basic issues of his time and their final solution. When a public orator delivered a panegyric in honor of an imperial victory he would refer to the toilsome and dangerous road which had led to the present heights. The extent of the contribution was measured by showing how dire had been the extremity from which the victor had given deliverance and how much gratitude he therefore deserved. The panegyric served only to enhance the reputation of the one celebrated and did not go beyond the achievement, which left nothing more to be desired or done.

But such was not the case with Constantine. His mission lay

5. On Constantine as "God's servant" see VC, II, 28; II, 29; III, 20.

like a great arc, spanning the past and the future, and over-arching the present. The ordinary panegyric would have covered the decline of the empire, the civil war up to the peace, and would have stopped with the universal monarchy. But now the arc stretched from the persecution to the renewal of the world. The past was adduced, not to exalt the present but to show what still remained to be done. Here for the first time we have the full context, which makes use of the past for the future and only by reference to that future can grasp its own meaning.

Constantine's review starts with the great persecution and the dark background of subsequent events, tarries over the martyrs, and comes to a climax with the fall of the persecutors. Whatever the relation of the political and the religious may have been at the outset, by now they were inextricably bound together. The persecution, not the disintegration or the political debility of the empire, was the deeper cause, rather than the apparent occasion which prompted God's saving intervention and the sending of His servant. The "dragon driven from the leadership of the state" was more than a mere tyrant. This shows how Constantine interpreted his own life's history. His mission and his under-standing of the past corresponded to the decision he had made in the great conflict of his age. This also determined his stand toward the Roman past. Whereas on the triumphal arch he had been placed between the good emperors Trajan and Marcus Aurelius, Constantine now appealed to none of his predecessors. The only one who still meant anything to him was his own father, because he was no persecutor and could therefore be included by his son in the new era. This is quite a fresh interpretation of history since the very emperor who considered that he had restored the Roman Empire made no reference to the great figures of the Roman past. At the same time, this concept of history in terms of a great religious decision produced consider-able freedom since Constantine felt constrained to reject only the pagan element in the old culture. Therefore, while condemn-ing Diocletian as a persecutor, he nevertheless could take over what Diocletian had done for the consolidation of the empire and the army to such a degree that he can be regarded as the fulfiller of Diocletian's work.

If Constantine had been only a military emperor he might have rested on his laurels or, like Alexander, he might have looked for more worlds to conquer. Had he been only an administrator he might have been content to repair the damages of the civil war and build up the internal organization. But then he would not have fulfilled what his age required of him and what his mission demanded. He understood well and publicly declared that his task began at the very point where others considered it to have been completed, when by overcoming Licinius he had recovered the unity of the empire in the year 324. Precisely because this date marked an epoch both for the empire and for himself, Constantine felt called upon to grasp the significance of the hour and to consummate his mission.

This is the burden of the ruler's speech to his subjects—of one sent by God speaking to those who were entrusted to him: they should follow him on the way of the new era. They, too, must understand what his mission involved and what the time demanded. On the basis of personal persuasion the people, too, should essay this venture, and not simply obey a command promising a golden future. At the point where power and command are insufficient, there free decision and trustful cooperation are called for. This had to be set forth in words because only by intelligent confidence could the ruler's goal be achieved. Now that the subjects understood the past and grasped the present, they should renounce the old error and turn to the truth. For them also the work and the mission of Constantine set the horizons which both in retrospect and prospect invested this point of time with such significance. The great addresses in which the emperor summoned his subjects to join him on the way would be unthinkable at any other time, but at this point are highly necessary because his clarification brought out the meaning of the hour which would otherwise have been missed. Constantine's mission called for the word as well as the deed.

Three factors combined to confer greatness on the historical point whose significance we have been probing. The first was the victory which restored the empire. The second was the comprehension on the part of the victor of the significance of what was happening and consequently of his own misson. The third was the appeal to his subjects to enter, of their own accord, with him upon the new path.

The most enduring monument Constantine erected to his name
was the new capital.

VII. Constantinople

The most enduring monument Constantine erected to his name
was the new capital. What Alexandria was for Hellenism, Antioch
for west Syria, and Seleucia for east Syria, Constantinople was for
the later Roman Empire. It was not only the center of the empire
but simultaneously the seat and symbol of an entire culture.
How did it come to be founded?

In 326 Constantine had made another visit to Rome to celebrate his twentieth anniversary, his first since his residence in the
liberated city during 312–13 and a brief return in 315 for his
tenth anniversary. It was also his last visit. When the Senate,
which at first received him as a liberator and thanked him for
the confirmation of some of its honors and rights, was not accorded its customary political importance and when Constantine
embraced the new faith as well, relations became strained.
Constantine departed, leaving the ancient mistress of the world
to solace herself with dreams of former greatness.

In the same year that the emperor fully achieved his goal,
tragedy darkened his own household. His eldest and most promising son Crispus came under his father's darkest suspicions.[1] The
court pronounced him guilty and he was executed at Pola. But
then his stepmother, who had accused him, came under the

1. According to the most trustworthy relation, Crispus was accused of
adultery with his stepmother, Fausta (Gen. 39, 7ff). About the divergent
sources, compare O. Seeck in footnote no. 2.

judgment of her husband. We are not in a position to determine innocence or guilt. Was Constantine an autocrat jealous of the competence of the young man? Did the emperor, who had issued several edicts in that very year on marital infidelity, treat more severely a dereliction in his own household? In any case the severe sentence was a misfortune also for the empire. The sons of Fausta were not able to carry on the work of the father as Crispus could have done.[2]

The heathen historian relates[3] that in consequence of his son's execution Constantine was so hated in Rome that he decided to build another capital. At the same time Constantine's conversion to the new faith was explained on the grounds that the Christians were the only ones who would forgive his blood guiltiness. Yet this historian did not refrain from portraying the new founding with occasional pagan embellishments. Eusebius, on the other hand, ascribed Constantine's resolve to his desire for a capital free from all heathen associations.

As a matter of fact Constantine had never considered making Rome his capital any more than Diocletian had. The importance and the imperiled position of the eastern regions demanded the presence of the regent and the transfer thither of the central point of the imperial administration. Neither Sardica nor Nicomedia could have fulfilled the role played for centuries by Constantinople. It lay precisely at the point where the land route from Europe to Asia crossed the sea route from the Mediterranean to the Black Sea. What Constantine had in mind is disclosed by the report that he had thought of building on the site of ancient Troy, whence Aeneas had set forth to found Rome. By selecting the very site of Rome's origin he could erect a sister city equal in dignity. Some think that the soldier's eye settled for the place

2. On the so-called "murder" of Constantine's relatives consult O. Seeck, *Die Verwandtenmorde Konstantins des Grossen* (1890). Though by no means tender toward Constantine, he does not use the word "murder" with reference to any of the executions. In point of fact the amount of blood shed under Constantine by no means equalled that under his predecessors.
3. Zosimus, II, 30.

whose strategic strength he had already experienced. Certainly from the political and the economic point of view the choice was eminently felicitous. It has been well said that the building of this city would have of itself sufficed to rank Constantine among the great figures of history.

Constantinople[4] was a new city of great distinctiveness and yet closely bound to the noble memories which she felt called upon to preserve. This was true also of the traditions attached to the locality. The imperial city was not in every respect a new foundation. The old Greek colony of Byzantium had proved its worth even under the Macedonian and Persian overlords and at the beginning of the third century had compelled Septimus Severus, the demolisher, to build it up again. Similarly, immediately after the successful siege, Constantine had repaired the damage. Shortly thereafter he conferred on the city its even greater role.

A wall from the Golden Horn to the Sea of Marmora protected the city, four times enlarged, against attack from the continent. The plan maintained the contours of the old Byzantium and, at the same time, imitated Rome. It was built on seven hills, divided into fourteen districts, with a forum, a senate chamber, and an imperial palace. Although this was a Greek city the inhabitants called themselves "Romans."

The old market of the Severi, with its hall of columns, in enlarged form remained the center of the imperial city. In honor of Constantine's mother, Helena, the place was called *Augusteion* and was adorned with her statue. The Church of Sophia was built on the northeast side. To be sure, the great Hagia Sophia dates back from the time of Justinian, but its predecessor, a basilica, dates from the time of Constantine and was finished by his son Constantius. Constantine himself enlarged the old

4. Compare A. M. Schneider, *Konstantinopel. Gesicht und Gestalt einer geschichtlichen Weltmetropole* (1956). This work, which appeared only after the author's death, is a beautiful description of the physical and spiritual life of the city. Also R. Janin, *Constantinople Byzantine* (1950).

Christian meetinghouse on the Acropolis. Perhaps at this time it was given the name *Irene* (peace), that after the long wars it might proclaim and foster the peace of the new age. The eastern end of the *Augusteion* was marked by the curial senate building with its marble colonnades.

On the long southern side the Hippodrome and the forecourt of the imperial palace divided the space. The gardens pertaining to the palace and the smaller buildings reached to the shore of the Sea of Marmora. We can form some idea of the appearance of the palace on the basis of ruins recently discovered of another palace of Constantine at Trèves, but we cannot distinguish very well from the ruins at Constantinople those portions for which Constantine was responsible. Eusebius restricts himself to a description of the "guardian sign of the empire." A cross in gold mosaic inlaid with costly stones occupied the middle of the ceiling of the great throne room.[5] As at the beginning of his conquering course, so at the pinnacle, the Cross watched over his entire rule. The same spirit is enshrined in the inscription which once graced the lintel of a door leading to the sea. A part of it was found in the ruins of the wall of the palace building directly on the seashore.[6] The inscription is addressed to Christ, who, because of Constantine's constant veneration of the Divinity, had helped him to extinguish the fire of the tyrant and had granted him lordship over the whole earth.

By going through four gates one passed from the *Augusteion* to the Hippodrome. Constantine completed on a greater scale a structure begun a century earlier by Severus. The chariot course measured four hundred and forty yards to the turning pillar. The Dioscuri, whose temple was brought into the area, watched over the lists. The long-famous serpent column from Delphi, dedicated by the victors at Plataea, was transported and erected on the broad wall between the chariot courses in the center, against

5. *VC*, III, 49.
6. Compare E. Mamboury and T. Wiegand, *Die Kaiserpaläste von Konstantinopel* (1934), pp. 7–9 and Fig. 16.

the emperor's lodge, where it still stands to this day. Of the heads which were knocked off in the eighteenth century only one has been found, and this one imperfect, but it is enough to show that the pillar was a work of artistic distinction.

On the west side of the area was the *milarion* (milestone), the hall of the gate from which, as from its Roman model, the miles of the imperial roads were reckoned. No longer could one say that "all roads lead to Rome." In the northwest and somewhat to the rear stood the basilica in which the newly founded university held its classes. The library was constructed close by at a later date.

Above the northern hall of pillars on the *Augusteion* stood two temples. The one belonged to *Tyche* (Fate). Constantinople from now on was, like Rome, to have its goddess *Fortuna* depicted on the coins. The other was dedicated to Rhea.[7] The full-length statue, gray with age, of *Magna Mater* and her two lions had previously stood on the south shore of the Sea of Marmora on the eminence above Cyzicus where the mariners could invoke her aid, but now, in her new position, the arms which had kept her lions in leash were raised in prayer to heaven. From the goddess to whom prayers were addressed she had become herself the intercessor, to beseech divine favor on the city. This is an amazing transformation. How can it be interpreted? Doubtless a statue of a god was not moved to a new location simply as a work of art. Nor was she given a new name, as Isis, for instance, became Mary, nor adopted into a sort of Christian pantheon. She had divested herself of all her power and had entered into the service of the new God. Since she kept her name and watched over the city only through her intercession, she had come to play a role comparable to that of an angel. This, of itself, precluded any sacrifice to her but did not forbid the adoration offered to the saints, who also were intercessors. To the

7. Zosimus, II, 31. According to Hesychios (VI, 4), Constantine found an older temple already there. In that case he built on an older tradition in order to rear on the site a new cultus.

pagans this must have appeared as a dethroning of the Divine Mother. Zosimus reproached Constantine with irreverence. Constantine however did not view this transformation as a pedagogical device, that is, as a gentle way of leading the pagans to the new faith. Nor could he admit the new goddess in the style of the syncretism of late antiquity. For him the statue in her new position meant that the goddess herself had been converted. From the uplifted arms of Rhea we can perceive the significance which Constantine attached to intercession as one of the pillars of his religion.

Leaving the *Augusteion,* around which the most important buildings were clustered, and going through the portico into the new portion of the city, one reached the Forum of Constantine, begirt by a circle of columns. In the center rose a porphyry column nearly a hundred feet in height.[8] According to fifth-century accounts, this was surmounted by a gold-bedecked statue of the emperor. The diadem was believed to include a nail from the Holy Cross and the column had, in addition, a piece of the Cross for the protection of the city. The claim to be the new Rome was indicated when Constantine set the palladium of ancient Rome beneath the column. All three: the adoration of the Cross, the pride in the symbol of ancient Rome, and the continued remembrance of the founder of the city, were combined in the porphyry column which for a thousand years distinguished the center of Constantinople. Until the fall of the city it was the ground and hope planted in the hearts of the inhabitants. Called "the burned column," it still stands today. If we go down the main street, called the *Mese,* which runs parallel to the sea coast, we come to the broad square known as the *Philadelphion,* adorned with a high cross and statues of the sons of the emperor. South of the *Mese,* near the harbor, where the commercial life

8. This pillar in the course of the centuries has been covered by a rank growth of legend, pagan and Christian. Suffice it to mention some of the literature. The thesis of Preger that Constantine was a "sun emperor" (T. Preger, "Konstantinos-Helios") has been refuted by J. Karayannopulos, "Konstantin der Grosse und der Kaiserkult" (1956).

of the city pulses, we come upon several churches and great memorials to the martyrs. According to Eusebius, Constantine had dedicated his city to "the God of the martyrs." We may well believe the report that in this new section of the city no more bloody sacrifices and burnt offerings were practiced. But in the remaining temples of the old city the pagan rites continued undisturbed.

From the *Philadelphion* the street branches off and takes us to the northwest edge of the city, to an imposing structure on one of the hills, the Church of the Apostles. With this church Constantine combined both his family's and his own mausoleum. Corridors of pillars in a broad expanse surround the church. From the outside the eye is dazzled by the gold-bedecked roof and the artistic trellis. Only the inside discloses the full beauty of the "inexpressible height" of the sanctuary. The walls are inlaid with stones of many colors and the gold of the ceiling arches over the space with indefinable charm.

Many of the buildings with which the emperor sought to embellish his foundation are features appertaining to any ancient city: aqueducts, cisterns, and baths. A horde of statues assembled from all parts of the empire adorned the market place and the streets. A motive for their placement may have been to profane statues previously standing in temples.[9] To be sure, only the impotence of the gods was disclosed by thus bringing them out into public gaze, rather than, as the Christian Eusebius believed, that the people should be repelled by their ugliness. Constantine himself certainly had no such thought. He appreciated their loveliness and his chief desire was to beautify his city. He removed the Muses from their temple at Helicon to his palace—certainly not for the sake of profaning repulsive idols.

Inevitably the light which shone so brilliantly on this city cast its shadows elsewhere, for the cities despoiled of their treasures

9. Socrates has only this to record, that pictures and a tripod were brought to Constantinople "to destroy the superstition of the heathen." *Hist. Eccl.*, I, 16.

did not relish the loss, nor were the pagans very happy about it. A critic from the old faith taxed Constantine with squandering public funds and building shabbily in his haste,[10] for some edifices had to be propped up or reconstructed. And indeed the Church of the Apostles was so far restored by Constantine's son that he was later regarded as the real builder.[11] Private buildings financed by voluntary munificence or at imperial command were added to those constructed by the emperor. Reduction of taxes and transfers of population filled the city with men. Christians were in the majority but there were also Jews and pagans. The emperor invited Roman senators to transfer their residences and built stately houses for them. Few of the old families responded to this invitation, which was accepted chiefly by the Christians. The new Senate, recruited from the Greek cities, enjoyed social rank though not political powers. But well into the Middle Ages this Senate boasted of its Roman origin and the late Byzantine rulers called themselves the emperors of the Romans.

Although the second Rome had an active manufacture and a lively commerce, it confronted many of the same economic difficulties as did the first Rome—and met them no better. Here, too, the populace of the new capital assembled in the forum only to receive doles of wheat, which here, as at Rome, sustained the masses in life and good humor. And in Constantinople, too, it was a case of *panem et circenses,* bread and circus. In the Hippodrome, the Byzantine *circus maximus,* the masses thronged toward the chariot courses; here the emperor showed himself in his lodge to the people and received their acclamation. Sometimes the cheers were mingled with petitions, and on occasion, complaints.

10. Zosimus, II, 31.
11. G. Downey, "The Builder of the Original Church of the Apostles at Constantinople" (1951). André Grabar *Martyrium,* 1, (1946), 228ff. interprets the Constantinian structure as modeled on tombs of the Hellenistic founders of cities, but Constantine's mausoleum lay on the outskirts, not at the center of the city, at a considerable remove from the imperial palace, not close to it as in the case of Hellenistic "heroes."

However questionable we may think the policy of supporting the capital populace on doles, we must remember that the city was not just a cluster of huts inhabited by begging hordes. Constantinople acquired character. Although at first the people shared few responsibilities, nevertheless in future emergencies they showed solidarity. The walls which cut them off from the outer world were also defended against attacks with advanced techniques and exemplary courage. Daughter and rival of Rome, Constantinople competed with the mother in vitality and capacity.

On May 11, 330, the city was officially dedicated, although the construction was by no means complete. Zosimus tells us that the nativity of the city was celebrated with astrological rites of dedication and that the Neoplatonic philosopher Sopatros participated. One should not be surprised if Constantine were not emancipated from astrological superstition—and one should not suppose that he retained ancient usages merely with regard to public opinion. The other rites, however, were Christian, for we read that processions went up from the Constantinian forum singing *Kyrie Eleison* to solemnize the services of religion. In the Hippodrome chariot races took place and the baths of *Zeuxippos* were opened. A specially minted silver coin expressed the significance of the day for the empire. It shows on the imperial scepter a union of the cross and the circle of the earth. The capital of the world began its rule under the Christian sign. Two other coins were minted, one of Rome, the other of Constantinople. They correspond to each other but only the second has the laurel. Whereas in another pair of coins the city of Romulus has the wolf, the city of Constantine has the *Victoria*.

The emperor founded the city "at the command of God."[12] He gave to it an "eternal name," for the "Eternal City" was its title—a title which to us seems shockingly pretentious. But Constantine was persuaded that there was no arrogance here because he had acted in obedience to a higher will.

12. Theodosianus, XIII, 5, 7, *"pro commoditate urbis, quam aeterno nomine iubente deo donavimus."*

VIII. The Organization of the Empire

How, in a time of intense crisis, can an empire be ordered? After a period of uncertain probings and disillusioned efforts there may well be an attempt to restore the tried and proven. If, however, those long outlawed come into power they may be expected to sweep aside the shattered structure and start all over again. But neither restoration nor revolution does justice to things as they are. A third, more sober approach takes full account of what has happened, realizes what is now called for, and does what can be done. This is the more realistic method, however varied the insight, capacity, and spirit of the participants.

Constantine often referred to the "ancient law," yet we cannot think of him as merely a restorer, in view of the reproach of Julian the Apostate that he was a "wrecker of the old order";[1] nor, on the other hand, can we regard him as a revolutionary lacking in a sense of tradition, for he retained doggedly the basic administrative scheme of Diocletian. Constantine in fact took the third course. How he did so is made apparent by what he retained and what he rejected.

The very hub of the late Roman Empire was the emperor.[2] In his person all power was concentrated and all duties converged. The uncontested conviction of the age was that the unity and stability of the entire structure depended on him. None of

1. Ammianus Marcellinus, *Rerum Gestarum Libri*, XXI, 10, 8.
2. Ensslin, "Gottkaiser und Kaiser von Gottes Gnaden" (1943).

the old administrative organs sufficed. The need to defend far-flung frontiers required an increasing army, which in turn necessitated coordination of all parts of the empire, not the least with respect to finances. The old organs of government were deficient and the frontier provinces were not able to defend themselves unaided. In consequence the process whereby they came to be merged and forfeited their local qualities was accelerated. In every area the need was apparent to bolster and direct residual forces. In the imperial office the need found its help and the question its answer; increasingly, throughout the late Roman Empire the conviction deepened that the well-being of society depended upon this power. The more, then, the hopes and expectations of the people fastened themselves upon the person of the emperor, the greater must be his own inner resources. No longer could he be carried along by the firm structure of the old order. He must himself create and ensure a viable structure.

Diocletian had established the full independence of the imperial office when he emancipated it from military control. There was no need of emancipation from senatorial control since the Senate was now impotent. Only after Constantine had invested the imperial office with undisputed authority could the empire confront the new era without fear of inner disintegration. Constantine appeared to be nullifying his very intent when he refused any longer to allow his image to be set up in temples and forbade all sacrifice to the emperor. This was the decisive change.[3] He ran, thereby, a great risk, for a lowering of prestige was dubious even when the state was running smoothly, and to demean the luster of the throne while instituting a new order might well prove disastrous. That Constantine was able to keep the dignity of the imperial office intact and even to enhance its power and glory explains how he managed to discharge his historical task. He knew how to persuade men of his divine mission. He kept intact the prerogatives of his office, and united both the

3. *VC*, IV, 16, and II, 44.

name and the claim of his dignity through the sheer power of his personality which induced even opponents to follow his course. They recognized his contributions and even the rage of his enemies testified to his greatness.

The emperor's palace in the new capital was the hub of the empire from which all administration radiated. The civil servants became courtiers. The officials met in the *consistorium* which surrounded the throne. The *comites*—we might almost call them the cabinet—in whose hands lay the administration of the empire, were the emperor's private servants who executed his will alone. The *quaestor sacri palatii,* minister of the sacred palace, drafted the laws. The finance minister bore the title of *comes sacrarum largitionum.* His chief assignment was to distribute the largesses bestowed by the emperor's generosity and regularly expected by officers and officials. The *comes rerum privatarum* looked after the emperor's private exchequer and received the revenues from the crown lands. The *magister officiorum* was the chief of the emperor's personal bodyguard. He was also the master of ceremonies for great functions and headed the corps of domestics. He also supervised the body of notaries (*schola notariorum*) and the Emperor's commissaries (*schola agentium in rebus*). In control of the local administration and frequently in charge of the secret police,[4] these commissaries enabled the emperor to implement his will quickly in any part of the empire, despite the complexity of the administrative machinery. For particularly important missions he could also send out some of the *comites* from his immediate circle. The once so-powerful Praetorian prefects lost their place at the court. In the days of the military emperors they had attained the greatest political significance as commanders of the guard and often enough usurped the purple. Now they were deprived of their military command and placed at the

4. In this function they made use of informers. Constantine detested the informers but found like other emperors that the system could not get along without them.

head of the civil and juridical administration, above the governors of the provinces and dioceses. In every other respect, too, the civil and the military were sharply differentiated.

The administration, thus concentrated in the palace, bore a distinctively Constantinian stamp. And traces of Constantine's reorganization are to be discovered also at many other points. Taken as a whole, however, this was still not a new empire or a new system of government. The great administrative machinery of the late Roman state continued its course. The fiscal system and the bureaucracy followed their own laws without being essentially altered even by so energetic a single ruler. The basic lines of Diocletian's initial reform remained under his successor, who merely moved more rapidly along the highway already mapped out. When the spirit of the new ruler comes unmistakably to the fore it is usually in the area of specific enactments. Here and there Constantine injected a new dynamism. At one point he mitigated, at another increased harsh measures, when confronted by emergencies which he could not bend to his will. His legal enactments best disclose his measures of relief. They left no branch of the administration untouched, without, however, instituting a thoroughgoing reconstruction.[5]

In his new enactments Constantine appealed to the ancient law,[6] and the changes, deep as they were, never broke with legal tradition. The juristic order was emphatically maintained and protected against encroachment. His statement that "public justice must hold to its established course," though directed to a spe-

5. It goes without saying that the emperor's personal share in the edicts issued in his name is difficult to isolate. But when one finds characteristic expressions and ideas of frequent recurrence one may assume that they go back to him and this is doubly so in the case of passages with a passionate tone issued in the name of an emperor who was not inclined to commit himself to secretaries. But the question of genuineness is complicated by the intrusion in this period of "rhetoric" in the drafting of laws, so that harsh enactments were couched in more humane terms.

6. A collection of Constantine's enactments is given in *Dö.*, pp. 162–207, 266ff.

cial case had, at the same time, a universal validity. The justice of a sentence of imprisonment must be evident to all. Bounds must be set upon "raging judges."

Constantine was personally and passionately concerned to check the system of denunciations. A large number of laws dealt with this point, so that no official could be in a position to utilize any, perchance all too welcome, denunciations. The sordid documents were to be promptly burned. If one "of the accursed horde of talebearers" were detected, his tongue should be torn out before execution, in order to eradicate this "evil, among the greatest afflicting mankind." This is a striking example of the contradiction between an entrenched system and the personal will and feeling of its ruler. A bureaucratic state could not dispense with secret agents to check on the attitudes of the officials and of the populace; nevertheless, the ruler took umbrage every now and then over flagrant instances of abuse, without making clear to himself to what extent they were conditioned by the whole administrative method of late antiquity.

A number of laws had to do with the securing of evidence. Torture was still used, especially upon slaves. The testimony of an eyewitness was not to be accepted without corroboration. A single witness would not suffice, and along with oral testimony written documents were admitted. Cruel abuses of official authority were severely punished, to the point of burning the offender. Even those in the emperor's immediate circle enjoyed no immunity. Constantine encouraged any who felt themselves aggrieved to appeal directly to him and if the charge were substantiated he would not withhold vengeance upon an assumed but faithless friend. His own welfare and that of the state depended upon the integrity of administrators. The emperor protected the juridical system against himself as well. His ordinances show that the absolute monarch was not arbitrary, even though legally no area was beyond his jurisdiction.

But conservatism and caution were not characteristic of Constantine's legal enactments, as they had been in the case of Diocletian.[7] The lack of parallels in Constantine's time to the legal decisions of his predecessor was not due simply to a decline in legal competence. Constantine himself was of no mind to disentangle legal snarls and hence his impatience cut through stacks of regulations. Whereas Diocletian had issued rescripts, Constantine simply enacted new laws. The result was that where Roman jurisprudence had proceeded with caution and moderation, Constantine's indignation blazed out against corrupt officials, sneaky delators, brutal draymen, and inflicted sharp penalties. The rage of the ruler was not always restrained within the bounds of reason, nor did the punishment necessarily fit the crime. The norms of law and morality were not always properly distinguished. Thus, the emperor revived an antiquated law that a parricide should be sewn into a sack filled with serpents and thrown into the sea! By means of terroristic severity he attempted to bring disintegrating morality under discipline: the abductor of a bride, and the lady, if she had consented, were to be executed; a nurse who abetted the plot was to have molten lead poured into her mouth; a slave accomplice was to be burned.[8] This was the time when the clarity of the old Roman jurisprudence began to be dimmed. Rhetoric invaded law, the language was barbarized, and legal concepts were coarsened. All of this signified not merely the breakdown of the juridical system but

7. F. Wieacker informs me that the revolutionary touches as against old Roman legal concepts predominate in Constantine. He sets equity against law, stresses the social import, and scorns the formalism of the old jurisprudence. Compare F. Wieacker, "Vulgarismus und Klassizismus im Recht der Spätantike" (1955). His penal legislation goes utterly counter to classical law.

8. In passing judgment on the inhuman severity of such penalties, of which this is not an isolated example, one cannot apply either modern or old Roman legal concepts. Constantine has been affected by the cruelties visited upon the Christian martyrs. The genuine acts show us that the barbarity of Roman "justice" cannot be exaggerated. And what shall one say of making a public holiday out of executions at the hands of gladiators or beasts?

also the indispensable needs of the time, for which the old system was no longer adequate.

A man rooted in the past will see in the passing of an era only degeneration. How can one contemplate the passing of the age of chivalry without a pang of nostalgia? But shall we then grumble over the new and fail to see that the past, however attractive, is outmoded and incapable of meeting demands which are not simply arbitrary? Do not the representatives of the old order often stand in their own way? The very loyalty which gives them their charm leads them to thrust aside the inescapable questions for which they have no answer.

An example will indicate the feeling for realism in Constantinian laws. Diocletian was so firmly persuaded that freedom is an inalienable right that he would not allow a father to sell his child into slavery. But when its parents could not bring up the child Diocletian had to allow exposure instead. Constantine, following the custom in the East, allowed the sale of the child in extremities with a provision for re-purchase. At the same time he tried to stop exposure. He not only took measures personally but also through the state to save parents from such extremities, and regarded it as the emperor's particular duty to see to it that citizens were not so reduced. Anyone who did expose a child, however, lost all right of reclamation, even though the babe had been picked up and reared in slavery, because under the new circumstances there was no stringent necessity to dispose of a child. Constantine branded exposure as murder, in accord with the judgment of the Church, whether on Roman or later on German soil. In his recognition of his own duty and his admonition to parents we can see what was new in Constantine's public legislation. For him, law was indissolubly bound up with the moral commandments, with the demands of community living, and with regulation by the state of the population problem.

Many laws looked to the defense of the weak. The emperor would himself vindicate the oppressed and bring down the mighty, if provincial officials were remiss. Under no circumstances should the weak be called upon to bear the burdens of the strong. If the heavy load of taxes could not be lightened, exploitation on the part of the tax collectors was all the more to be punished. There was to be no feathering of nests! "Extortionate bleeding and greedy cheating" of taxpayers by the fiscal officials were scathingly rebuked under threat of the direst corporal punishment.

There is a humanitarian note in the edict for the relief of those imprisoned pending trial. The emperor called for speedy justice that the innocent might be freed and the guilty punished. He forbade galling chains and imprisonment in darkness; at dawn the prisoners should be brought out to the light. A Christian influence is discernible in the prohibition of branding on the face, "the countenance, created after the image of the heavenly beauty, is not to be defaced."[9] He broke with repulsive practices, even those long rooted in popular esteem such as gladiatorial combats. Men guilty of crime, instead of being condemned to the arena, should be sent to the mines so that "without bloodshed" they might expiate their offense. Ten years earlier Constantine himself had sent kidnappers of children to the arena.

The great codification of the law made under Justinian lifted from the enactments of Constantine one isolated provision and introduced it, even without an appropriate context, for its intrinsic worth: it asserted the principle of freedom from law—"In all instances justice and equity must take precedence over the letter of the law."[10] This is a statement with dangerous implications, dangerous because it opens the door to a weakening of justice. Administered by those not committed to the law it could indeed supplant justice. At the same time it tended to uphold

9. On this question of Christian influence compare J. Vogt, *Festschrift L. Wenger,* II (1945); J. Gaudemet (1947); and A. Ehrhardt, "Constantin der Grosse. Religionspolitik und Gesetzgebung." Theodosianus IX, 40, 2 (315 (316?) March 21).

10. Justinianus, III, 1, 8 (314, May 15; Seeck, May 13); Theodosianus, XI, 39, 1 (325, September 17).

the law, because that law which exceeds its proper domain forfeits its binding authority. "Man is more than law," claims Constantine. As a claim this is subversive of law, but for one loyal to law it serves as a guide in its application. A century later another emperor interpreted Constantine's saying in these words: "Still higher than legal justice is humanity."[11]

Legal development in Constantine's day was anything but tranquil. The great jurists had died out who alone could have cut through the snarl of enactments to recover the original sense and to draft it afresh. The lesser figures of his time, though versed in the minutiae, did not know how to inspire confidence in the justice and finality of their decisions and were not able to prevent those whose claims were denied from making interminable appeals. The courts served as arenas for the lawyers and gambling tables for the contestants, ever ready to make another throw for their luck. The devices used for eliciting the truth seemed to the emperor utterly inadequate and he was less and less persuaded that judgments were just no matter how legally correct. This is evident in that he overrode the courts of civil justice and conferred full authority upon the courts of the bishops.

Disputes from the earliest period had been reconciled or adjudicated in the Christian congregations. St. Paul had long since found it unbecoming that Christians should go to law before pagan judges. Consequently, we find deacons, presbyters, and bishops active in settling quarrels small and great. A Church order of the third century shows the procedure.[12] The priest or bishop should summon the contestants before him. The ecclesiastical judge must take into account not only the case but also the people involved. The sentence should be moderate, designed to bring peace, not retaliation. Thus the juristic duty of the bishop merged with that of his pastoral care. When a decision

11. *Const. Sirm.*, 13; Theodosianus, IX, 45, 4.2. Compare Fritz Pringsheim, "Römische Aequitas der christlichen Kaiser," *Acta Congressus Juridici internationalis,* I (1935).

12. *Didascalia,* II, 46ff.

must be rendered, the ecclesiastical court had an eye less to strict justice than to the integrity of the congregation. The bishop might even exhort the aggrieved person to renounce a just claim.

Thus we see that Constantine was giving recognition to a long-established practice. He decreed[13] that anyone involved in a legal case could take it to the bishop's court and that the bishop's ruling must be accepted as "sacred and honorable," to be carried out by the civil judge. Thus the bishop's court was indirectly given civil authority. No statesman could fail to see that the ecclesiastical court to this degree infringed upon the civil court. When Constantine nevertheless decided to adhere to his earlier ruling he must have had solid reasons. Some modern historians explain this by pointing to the corruption of the civil officials as opposed to the integrity of the Christians, but the law itself does not give this as a reason. Another explanation is more plausible: could Christians expect to receive justice from judges who, under the old régime, had been their persecutors? This reason would hold, however, only so long as these judges were alive. Yet after their generation was passing, Constantine, in his last years, inculcated the ruling. The proper explanation must be that he was confronted by a difficulty which the legal institutions could not resolve. How is the judge to get at the truth? There is much, he said, which entangling legal procedures do not bring to light. Such evidence is disclosed by "the holy virtue of religion."

Did he credit the bishops, as he did himself, with the ability to see through men by reason of a higher insight? Did he think that respect for the bench, divinely guided, would drive men to tell the truth? This assumption initiated by Constantine continued to be operative throughout the Middle Ages and was brought to its peak in medieval Germany where appeal was made to God when guilt could not be otherwise determined; a miracle would disclose what the eye of man could not discern. Constantine hardly went so far. He was not looking for a miracle, but he did

13. *Const. Sirm.*, I (333, May 5). *Dö.*, p. 197, no. 123.

place his confidence in the particular authority which he thought to have been invested in the clergy and in the holy fear it would evoke.

Directly connected with this confidence was the hope that the bishops could stem the flood of legal cases. "We desire to suppress the sinister seeds of strife, that miserable men, involved in an almost endless chain of litigation, in due time may desist from undue claims and perverted desires." The Church courts had always aimed at adjustment and reconciliation and probably often achieved it. So long as this was true, these courts were wholesome and their defects could be overlooked. There were defects not only in the orderly administration of justice but also in the Church itself. The principle that equity should supersede strict application of the letter of the law led inevitably to abuses when applied by bishops who, however careful, still operated without rules; and the character of the Church's judgment must necessarily alter when sustained by the coercive power of the state. Enforced obedience did not convert the contestants into brothers and the intervention of the state did not restore the fellowship of the community. Moreover, the selection of Church officials was affected by their judicial function. The more bishops were called upon to render legal decisions, the more must they be selected for their legal qualifications. Undoubtedly Constantine entrusted the bishops with civil duties and conferred upon them civil authority because he held them in such high esteem. This is evident in that section of the law which places a higher value on the testimony of a bishop than on that of the *honoratiores*. The word of a bishop was unimpeachable because one could expect him to be conscientious. "For that which is spoken by a holy man of good conscience has the incontestable authority of truth." This uncommon confidence rested not least on the reputation for steadfastness on the part of officials of the Church. There is a close connection here with the period of persecution and with the personal experiences of the emperor. If the steadfastness of the bishops under trial made them more trustworthy, still the main point was that their discharge of the legal function was in fact so exemplary.

The laws concerning the ecclesiastical courts strengthened a specific institution within the structure of the Church but also took it into the service of the state. The reciprocal relationship had important consequences for both. The Constantinian administrative system scarcely altered the social structure. Ordinarily political and religious changes tend to raise new classes and diminish or extinguish the old ones, but the old Roman aristocracy had actually lost its political influence long since. Constantine, however, did not threaten their status but, on the contrary, left their privileges intact and even granted new favors. The governors of the single provinces were drawn from the senatorial and equestrian ranks. The privileges of the old ruling class were preserved, particularly in Rome. Generally, the *praefectus urbis* and the consuls were recruited from these ranks. The former had jurisdiction over the senators; the latter gave their names to the year, a social distinction without political importance. The highest rank in the aristocracy was held by the *patricii*, who were "relatives" of the ruler or were elevated to that status.

The other classes in the society also remained. If their rights were constant and their duties enlarged, the reason was the increasing imbalance of the bureaucracy which threatened local government. Basically the trouble lay in the unforeseen result of the mounting needs of the empire. The court, the army, and the administration all called for large sums. Though attempts were made, no sucess was achieved in distributing the loads.

The hierarchy in the social structure had a corresponding scale of burdens. Taxes and civil duties pressed hard on the largest portion of the population. But the aristocracy into which the officers and the officials were elevated could amass riches, even though they were not relieved of duties; and landlords were responsible for delivering the levies laid upon their tenants and estates. The burden fell more heavily on the upper brackets in the towns, the members of the councils. At one time membership in the *curia* had been a coveted honor, but no longer, because the *curiales* were responsible out of their own resources for the basic tax in their area. Membership in this class was hereditary and was augmented by impressing into it men of substance. Many sought to escape the burden by entering the army or the Church. But Constantine in several decrees closed this door. Only appointment to the highest posts or transfer to the court brought relief. Still, the *curial* class continued to be a grudging but still workable support of the empire until the seventh century when it finally collapsed.

Commerce and small manufacture were also burdened. Every five years the crown gold, to be paid as a thank-offering, bore heavily on all propertied men. The levy was not altogether unwarranted. Merchants and craftsmen shared in the noticeable, if not phenomenal, economic improvements due to the peace within and the protection from without afforded by the emperor. The gold *solidus*, of high value, minted after several unsuccessful attempts in 324, bore witness to the unity of the empire. These coins continued to be valued for another seven hundred and fifty years.

The taxes fell most heavily upon the agricultural population. For a long time the arable land had been particularly burdened. The reform of Diocletian treated the farm and the farmer as if they were one. This system commended itself by reason of its simplicity; to render the link indissoluble was so obvious as to come immediately to mind. Constantine was not the first to start binding the farmer to the farm in order to arrest the flight from the land. The late Roman *coloni* were the serfs of the Middle Ages. From the time of Constantine other occupations also were "frozen." The sailors, on whom depended the importation of food for the chief cities, could not leave their rudders, nor could the bakers in Rome and Constantinople desert their ovens. The coin minters, too, were made into an hereditary profession, though some of these artistic and technical callings acquired rights along with duties.[14] Their practitioners were not to be troubled during the period necessary for the training of their sons and were excused from lower civil services. Such immunities lightened the load of public obligation for particular classes, while others whose work was of especial importance—such as doctors, grammarians, and other teachers—could be excused. The student of architecture received consideration from the ruler with his passion for building. And Constantine's respect for culture led him to give places of honor to professors of literature. Those who earlier had occupied these posts, such as the priests in the provinces and the *duumviri,* were permitted to retain their privileges. The sons of soldiers had long been obligated to continue in their fathers' career and now the officials were made into a sort of militia on the same terms. The careful planning which regulated the mechanism of the state aimed to keep up the succession of ranks and classes.

Disaffection to the point of rebellion did not occur within Constantine's empire. There was no parallel to the revolt of the Gallic peasants, the *bagaudae,* which had led to the appointment of Maximian, nor to the revolt in Egypt which Diocletian had put down in blood. Only in Cyprus was there a brief usurpation and in northern Africa a religious social movement connected with Constantine's religious policy. The populace desired nothing other than an absolute monarchy, able to give stability to the empire which was their world. They were ready to pay the price.

14. Immunities for palace officials: Theodosianus, VI, 35, 1 (314, October 29); Theodosianus, XII, 1, 22 (336, August 22); veterans: Theodosianus, VIII, 4, 1 (315 or 324/325?, April 28); sailors: Theodosianus, XIII, 5, 5 (326, September 18), Theodosianus XIII, 5, 7 (334, December 1); artifices artium: Theodosianus, XIII, 4, 2 (337, August 2); students of architecture: Theodosianus, XIII, 4, 1 (334, August? 27?); physicians, grammarians, and teachers: Theodosianus, XIII, 3, 1 (321 or 324, August 1); physicians and *professores litterarum*: Theodosianus, XIII, 3, 3 (333, September 27); provincial priests, *Duumviri*: Theodosianus, XII, 1, 21 (335, August 4), Theodosianus, XII, 5, 2 (337, May 21); Jews: Theodosianus, XVI, 8, 3 (321, December 11), Theodosianus, XVI, 8, 2 (330, November 29).

The judgment of a British historian with regard to the late Byzantine era is valid also for this period, that any move toward a distribution of power was regarded as a sign of disintegration: "In East Rome 'democracy' meant revolution, civil war"; "to the Byzantine the mere word 'democracy' spelt chaos." [15] Under the conditions of that world, within and without, such persuasions were realistic, just as under other circumstances they have lost their meaning and their right. At that time only a unified state, able to deploy its power in every direction, had any hope of holding out against the decline of capacity within and the threats of barbarians from without.

15. Norman H. Baynes, *Byzantine Studies and Other Essays* (1955), p. 35.

IX. Slavery

Constantine did not overturn the system he inherited, nor did he abolish slavery—which so offends modern sensibilities.[1] Would not this have been the proper place for a Christian emperor to put his faith into practice? Instead, Constantine in his laws strenuously maintained social distinctions.[2] A free woman who forgot her birth and married a slave lost freedom for herself and her children. Later on this edict was made more severe, the penalty being death. In his last years Constantine still resisted many attempts to legitimatize the son of a slavewoman and he secured family estates from diminution by giving portions as presents to illegitimate children and their mothers. This was regarded as "unseemly generosity." Nor did Constantine alleviate the severity used in antiquity against runaway slaves, who were threatened with torture and imprisonment. Those caught escaping to the barbarians were mutilated and placed in the mines.

1. F. Overbeck, "Über das Verhältnis der alten Kirche zur Sklaverei im römischen Reiche" (1875). H. Wallon, *Histoire de l'esclavage dans l'antiquité*, 3 vols. (1879²). R. H. Barrow, *Slavery in the Roman Empire* (1928). J. Vogt, "Sklaverei und Humanität," *Studien zur antiken Sklaverei und ihrer Erforschung* (1965).

2. *Dö.*, pp. 275ff. On the woman and the slave: Theodosianus, IV, 13, 1 (314, April 1), Theodosianus, IX, 9, 1 (326, May 29); stealing a bride: Theodosianus, IX, 24, 1 (320, April 1); stealing a child: Theodosianus, IX, 18, 1 (315, August 1); runaway slaves: Justinian, VI, 1, 6 (332, October 17), Justinian, VI, 1, 3 (314, April 1), Theodosianus, XIII, 3, 1 (321 or 324, August 1), Theodosianus, IV, 11, 1a (326, April 13), Theodosianus, IX, 5, 1 (314, January 1).

Could Constantine have changed this system? The slaves had their fixed place in the structure of ancient life. The imperial domains and the huge estates in south Italy, Sicily, Africa, and Egypt were operated by slave labor. Without the produce of these farms the great cities could not have survived. The very existence of Rome and Constantinople depended on them. The big industries and the state armories which supplied the troops used slaves. They were thus indispensable.

To keep up the quota of slaves became ever more the duty of the state as the supply diminished. Kidnapping by pirates—the curse of the ancient world—had been suppressed. The slave merchants no longer followed the armies on the German frontiers. Constantine purchased the prisoners from his own soldiers and then settled them on abandoned farms or used them to replenish his legions.

The strict maintenance of the institution of slavery did not, however, exclude all humanitarian considerations. Certainly, callous custom disregarded the lot of an entire class in the society, and rulers, obligated to place the whole above its individual parts, could not dispense with severity. Still the emperor did not treat the slaves solely with an eye to what he could get out of them. The role a slave might play in a household is shown by a law giving explicit details: slaves watched over the property of the children of the dead master—often enough their care saved the lives of orphans. The guardian was forbidden to sell the parental home of his ward. When the father died the household must be kept together, that household where childhood had been spent, where the images of the ancestors were conserved, and to which no less the inherited slave families belonged.[3] Constantine maintained the patriarchal relation in the homes of the aristocracy and required of the domestics not only ordinary services but also continual care for the young heirs. Respect for the human rights of slaves is shown by another law providing that slave families were not to be separated when an inheritance was

3. Theodosianus, III, 30, 3 (326, March 15).

divided. "For who can tolerate the separation of children from their parents, sisters from their brothers, wives from their husbands?"[4]

To Aristotle a slave was not a man, merely an animated tool, as in Roman law the slaves were simply property, not people. Plato, on the other hand, considered that among the Greeks no one was designed by nature to be a slave; yet he did not extend the same egalitarianism to the barbarians. The Stoics went further. One of their most distinguished representatives, Epictetus, was himself a slave. They held that all men are of the same nature and recognized that actual servitude does not preclude the inner freedom of the mind. This attitude tended to ameliorate the treatment of slaves, but did not alter their status. The few protective laws on slavery in the imperial period did no more than ensure the life of the slave against the caprice of a master. The death of a slave through maltreatment was accounted murder. Nevertheless, slaves could still be scourged.

Humane treatment of the slave, together with an unmodified retention of the system of slavery, was Stoicism's contribution to society. We may well wonder whether Constantine's legislation does not belong within this framework, insofar as it did not introduce any completely new attitude. Several of his laws opened the door, however, to emancipation. "It is good and laudable," he said, "to do something pleasing to God on Sunday. Therefore all shall be permitted on this day to emancipate slaves."[5] For that reason the offices of the registrars were to be open, despite the public holiday. As if that were not enough, he who "with pious intent" wishes to free his slaves may turn to the church as a particularly appropriate place. The emancipation, whether conducted before an entire Christian congregation or before the bishop alone, would be as legally valid as if performed

---

4. Theodosianus, II, 25, 1 (334?, April 29).
5. Theodosianus IV, 8, 1a (313, June 8), Theodosianus, IV, 8, 1 (321, April 18). Compare Dö., p. 182, no. 68 and Fabrizio Fabrini, *La Manumissio in Ecclesia*, Milan 1965, pp. 48–89: Le Costituzioni di Costantino.

before a civil magistrate. On their deathbeds clerics might free slaves without a witness and without a written document. This is the first time in history that emancipation is praised as godly work and encouraged by an emperor.

How did this come about? Emancipation, of course, was recognized in various forms by Roman law. A slave might be freed as a reward for loyal service, or to cut down the cost of his maintenance. But at this point the state had misgivings. Augustus did not wish to increase the proletariat fed at public expense, nor to introduce foreign elements into the Roman citizenry. A later law permitted the emancipation at the most of only one third of a slave household. Perhaps such reservations were not universally enforced; there may have been regional differences. But what is quite clear is that Constantine's legislation diverged from the principles of the old Roman law.

The source of his legislation is indicated by the choice of the man to whom the directive on emancipation was addressed. Ossius, bishop of Cordova, an ecclesiastical adviser to Constantine, appears as the advocate of this enactment. Was he, then, the mouthpiece of a universal Christian demand and was Constantine merely implementing what the Church had long demanded? What was the attitude of the Christians to slavery?

In the Christian congregation there was "neither Jew nor Greek, slave nor free" (Galatians 3:28). Since the Lord of the Christian Church had "emptied himself and taken the form of a slave" (Philippians 2:7), slavery was no longer shameful. In the congregation there was no distinction. "For us there are no slaves and we call them all brothers in the spirit and, as to religion, fellow slaves."[6] Indeed, the earliest Christian congregations contained more slaves than masters. To be sure, the masters were numerous enough to receive special admonitions in the sermons and letters, but they were given no pre-eminence. Discrepancies between rich and poor indeed remained but they had no influence on elevation to ecclesiastical office. There were bishops who

6. Lactantius, *Institutiones,* V, 15, 3.

had once been slaves—among them Callistus, an eminent Roman bishop. Thus a congregation as outstanding as that at Rome was no exception. In the Greek world, likewise, there were religious cults which admitted slaves; but no one drew any deductions from this religious equality as to social equality. Here the class distinctions retained their full force, which is not surprising, for the more a religion regards itself simply as a cult the less is it bound to transform the structures of human community.

But would not the situation differ for Christians for whom morality belongs to faith and faith creates a new fellowship? If one expects this to create new social structures one will be disappointed. The old remains as it was. But what if the real effect of the renewal is to be sought in the area of personal relations? Here the change is deeper than any mere altering of institutions can either effect or express. The bonds which bind men to their world receive a new meaning. The mere legal regulations embody a living relationship in which giving and taking exchange places. There is then no need to alter the social structure, but rather to renew its content. The Stoic asserts his nobility independently of fate and circumstances. They cannot touch him. The Christian gains his dignity precisely in his relation to his neighbor, as much in serving as in ruling.

The master must regard his slave differently when he looks upon him not as "an animated tool" but as a brother, fully his spiritual equal, even though physically under his care. He must treat his slave as he himself would wish to be treated. No less the relationship of the slave to the master is altered: "Serve willingly as to Christ, and not men."[7] The frequent injunctions in this vein point to an increased and deeper service. Even the evil master has a claim to fidelity,[8] but there is here no "slave morality" which adds inner to outer servitude and ends in cringing suspicion delivering the slave to the mercy of his master. The obedient slave does not forget that in serving the earthly lord

7. Ephesians 6:7.
8. I Peter 2:18.

he is bound to the heavenly. The slave does not look upon his master as a device to provide him exercises in humility; instead, the master is taken seriously as a man and in him the slave encounters the demands of God which determine his own life. Thereby the slave escapes also the danger of Pharisaic self-righteousness which by submissiveness seeks to demonstrate its own piety.

The slave was not given to feel that he had a claim to emancipation and there is no suggestion that the owner was obliged to set his slaves free. It is true that the New Testament talks of ransoming and emancipating, but these were figures of speech applied to the redeeming of captives from the bondage of sin and the Devil. Only one small letter in the New Testament refers to emancipation in the literal sense. Paul is writing to Philemon, a slaveholder, on behalf of his runaway slave Onesimus. Onesimus had managed to escape detection in the great city, had been converted by Paul, and was now himself the bearer of the letter which returned him to his master. True, he came back as a different man, ready now to render willing service. His master should determine whether it should be for life. Paul not only requests that Philemon forgive the runaway but that he permit him to serve the Apostle in prison. This implies that Philemon should renounce his right and set Onesimus free. The law is thus given its due. The slave has returned voluntarily to his yoke but the Christian master is exhorted to do what no law requires and no general rule achieves.

The New Testament gives slaves no claim to emancipation; but before long, the claim was being made. It was sharply rejected by the martyr bishop, Ignatius of Antioch, when slaves demanded that their freedom be purchased at the expense of the congregation. The bishop saw here the danger that Christianity would be misconstrued in terms of social advantage. "They are not to be puffed up but the more willingly to serve to the glory of God, that from God they may receive a higher freedom. They are not to ask the Christian congregation to set them free lest they appear as slaves to their desires."[9] The bishop repells the misuse of the Christian confession by subordinating social freedom to another of a higher order and by setting moral servitude over against outward slavery. The more faithful the service, the more one is truly free, whereas emancipation at the expense of others brings one into a deeper servitude.

From this point of view it is but a short step to the position held by Tertullian, for whom the difference between slavery and freedom in the world has disappeared. "The true slavery consists in sin, the true freedom in righteousness."[10] Therefore, the whole fire of devotion should be accorded to true freedom and the whole power of rejection applied to genuine servitude. Why should one trouble to throw off a slavery which means nothing and strive for a freedom which is only an appearance?

Although there were callings incompatible with the Christian faith—the Apostolic Constitutions mentioned not a few—no single social status was considered intolerable. Tertullian boasted that there was no walk of life in which Christians were not to be found. The statement of Homer, that when a man loses his freedom he loses half of his virtues, could not be repeated in Christian circles. The new value attached to service opened the eyes to what was possible for the servant, yet was not blind to the danger involved. The slave was driven all too easily to rancor and bitterness. During the day he had to work with a slave gang and during the night he was locked up with them, subject to their demoralizing brutality. Yet the great preacher Chrysostom pointed out that true freedom could shine in the midst of slavery. "He has but a small grasp of the power of the faith who thinks that it is not equal to the distress and misery of slavery."

That the master was endangered not only by his wealth in general but also by the possession of slaves was not overlooked. Clement of Alexandria pointed out that many slaves tempt one to luxury and in the end make the master incapable of helping

9. Ignatius to Polycarp, IV, 3.
10. Tertullian, *De Corona Militis*, XIII.

himself.[11] On another occasion, Clement asked how one could tell a slave from a master if they were dressed alike. Only by this, he answered, that the master is weaker and more effeminate. The masters are dependent to a degree which robs them of their freedom.[12] Chrysostom, who saw the highest triumph of freedom in the chains of slavery, found the most degraded slavery in the arrogance of the master who parades with a great retinue of slaves.[13]

One looks in vain in the early Church for a model for Constantine's Christian motivations in his laws on manumission. There were indeed many favorable prerequisites. But the Christians had no well-developed social program waiting to be enacted and the conviction had not emerged that emancipation was a duty to God and a right of the slave. If we ask why this came later to be assumed, the explanation is to be found partly in the growing demands upon the clerical office—as revealed in the regulations of some of the councils. A slave could be received into the clergy only if he were emancipated and thus able to dispose of his own time.[14] The requirement of prior emancipation did not imply a disparagement of his status, but had respect only to his freedom to discharge his functions. The same reason led to the enactment that priests should not engage in business which might entail long journeys.[15] The meaning of the regulation on slaves could, however, shift imperceptibly: the bishop was expected, even outside of the Church, to have a good reputation, which could readily be taken to mean social prestige as the leader of the congregation. Just before Constantine a Spanish council required that a freedman could not hold a Church office unless his onetime master were dead,[16] lest there be any living reminder of his former servitude. The reason assigned for this regulation, so akin

11. Clement of Alexandria, *Paedagogus*, III, 4, 26.
12. *Ibid.*, III, 6, 34, 2.
13. Chrysostom, *De Lazaro serm.*, VI, 8.
14. *Constitutiones Apost.*, VIII, 47, 82.
15. Council of Elvira, canon 19.
16. *Ibid.*, canon 80.

in its form to the one mentioned above, shows what forces of transmutation were at work. The distinctions which for the early Church had meant nothing began now to be taken seriously. This tendency could not but increase in the time to come. When Constantine gave the bishop a status equal to that of the most prominent men in the empire, the Church naturally wanted to name someone who could move among senators and statesmen.

Far more important was the delegation of new duties to the officers of the Church, which they could not refuse. The Church courts called for judges who, even if not trained in the law, were at any rate men of discernment; and such persons were to be found most readily in circles of culture and tradition. If the Church paid attention to social distinctions in the clerical office, then she must make emancipation a matter for ecclesiastical concern since, if social distinctions persisted in the Church, then equality within the congregation would be forfeit.

Our concern is to make Constantine's legislation intelligible, not to discover its immediate derivation. The ideas were of Christian origin but until then had been without implementation. The insight that new occasions demand new solutions is often the unintentional result of a great endeavor. It was not Constantine himself but the Christians of his time who elaborated the assumptions by matching their faith to the demands of the period. Their attitudes were so impressed upon Constantine that he then embodied them in his legislation.

Yet universal emancipation was not in itself regarded as a work of piety. The slaves emancipated on Sundays and in the churches were simply being rewarded for their faithful service. A sermon of Augustine's gives us the procedure. The owner took the slave to the church. There he submitted a document or expressed his wish orally to set the slave free. Because he had served in all fidelity he was to receive the reward of freedom.[17]

The course set by Constantine was followed by many. Subsequent history shows that his pioneer legislation corresponded to

17. Augustine, *Sermo*, XXI, 6.

the best insight of the time. His laws set the pattern for the practice of Church and state, although the development was admittedly slow and sometimes ran into reverse.

Monasticism must be reckoned among the great forward-looking movements of the fourth century. The decisiveness with which it brought the contemporary world under the demands of the Christian ethic shook not a few out of their complacent addiction to injustice. This makes it all the more remarkable that one of the great proponents of monasticism, Basil of Caesarea, refused to condemn slavery outright. To be sure, he argued, no man is a slave by nature; historical circumstances, such as war and poverty, have brought him to it. But this does not explain everything. There is a hidden and wise Providence at work which causes the inferior brother to serve the superior. Servitude, then, is to be understood not so much as a punishment as a benefit. He who is not in a position to rule himself must be under the direction of another.[18]

Basil was no defender of private property. For him everything should be determined in accordance with biblical norms. The judgment he rendered in a particular case serves as an example: What should be done with a slave who runs away from his master to enter a cloister? He should be reproved and sent back like Onesimus. That is consistent with Paul's procedure. But suppose his master commands him to do something forbidden by the law of God? In that case the monks should equip him for a steadfast refusal. But if he is not equal to it? Then he should be admitted to the cloister lest he lose his soul and suffer eternal punishment.[19] In this case the law, otherwise so stoutly upheld, was set aside for the sake of the endangered brother. No claim is laid to exemption from the law, but the punishment that hung over the brother will be assumed willingly by the cloister. This is an admirable freedom, which acknowledges the law while going beyond the law. It shows Basil's loyalty to the old order

18. Basil, *De Spiritu Sancto*, XX.
19. Basil, *The Rule*, long recension XI.

in a new light. The law does not have the last word; rather, concern for the human being triumphs. He who has this concern can fulfill the law by breaking the law.

Monasticism required that its novices renounce completely all property, including their slaves. When Melania, the young disciple of Jerome, followed her teacher from Rome to Palestine, she distributed her whole rich inheritance to monastic establishments and emancipated thousands of her slaves. But not all of them relished freedom and many voluntarily transferred themselves to her brother's service, preferring security under a wealthy owner to precarious independence.[20] Thus there was at least a semblance of propriety in the attitude of the rich in Chrysostom's congregation who, when he exhorted them to free the excessive number of their slaves, pointed out that the slaves were cared for and that, if freed, would be exposed to dire need. Chrysostom then indicated a better way: let all the slaves be taught trades so that they might care for themselves. He agreed, however, that one or two slaves might remain with the master.[21] There was no thought here of abolishing slavery altogether, only that its extent might be voluntarily restricted.

The attitude of the early Christians toward slavery followed a consistent principle. The institution itself was not called into question; a responsible statesman would have set himself sharply against total abolition. But we are not to infer that the Church simply accommodated herself to the position of such a statesman, any more than that she made herself the mere advocate of the existing institution. Rather, she took an independent course, with an eye both to the social situation and to her own principles. And the emperor followed her lead. On the question of the humane treatment of slaves, the statesman and the Christians were of the same mind. A legal enactment of complete emancipation in accordance with the Stoic principle would have overturned the social order. The Christian procedure of dealing with concrete

20. Palladius, *Historia Lausiaca*, ch. LXI.
21. Chrysostom, *Homily* on I. Cor., XL, 5.

situations as they arose, without insisting on a preconceived plan, may well seem to be inconsistent with Christian principles but it did give the legislator the possibility of gradual amelioration. In fact, it is amazing that the Christian faith could dare to cut into the relation of master and man and confer upon it a moral quality at all. Master and servant became related to each other as father to son, brother to brother. Attention was focused on the demands laid alike upon the owner and upon the slave, each in his station. St. Augustine had occasion to tackle the problem in connection with the Gospel injunction to suffer the despoiling of one's goods (Matthew 5:40); this might include the slave because according to law he was property. So Augustine ruled that slaves are not goods like any other property. Although, therefore, a cloak or money may be given up, in the case of a slave one must consider into whose hands he will fall. Whoever gives him up has a responsibility for what will become of him, "because a man should love a man as he would himself."[22]

The short letter of Paul to Philemon contains only a subtle suggestion, not a direct counsel, let alone law. Paul asked only for that which could not have been done save in full freedom: that Philemon should have regard for a man as a human being. This demand runs persistently through all subsequent Christian history, like the violin carrying the words of the Lord in the *St. Matthew Passion*. It is not the cry of the oppressed demanding their rights, but the overtone which touches human consciences whenever men are degraded to mere objects. It may cause the overthrow of established institutions and bring in a new order. But the new and better order is never the ultimate good, and this voice is still not silenced. It speaks for those needs of man for which laws can not provide. As times and conditions change, it finds new ways of expressing what Paul asked of Philemon: to accept Onesimus "no longer as a slave but as a dear brother."

---

22. Augustine, *De Sermone Domini in Monte*, I, 59.

X. *Military Service*

In the matter of slavery Constantine gave expression to Christian
sentiment without breaking with the institution. But in other
areas he did introduce thoroughgoing reorganization of his own.
The army was radically overhauled. He was able, to be sure, to
build upon the work of Diocletian; but the great military reform
was his own.[1] The security of the extensive frontiers, with their
walls and castles, was now entrusted to garrisons built around the
core of colonized veterans, but the legions were removed from
the frontiers and stationed at the intersections of military high-
ways. In this way a mobile force was constantly available, able
in short order to reach points in danger. The armed services included the *palatini,* the imperial guard. A new feature was the
division into infantry and cavalry units which made it possible
to withstand barbarian cavalrymen, and for that very reason
Constantine increasingly also incorporated German cavalrymen
into his own forces. The Illyrian contingent diminished. The
introduction of many Germanic recruits into the Roman army and
the settlement of whole tribes on Roman soil became more and
more the policy of the late Roman Empire, and this was initiated
by Constantine. Both his reorganization of the army and his distribution of its units were timely and resolute. The success of
these measures was soon apparent on the German and Sarmatian

1. Van Berchem, *L'Armée de Dioclétien et la réforme constantinienne*
(Paris, 1952).

frontiers. In 332 the Goths experienced at long last the superiority of Roman arms and this was to dispose them the more readily to accept the religion of their conqueror.

Constantine was, to the end, a soldier-emperor and retained his claim to the warrior's laurel crown which, however, on his later coins was left to the Caesars. From his military laws a few provisions[2] have come down to us which vindicate the rights of veterans, set penalties, establish rules, protect welfare, and in general show the concern of the emperor for his soldiers. A veteran of twenty years was to be relieved from civic duties. Where such military rights had fallen into desuetude they were restored. The only other men who shared in the favors given to warriors were the members of what might be called the traveling cabinet of the emperor, because they were not far from the "dust and hardship of the camp." But the pretensions of other officials to military privileges were sharply rebuffed. The literary hacks who hung around the offices were regarded with soldierly contempt. They had never seen a battle, nor a standard, and had never held a weapon in their hands. Such expressions of his soldierly feelings, however, did not keep the emperor from resenting the excesses of the soldiery. Special military claims must give way to the general walfare.

In reorganizing the army, the problem of Christian soldiers had to be met.[3] Constantine restored those who had been unjustly dismissed by the severity of his persecuting predecessors; but these Christians could be given an honorable discharge if they preferred, in recognition of their steadfast adherence to the faith.

2. Regulations prejudicial to the military were repealed: Theodosianus, VIII, 4, 1 (315 [324/5?], April 28); privileges for veterans: Theodosianus, VII, 20, 2 (320?, 326?, March 1); no curial duties for soldiers of twenty years' service: Theodosianus, XII, 1, 13 (326, May 17); soldierly pride in Theodosianus, VII, 21, 1 (313, August 10).

3. Cecil J. Cadoux, *The Early Christian Attitude to War* (1919); Roland H. Bainton, "The Early Church and War," *Harvard Theol. Rev.*, XXXIX (1946), 189–212; Hans Frhr. v. Campenhausen, "Der Kriegsdienst der Christen in der Kirche des Altertums," pp. 203–215; H. Karpp, "Die Stellung der Alten Kirche zu Kriegsdienst und Krieg" (1957).

Why did Constantine offer this second possibility? Did he assume that some had scruples of conscience about military service? The emperor himself certainly had none. Not only was he responsible for the defense of the empire but he had experienced Christ's help in battle and had instituted Christian worship in the army. But were all Christians as fully persuaded as he of the compatibility of their faith with military service? Christianity, unlike Mithraism and the cult of the unconquerable sun, was never the religion of the camp (Mithraic caves and altars to the sun are frequently found in the ruins of frontier encampments). Although from the very outset Christian literature is replete with military imagery—the New Testament speaks of the helmet of salvation, of the shield of faith, of the sword of the spirit (Ephesians 6:16)—Christian sermons were not directed especially to soldiers, and soldiers were not the ones who propagated the faith. At the same time the new faith did not remain outside the camp. There were Christians in the ranks, but they had to examine closely the compatibility of military service with their faith. One objection was to the shedding of blood, another to contamination by heathen religion; the military standards could be considered holy because fraught with religious significance. The chief stumbling block for the Christian was sacrifice. Of course the whole of everyday life, public and private, was shot through with pagan practices. Every holiday had religious accompaniments and the very meat on sale in the markets had first been sacrificed to the gods. Hence, the taint of heathenism was inescapable if heathen rites were conjoined with miltiary obedience. One Christian soldier-martyr declared, "The Christian soldier is forced to sacrifice to the gods and to the Emperor."

A striking example of the Christian's dilemma is given in the acts of the martyr Julius.[4] The magistrate was examining Julius for his refusal to sacrifice. The judge was not a fanatical opponent of Christianity and the soldier did not reject military service as

4. *Ausgewählte Märtyrerakten*, ed. R. Knopf and G. Krüger (1929³), no. 27.

such. He had fought in seven campaigns and had been behind no one in valor. The judge did his best to save him. The examination centered on sacrifices to the emperor. "What is the harm in sprinkling a pinch of incense and then doing as you please?" asked the judge. But such compliance to the Christian meant renouncing God: "After I have served the Emperor faithfully for so many years I cannot despise God's command and thus show myself faithless in a higher service." The judge made one more attempt to save Julius by taking the responsibility upon himself. "I will use force so that it will appear that you have acted under duress. Then you take your wages and go home and no one will be the wiser." But the Christian considered all this a device to seduce him. He stood firm and willingly accepted the sentence of death. The account shows that for this particular Christian the line of refusal was drawn not at bloodshed but at sacrifice to the gods and the emperor. On the other hand, the judge regarded the religious question only from the point of view of unconditional obedience. His statement, "If you think this is sin put the blame on me," sounded much like the attitude of some in our day who have assumed that the command of a superior relieves the individual of moral reponsibility. In the more tranquil period before Diocletian, unpalatable regulations were not unduly pressed upon the Christians. Only officers had to sacrifice and those in the ranks could feel that they had not participated. Elevation to the rank of officer would thus often provoke the issue of open confession.

But although for some Christians the objection was to pagan rites in the army, others rejected military service per se. We have from Africa the acts of the martyr Maximilian,[5] who refused the requirement that as the son of a soldier he should follow his father's profession. Said the boy, "I cannot be a soldier, I cannot do wrong, I am a Christian . . . I serve in the army not of the world but of my God." The proconsul pointed to other Christians who were serving without scruple; he could even call upon the

5. *Ibid.*, no. 19.

boy's father, standing at his side, that he try to bring the lad to his right mind. But the father's answer left the son free. "He knows himself what is true and right for him and can decide." Finally, to the question: "What sin is there in serving in the army?" the boy responded, "You know what is done." The determined tone of the refusal ended the examination. The proconsul could do no other than pronounce the inevitable penalty. "Maximilian is to be executed because he has insolently refused the oath of allegiance." The judge by pointing to the Christians in the army had thought to remove the question from the realm of religion; the father respected his son's decision although he did not share it; for the son, his Christian faith forbade all use of violence.

The boy's body was brought by the mother to Carthage and interred near the remains of the martyred bishop Cyprian. This was fitting because Cyprian, executed in 258, had shared the same beliefs. In one of his writings he undertakes to describe the world as it really is. He summons those captive to earth to climb a peak and survey the scene. On the roads robbers lurk, pirates infest the seas, the whole earth is soaked with blood. If such bloodshed is private it is considered a crime, if public it is regarded as honorable. The extent of the damage exempts crime from punishment rather than innocence.[6] In that very same Carthage, half a century earlier, Tertullian had branded military service as absolutely incompatible with Christianity. "How can one even be a soldier in peace without wielding the sword which Christ took away? And although the soldiers who came to John the Baptist received instructions as to their duties, and though the centurion Cornelius was converted, Christ later disarmed Peter and thereby every soldier."[7] "One cannot at the same time serve God and men. One cannot combine the sign of Christ and the sign of the Devil, the camp of light and the camp of darkness.

6. Cyprian, *Ad Donatum*, VI.
7. Tertullian, *De Idol.*, XIX.

One cannot serve both God and the Emperor."[8] The renunciation applied not only to war but to the whole system of justice and the coercive power of the state. Tertullian could only say ironically that a Christian might hold public office "provided he pronounce no sentence touching life, death and honor; provided he condemn no one, suffer no one to be chained, imprisoned or tortured—if this is conceivable—then there is no objection."[9] The Christians knew that they belonged to a different order whose laws they must obey. The conclusion was easily drawn that to a point the Christian might submit to the ordinances of the state, but could not utilize the powers of the state against others, nor place himself at its disposal.

We need not be surprised that the ancient world has no understanding of the Christians' position. A flat contradiction had already been voiced in the second century by Celsus in his *True Word*. "If everybody did as you," he said, addressing a Christian in an imaginary dialogue, "nothing would prevent the Emperor from being left alone and deserted and the world would succumb to the most lawless and wildest barbarians and then there would be nothing left either of the Christian religion or of the true philosophy."[10] Celsus then pleaded for helping the emperor to the uttermost, fighting for him, fighting beside him for righteousness.[11] In order to maintain law and religion, let Christians assume political duties.

These are persuasive words, which found a wide echo and stirred the great theologian of the third century, Origen, to make a reply. "We help the Emperor," said he, "in his extremities by our prayers and intercessions more effectively than do the soldiers. Just as the priests must keep their hands unsullied for the sacrifice, so also must the Christians, who are all priests and servants

8. *Ibid.*
9. *Ibid.*, XVII.
10. Origen, *Contra Celsum*, VIII, 68.
11. *Ibid.*, VIII, 75.

of God, keep their hands unstained by blood that they may be able to pray for the Emperor and the army in just cause. In this way we overcome the real disturbers of the peace, the demons. Thus we fight for the Emperor more than the others, though we do not fight with him, nor at his command. We constitute an army of piety by our intercession with the Deity."[12] This was more than a contribution to the *pax romana*, it was a spiritual support of the war. As a nation of priests the Christians, like the pagan priests, must keep their hands clean the better to support the army at war. Here was a secret and mighty auxiliary for the emperor in a just war. Origen could point to the actual prayers of the Christians for the emperor and the army, for which we have other evidence. Reference to the pagan priests brings this Christian intercession close to the idea of a crusade and suggests that the renunciation of weapons is a matter of cultic purity, quite apart from the fact that the unreserved intercession makes all the other reservations sound like a spiritualistic withdrawal from all the realities of the world.

Similar in tendency are the words of another Alexandrian teacher, Clement, although he did not expressly reject military service. "Till the ground if you are a husbandman," he said, "but recognize God in your husbandry. Sail the sea, you who love seafaring, but ever call upon your heavenly Pilot. Were you converted while serving as a soldier, then harken to the Commander who signals righteousness."[13] Everything, then, depends upon the recognition of God. Worldly callings are not of sufficient importance to be worth renouncing.

One might suppose that Christian misgivings as to war applied also to the continuance of the empire, but the prayers for its maintenance show that this cannot be the proper interpretation. Origen linked the Church to the Roman peace. "In the days of Jesus justice came forth and the fullness of peace. God prepared the place for his teaching and arranged that the Roman Empire

12. *Ibid.*, VIII, 73.
13. Clement of Alexandria, *Protrept.*, X, 100, 4 (ed. Stählin).

should rule the whole world."[14] Only within the framework of peace under one emperor could Christianity have been disseminated; the Christians had a responsibility, therefore, to maintain this peace. If they could not contribute to the support of the empire against external assault, they were all the more obliged to strengthen it from within. The Christian command of obedience to rulers eliminated the danger that force on the part of the ruler and mistrust on the part of the ruled would vitiate their mutual relations. When the Christians formed bonds of fellowship with those afar off and unknown, they served in this way to hold the empire together at a time when the old order was breaking up. If the Christian attitude were to pervade the whole world, surely, assumed the Christians, wars would cease as well as all contention about mine and thine, and all injustice and violence would come to an end. Whether or not this hope within and without the Church was at all realistic, at any rate every step in that direction would be beneficial to the empire, even in its relation to the world beyond the frontiers. Hence Origen's answer to Celsus was not based on simple indifference to the perils, and the considerations adduced by the Christians might impress even a partisan of the state, especially since they were those of an ostracized minority.

Origen's statements were all made in the days of persecution. Constantine now confronted the Christians with a new situation. When, then, the head of the state was no longer a persecutor but was inviting the Christians to share in the administration, could they decline? The old answers were no longer adequate. On the other hand, the sound Christian core of those answers was not to be repudiated. There was, therefore, no easy answer and we need not be surprised when the answers actually given made this point plain.

At the Council of Arles in 314 the western Church tried to face up to the new circumstances. The question of military service and of holding office called for new rulings. The council inter-

14. Origen, *Contra Celsum*, VIII, 68.

posed no objection to the assumption of public office but the officials must be subject to the bishops, who could exclude them from the Church if they transgressed her norms.[15] One perceives that the permission to take office was not granted without some hesitation. Both consent and reservation had a recent precedent. A few years before there had been Christian magistrates in Spain. A synod there had ruled that during his year of office the Christian magistrate should stay away from church[16] because his office brought him necessarily into conflict with Christian principles. The Council of Arles gave up this halfway measure but not the concern by which it was prompted. If it was not proper to deny the demands of the common life, still there was need for great caution.

Still more difficult was the question of military service in which the coercive power of the state was most clearly evidenced. "He who throws down his weapon in time of peace," decreed the council, "shall abstain from communion."[17] Over against the principle of non-resistance, disquieting soldiers who became Christians, the council forbade leaving the service. Remarkable as this decision is, even more remarkable is the point at which it stopped; for although the Christian might not throw down his weapons in time of peace, he is not forbidden to do so in time of war. Maintenance of the state is commanded, but the objections to shedding blood in war are not set aside.[18]

An insight into the meaning of this regulation is afforded by the example of that most popular of all Christian soldiers, St. Martin of Tours, in the time of Constantine. Two years after his

15. Synod of Arles, canon VII.
16. Synod of Elvira, canon LVII.
17. Synod of Arles, canon III. Gibbon took the *in pace* to refer to the peace of the Church, which meant that the Christian was not to throw down his arms if the Church were not being persecuted (ch. XX, vol. II, 317 fn.).
18. Obvious contrast to *in pace* is *in bello*. If, then, the meaning is that the Christian might not throw down his arms in time of peace but was allowed by the Church to do so in time of war, we see plainly that such a provision must have originated with the Church and not with Constantine. The Church was not subservient.

conversion in the army he continued to wear his sword, yet when an actual battle was imminent he refused to use it but volunteered to rebuke the charge of cowardice by standing unarmed in the front ranks.

The decision at Arles was new but this does not mean that it was without precedent. A hundred years earlier in Rome it had been decreed that a Christian might be a soldier provided he did not kill. This forbade the shedding of blood but permitted the Christian to participate in the police functions of the army. In this way the Christian sought to fulfill public obligation without renouncing his own principles.[19] The Council of Arles was doing the very same thing. The reservation implicit in the decree shows that the limitation, once voiced at Rome, had not become obsolete, and St. Martin of Tours is the proof.

One cannot, therefore, look upon the decision at Arles as mere conformity to the will of the emperor. To see in this regulation the price paid by the Church for imperial favor is unjust, as if she were repudiating her principles. The Church could not give up her mission. But was she, then, to be deaf to the call of the new era? The Council of Arles tried to combine the two. Military service was not rejected per se and yet was not unconditionally endorsed. With reefed rather than full sails the Church embarked upon new seas.

That the tension still remained is not the only point of interest here. The decision of the council had the provisional quality of an initial attempt, which did not suffice for the next generation. The problem continued to occupy the theologians. It was felt even when war service was affirmed. Sixty years after Arles the Church Father, Basil, said that early Fathers did not regard killing in war as murder and did not subject those who had done it to penitential discipline. This did not mean that military service was a duty, let alone to be glorified. The point was simply that the soldier was not to be excluded from the Church. Basil, in fact, qualified his apology for military service by adding that it

19. Canons of Hippolytus, XIIIff.

was permissible only if in defense of morals and piety. This justification is not derived from considerations of temporal peace and political order but from concern for the realm protected by the state. Basil's attitude stemmed from the Church and the cloister. And despite his qualified approval of participation in war, Basil could not give it full endorsement. In a "canonical letter"[20] to a neighboring bishop who asked his advice on the point, Basil answered that those who fought in wars should abstain from communion for three years. Their hands were sullied and during that period they were in the position of penitents. This counsel was not altogether forgotten when, centuries later, a military emperor desired the Church to honor his soldiers fallen in battle as martyrs. The Church of his day laid before him the letter of Basil, even though it was addressed to a different situation. But the rule of Basil did not become canon law. The great Athanasius (293?–373) illustrated the point that every moral judgment must take account of circumstances by citing an example from military life. "Whereas," said he, "killing is otherwise forbidden, in war it is legitimate and even praiseworthy to kill enemies. He who distinguishes himself in this receives great honor."[21] That Athanasius should take this for granted shows that it must by then have been generally assumed. Not long afterward, only one hundred years later than the Synod of Arles, an imperial edict forbade entry into the army to all pagans. Military service was thus restricted to Christians.[22]

The final word of the Church was reserved for Augustine. He himself renounced the business of the world and encouraged his friends to do the like. This meant complete abandonment of the world, including marriage. But although this mode of life rated higher with God, nevertheless life in the world did have its claims. And in this area coercion and power have their place. To expect to live among saints before God's good time would be

20. Basil, *Epistula*, CLXXXVIII, 13.
21. Athanasius, *Epistula ad Amunem*, Migne P. G., XXVI, 1173 B.
22. *Codex Theodosianus*, XVI, 10, 21 (anno 416).

presumptuous. Christian morality does not condemn all wars, said Augustine, although certainly in a truly Christian world war would disappear. But in the meantime the clergy on the one hand and the laity on the other have each their function to discharge. The former fight with the arms of prayer against the unseen enemy, the latter make war against the visible barbarian. Augustine was enough of a Roman to think of the enemy in terms only of the invading barbarians, the lawless rebels. Against such the commonwealth must be protected and the invaders themselves need severity for their own good, as the sick man needs the surgeon's knife. To be sure, not everyone is permitted to bear arms. This is allowed only to an official of the state and to those under his command. The private man is to obey the Gospel injunction to "resist not evil" (Matthew 5:39), even if attacked by a highwayman. But fighting is a duty for the proper authority, which "seeks not its own" but the security of the state and the commonweal. The emperor and the army do difficult and important work. The soldier is the servant of the law. War of itself is neither good nor absolutely bad. All depends on the cause, the manner, and the aim. The object of the "just war" is to vindicate justice and restore peace. The warrior must be peace-loving in his heart; then it is necessity which does the killing, rather than will and desire. Obedience toward men is restricted by God's commandments. For Augustine they don't imply a general rejection of war, but they surely forbid any aggression. To wage war can be legitimate only insofar as the object is to bring the opponent all the more quickly back into the peace of a humane society—a society whose constitutive bond is justice.[23]

Augustine's answer thus distinguishes between the public and the private spheres, as well as between the clerical and the lay. The code for the varied callings both recognizes the obligation to keep the world from becoming a prey to the demons and at the same time does not forget that the Church has another role than blessing weapons. If this position is lifted out of the framework

23. Augustine, *Epistula* CLXXXVIII, cf. Ep. CXXXVIII and XLVII.

of Augustine's theology the result can be a graded morality and, with only a slight change, can be transformed into a war of religion, a crusade; but in Augustine's time it was an attempt to do justice to both the civil and religious obligations of the Christian.

A solution devoid of difficulties was never achieved, even by Augustine. The Christian no longer disclaimed the demands of the earthly society but recognized his obligation to assume a share of the burden. This included the office of the sword in war and justice, to which the Christian must be subject in obedience and faith. At the same time the Church did not forget that she is something more than an instrument of the civil order. She has continually born witness to defenseless love. She has always opposed self-seeking and the use of force, even when garbed in the robe of the interests of the state. Such love checks robbery and murder by confronting them weaponless. Danger lurks in two opposite directions, either to succumb to the world or to withdraw from the world in selfish unconcern. The irreconcilable contrast shows that among Christians there can be no rigid rule, universally binding. Each must respect the integrity of the other, and conscience cannot be relieved of responsibility, because the decision rests with the individual.

The question whether Constantine had in mind Christian scruples when he gave to Christians dismissed from the army during the persecution the option of reinstatement or honorable discharge required a far-reaching review of his entire policy. He can scarcely have had anything in mind more than that the fidelity of the Christian during persecution was equivalent to long military service and entitled the surviving martyr to the rights of a veteran. Still, a glance at Church history enables us to do more than differentiate the position of Constantine from that of the early Church. He agreed with Origen that the Christians did make a contribution to the maintenance of the Roman peace by their prayers. It was precisely their prayers that he craved to preserve the social bond. At the same time, it never occurred to him that arms and prayers excluded each other. Just as he employed both, so he expected the Christians to help him in the one as in the other.

XI. Sunday

The element in Constantine's legislation which reaches directly to our own day is the legal recognition of Sunday. It seems to us as obvious as day and night that time consists of blocks of seven days, headed by Sunday. It was not so evident in Constantine's day, when only the Jews had the alternation between six work-days and a day for rest, given by God, a reminder that God Himself after the six days of creation rested on the seventh. A different way of dividing the years and the months also had a venerable tradition. Stemming from Alexandria in the second century before Christ, the planetary week had spread through the Hellenistic and Roman world. The popular astrology of the time saw in the seven movable stars (including the sun and the moon) the powers of fate presiding over the hours and days. At first, the week was initiated by Hermes-Mercury; then by Kronos-Saturn, until at the beginning of the fourth century the day of the conquering sun god was the first, followed in astrological order by the moon, Mars, Mercury, Jupiter, Venus, and Saturn. They all survive in the Latin countries. In French, for example, we still have *Lundi, Mardi, Mercredi, Jeudi* (from Jove), *Vendredi, Samedi*. English has kept of these only Monday and Saturday. Some days were lucky, some unlucky, and superstition at all times has found here a rich field for selecting days and hours. The power of the stars to determine or settle the future lived on in popular belief even after the gods for whom the days were named had collapsed. Still for a long while the belief survived that the gods themselves were active on their respective days.

The planetary week spread beyond the confines of the empire. In the Germanic lands local deities replaced those of Rome. In English, for example, we have the names Tuesday from *Ziu,* Wednesday from *Woden,* Thursday from *Thor,* and Friday from *Freia.*[1] This does not mean that festivals were observed in honor of the particular gods on those days, any more than in classical antiquity. Only the Persian Mithras, now identified with the sun god, may have assembled his followers for a special service on Sundays,[2] but this was exceptional. In general, the particular god was supplicated on his day but without any worship in common. In other words, there was no holiday, or holy day, of weekly recurrence. But there was a yearly festal calendar in which certain days were annually observed. The most influential calendar was naturally the Roman, even though often restricted to the temples of the city. Throughout the empire the great temples had annual feasts, the cities commemorated the days of their foundation, and the countryside kept up its traditional seasonal observances. Holidays were especially popular in Alexandria and cultic practices retained their particularity throughout: the dignified ritual of Jupiter Capitolinus and the orgiastic rites of the Bacchanalia. The central feature was the solemn sacrifice, often accompanied by great celebration. Not all citizens had an obligation to participate, but shops were closed and work had to stop. "The

1. The English-speaking world uses still the Germanic names of the gods for the days of the week except for the seventh day, for which Saturn retains his place (Saturday), since for him there was no Germanic equivalent. In German he was replaced by the Sabbath (*Samstag*) or the Eve of Sunday (*Sonnabend*). Woden's day has been replaced by the colorless *Mittwoch.* Compare W. v. Wartburg, "Les noms des jours de la semaine dans les langues romanes," in his collected essays *Von Sprache und Mensch* (Berne, 1956), pp. 45–60.

2. But consult Arthur D. Nock, "The Roman Army and the Roman Religious Year," *Harvard Theol. Rev.,* XLV (1952), 233–234, where he brings forward objections to the current view that the *dies Solis* "counted for something in Mithraism."

festivals require that free men should abstain on these days from lawsuits and that slaves should rest from their labors."[3] This general principle was not carried out rigidly; any necessary work could be done. But this left plenty of slack. Punishment was meted out only to those who, in the view of the priests, disturbed the quiet of religious observances.

The worship of God characterized the holy day of the Christian week. From the very beginning the Christians had retained the Jewish week and, like the Jews, they gave the days no names but only numbers. But instead of following the Jewish Sabbath at the end of the week, they speedily shifted to the first day for their church service, the day on which Christ rose from the dead. We first encounter the day of the sun in Christian literature in Justin Martyr's *Apology*, addressed to the emperor about the middle of the second century. In order to make the celebration intelligible to the pagan, pagan terminology was deliberately used. For the Christians to call the first day "the day of light" recalled the Creation, for on the first day God said: "Let there be light." But more particularly this was the day when the "true sun" rose from the darkness of the grave and manifested himself to his disciples.[4] A half century later Tertullian had to refute the assumption that the Christians on this day were honoring the sun.

The day did not derive its import from the pagan world but rather from the Christians' own joy over the Resurrection. "We greet the first day of the week with joy," "for this is the day on which our life began."[5] On this day the congregations gathered for worship; this was the distinguishing feature. The day was not holy because set off from secular days by laws and abstinences. Origen said, "The perfect Christian does not need any special holy days, he is always living on the day of the Lord."[6] The Christians contrasted their day with that of the Jewish

3. Cicero, *De Legibus*, II, 29.
4. Justin, *Apology*, I, 16.
5. Barnabas, XV, 8, and Ignatius, *Ad Magn.*, IX, 1.
6. Origen, *Contra Celsum*, VIII, 22.

Sabbath, recalling the word of Paul against the Judaizers, "You keep days, months, feasts and years" (Galatians 4:10). The Lord's day, consequently, was not a Christian continuance of the Jewish Sabbath. Rest from labor applied only to the extent that one should not be kept by work from common worship. "On the Lord's day put aside your work and go to the church. What excuse will they have who, on the Lord's day, do not come together to hear the word of life?"[7] Thus it was worship rather than a general rule to lay down one's tools that precluded work. The step to transfer the traits of the Jewish Sabbath to the Christian and to enact Sabbatarian laws was certainly easy, but when this happened the meaning was changed and the day was subject to legalistic taboo with penalty and curse attached.

Thus Constantine found already among the Christians a day dedicated to worship. And this practice was what lay behind his Edict of 321 dealing with Sunday.[8] The law of March 3 read, "All the judges, the city folk and the handicraftsmen shall cease work on the venerable day of the sun. However, the farmers may continue their labors in the fields because often no day is more suitable for sowing and planting, that the auspicious moment offered by heavenly Providence may not be disregarded." Three months later a second exception was added, which clarified the meaning of the first edict. "As it is ignoble to be filled with mutual contention on Sunday dedicated to worship, even more is it appropriate on this day to do something well pleasing to God. Therefore, permission is given to free slaves this day and it is not forbidden to draw up the necessary papers."

These laws conferred on Sunday a legal status. Whatever was contrary to its nature should stop. That legal suits and the labor of slaves should cease on public holidays was Roman practice. Constantine added a sharp condemnation of such litigation

7. *Didaskalia* (ed. Funk), II, 59, 2.
8. Theodosianus, II, 8, 1a (321, March 3), *ibid.*, II, 8, 1 (321, July 3). Compare *Dö.*, p. 181, nos. 65 and 66, and pp. 322ff. Compare also C. S. Mosna, *Storia della Domenica dalle origini agli fino inizi del V secolo* (Rome, 1969), pp. 216ff.

which, for him, was incompatible with worship. The emperor was
not so much concerned to see justice done as to complain of the
rancor of the litigants whose endless and senseless contentions
violated the spirit of peace indissoluble in his mind from religion.
Similarly, Constantine sharpened the obligation to abstain from
work. This was not a humanitarian regulation. The point was that
the clatter of the workshop should be stilled. The permission to
the farmer to till the land and to the master to free his slaves
showed the character of the holy Sunday. The first carries out the
will of Providence, the second calls for a work pleasing to God.
Both are entirely in accordance with the worship which is the
primary reason for the day and the source of its dignity.

We find it noteworthy that a legal ruling about Sunday should
not simply decree worship and rest but should first forbid and
excoriate legal disputes on Sundays. A Church historian of the
fifth century, well acquainted with Constantine's Sunday legislation, spoke first of the closing of the law courts. This explains why
the code of Theodosius the Second of the same century entirely
omitted Constantine's Sunday law, because, if the primary point
of his legislation was the regulation of the courts, this subject
was more adequately handled in subsequent enactments.

Constantine's feeling about Sunday may be inferred from the
account given by his biographer. The emperor instituted a service
of worship in the palace at which he would read the Scripture
and give an address of his own.[9] He also introduced Christian
worship into the army. Eusebius relates how the soldiers honored
"the day of salvation which is also the day of the light of the
sun"[10] in a dual manner. The Christians could assemble unimpeded in the church, the pagans could assemble in the open
and recite a prayer composed for them by Constantine himself.
How far, in so doing, he took account of pagan assumptions will
be discussed in connection with Constantine's attitude to religious
liberty.

9. *VC*, IV, 29.
10. *Ibid.*, IV, 19.

"Sunday," not "the Lord's day," was the term used for the day declared to be a public holiday. This was the day which already had taken its place at the head of the week, and many Christians already used this name. When Constantine denominated it as "Sunday" he knew that the name would satisfy pagans as well as Christians; as the lawgiver he could not expect to impose upon all a name which would be offensive to some. But Theodosius did. He changed "Sunday" into the "Lord's day" and in so doing he appealed to early Christian usage. He could do so appropriately because by then he had caused the state Church to embrace all citizens. And he succeeded. In the Romance lands, though the pagan gods still give their names to the days of the week, the first day is the Lord's day: *Dominica, Domingo, Dimanche*. Constantine did not go so far. His intention was made manifest by the two forms of worship set up in the army, one for the Christians, the other for pagans. We have still, then, to ask what the day originally meant to Constantine. Was it the Christian Sunday or the pagan day of the sun, or a loftier combination of both?

Constantine's background would incline him to regard it as the sun's day. "His Apollo" had promised that Constantine would become the ruler; the sun had accompanied him in his victorious course. The Arch of Constantine in Rome was a monument to the sun cult. Up to the time of the Sunday legislation Constantine had had emblems of the sun on his coins. But at this precise point they disappeared, as did also the title "*Invictus*" for the emperor (a term commonly applied to the sun as unconquerable). Not long thereafter Constantine spoke in the sharpest words against Apollo. It would be strange if at this same time Constantine had emphasized the first day so strongly as the sun's day.

Some factors speak in favor of a syncretistic interpretation of his intention. The laws employ ambiguous terminology, such as "the heavenly Providence"; they speak of that which is "well pleasing to God"; and of "the day worthy of worship"; expressions by no means exclusively Christian. "Sunday" in any case was not of Christian origin and this point was not forgotten even if Christians did use the name. The contradiction was noted not merely by theologians like Augustine but also by the emperor Theodosius. This suggests that Constantine did not want to make a choice but, rather, to set up a universal day which all could accept. Was it not an appealing prospect for a ruler whose chief aim was to accomplish a religious union of mankind, to hit upon a plan whereby, week after week, all the subjects of the empire could raise their voices in perfect freedom to the deity? On the other hand, in the army—where a unified procedure could most easily have been introduced—the emperor tried precisely the opposite course. There pagans and Christians did not meet together but worshipped separately.

Yet the Christians' rejection of the sun's day may well have been what Constantine intended. Several details in his enactments point to this conclusion. The legal contests, so inappropriate to the day, were by a later law to be most surely reduced through the jurisdiction of a Christian bishop. And the emancipation of slaves, so in keeping with the spirit of the day, could take place in the churches. For what reason then in particular was the day itself to be venerated? For no other than that this was the day of divine worship. Now, this is the very heart of the *Christian* significance of the day, not the pagan. And when, further, Constantine himself established divine worship at the palace, one perceives very clearly the clue to his own understanding of his legislation. The Christian Sunday was his concern. He was implementing what he had written earlier in his letters to Africa, that the welfare of the state depends on the Christian worship of God. This worship was now to receive a place in public rites. Its observance should include all the inhabitants of the empire, even those who did not subscribe to its real meaning. It included everybody.

Justin Martyr in his *Apology* had used pagan expressions to make Christian concepts intelligible. But Constantine in his official language gave expression to what the day of Christian worship meant for the empire and what the empire owed to that day. Unlike Theodosius, he compelled no one to observe Sunday in a Christian manner. Still, in the person of its emperor the empire must respect the day, so crucial to its very life.

This meant bringing Sunday into the lives of the people. The day bore the marks of its founder. The experience to which Constantine gave expression in the letters to Africa—the concept of the day as one primarily of worship, the desire that all the urban communities should share directly in the worship, the persuasion that lawsuits are unseemly and emancipation of slaves godly, the religious sanction for farm labor—all these ingredients entered into the Constantinian Sunday and reached down to the very lowest of the subjects, often indeed in less refined form, just as the copper coins minted in bulk still revealed the artistic designs of the gold coins from which they were derived.

The stamp given to Sunday by Constantine was vigorous enough to reach down through the centuries. The consequences were of a threefold character. In the first place the fact that a law was promulgated made possible a legalistic treatment of the day, as if reversing the word of Jesus (Mark 2:27) and causing it to read that "man was made for the Sabbath and not the Sabbath for man." If in the Middle Ages Sunday became the "Sabbath" with which it had nothing to do, if it was then rigorously enforced by state and Church, Constantine is not to be held solely responsible, though of course any legal enactment may lead to legalism. Along with this danger the enforcement did have an educational value. The second point was wholly to the good. The Sunday rest gave a break from exacting labor while Church ordinances and sermons emphasized the relief which this rest afforded the slaves and *coloni*. The exception for the tilling of the soil by the farmer was soon repealed. The day of rest gave an opportunity for the development of the social character of Christianity. The third point was that public worship was made the prime purpose of the day. What that meant for the folk who participated in it cannot be measured. Sunday is the surviving monument of the age of Constantine. It could not have wished for a better.

In Constantine's reorganization of the empire old and new are hard to separate. He has been portrayed as a revolutionary and again as a conservative. If we judge by the outward aspects of his political achievement there is something to be said for each of these evaluations. There was no novelty in the existence both before and after Constantine of emperors, bureaucracies, nobles, and slaves, yet he did give evidence of a new empire through the transfer of the capital and the recognition of Sunday. Appearances, however, afford no adequate proof. *Plus ça change plus ça reste la même chose; plus ça reste la même chose plus ça change.* The perceptive words of the French statesman are fitting also at this point. There is no domain of life which does not thrust much behind it, yet in which, at the same time, the very oldest may not reappear as surprisingly new, and in so doing alter its character. Talleyrand in his famous epigram was thinking of historical forces which, regardless of the will of the actors, continue to operate. Without the will or the wish of revolutionaries much of the past is at work in their deeds; when the reaction comes, it is forced to realize many of the aims of the preceding revolution. If both, against their will, serve realities to which they have done violence, Constantine on the other hand brought his will into line with the reality and made himself its instrument. Between restoration and revolution he moved easily, independent of both, not compelled to retard progress, nor to give the new dangerously free scope. He knew how to conserve the past and assist the future to be true to its historical responsibility.

Constantine gives the impression of being decisive and swift. Laws flow from his hand and every one bespeaks his indefatigable activity. He showed something of the haste of the great reformer. One can compare the building of his capital with that of Peter the Great or his legislation with the tumultuous legal reforms of Joseph the Second. These men felt the greatness of the task and the shortness of the time. But the new world adawning must at least be circumscribed and measured. Constantine, sensible of the range of his task, was of no mind simply to overturn the old and bring in the new for the sake of novelty. The third way, of which we spoke earlier (p. 77), accomplished what the other two could not achieve. Because Constantine chose this third way, the period of crisis through which he passed became an epoch.

As we come now to the end of this section on the administration of the empire, we need to take a look beyond its frontiers. Writing to one of the proudest of the Persian kings, Shapur the Second, Constantine, toward the end of his life, put his finger precisely on the point at which they differed. In this letter[11] Constantine revived Rome's most shameful memory, the capture of Valerian and the frightful trophy of triumph left behind. The light in which he viewed this catastrophe gave him the courage to mention a disgrace to which he was far from indifferent. "The denial of the one God," he wrote to Shapur, "has brought many of our rulers to disaster and in particular the one whom the divine wrath drove hence and delivered as a mark of shame into your hands." Historians have sometimes flatly rejected the authenticity of this letter. They have not been able to bring themselves to believe that a Roman emperor could so betray a predecessor when writing to the arch enemy.

But if the letter is really from Constantine (and the arguments against its authenticity are not valid), then the emperor was laying himself open to the charge of traducing the honor of the Roman name. Without doubt his intention was to bring about the only possible vindication by showing that one standing under the wrath of God could no longer be Rome's representative and so God had used the Persian as the instrument of his justice. By

11. *Ibid.*, IV, 9–12.

this admission Constantine removed the point of contention with his enemy. If Rome had nothing to avenge, then Persia had nothing to fear.

But Constantine was not content merely to disown his predecessor. He repudiated fearlessly all those who "by their criminal orders had disquieted the people dear to God." Instead of proclaiming Roman solidarity, his resentment against the persecutors seems to have gone so far that he was willing to expose the spectacle of a divided nation to its deadliest foe.

The letter then goes on to overcome the intolerable offense such an admission would give to Romans of the old faith. Constantine, who owed the restoration of the empire to the one God, under whose sign he had conquered, invites the foreign ruler to follow in the same course. If Shapur were gracious to the Persian Christians, the God of Heaven would be gracious to him. What the true faith had done for the Roman Empire it could do also for the Persian. Diocletian had looked upon the missionaries of the Persian religion as infiltrators, softening the empire for conquest. For him religion and nation meant the same thing. But when Constantine, who attributed his success to heavenly assistance, invited his only formidable enemy to share in this aid, he broke new ground in quite another way.

Admittedly, he did not expect to wipe out the frontiers, but he did believe that the common service of the one God should level to human proportions the walls which religion had helped to raise to the very skies. The empire is not the ultimate value. There is a unity which transcends all boundaries, even if it does not obliterate them.[12]

Only thus is it possible to give and receive from other peoples more than land and booty. And this holds true not only for one's neighbors but also for posterity. It was in this fashion that the heritage of the ancient world was transmitted to the medieval world, and it was no accident that the Christian Church should have been the agent.

12. Leopold von Ranke, *Weltgeschichte*, III, 1 (1883), p. 531.

To perceive these implications in Constantine's day required a more comprehensive grasp than any of which he was capable. But his stature is not diminished because he could not grasp the full implications of his own letter. It was something that such ideas should be entertained and expressed by these lips. The words themselves make their own impact simply by stressing what was implicit in the faith to which his letter bears such eloquent testimony.

XII. The Church in the Empire

The administrative reform of Constantine showed at many points the operation of transforming forces whose origin has not yet been fully encompassed. The empowering of the bishop's courts indicated where the emperor looked for help in correcting the faults of civil justice; the reference to emancipation as "pleasing to God" did not rise from pagan assumptions. As for the sign which Constantine's soldiers bore on their shoulders, there could be no doubt on that score. The place of honor assigned to Sunday made a new holiday the mark of Constantine's age. But this was prompted not by individual Christian impulse but by the Church. What did the Church mean to Constantine?

At one time Constantine declared the chief points of Christianity to be "the veneration of God," "fellowship," "true faith"— in other words the cultus, the moral standards, and belief in God. The deity has a right to be reverenced and takes pleasure in proper worship. The new cultus should render what the old had vainly sought, victory and prosperity for the empire. For this reason the clergy were relieved of civil duties. They must be free, without encumbrance, to follow the requirements of their own law. Failure to render to God the service due would be like robbing a temple.[1]

This represented a new version of the old Roman concept of

1. *Donatismusurkunden*, no. 9 (312/13).

the dependence of the common weal upon the favor of heaven. The precise observance of the cultus and strict attention to all its obligations would ensure this favor. Carelessness or neglect would imperil the state. This was why the vestal virgins guarded the sacred flame. Were it to be extinguished, calamity for Rome could be averted only by the expiatory sacrifice of the one at fault. Religion here was not assessed from the point of view of inward devotion but of the outward act of worship, which must be performed at a specific place, at a given hour, by a qualified person.

We can understand, therefore, why Augustus should have thought it incumbent upon him to provide a fitting and precise cultus of the gods of the state. Because he was responsible for the empire he assumed the title of *Pontifex Maximus*. Constantine evoked reminiscences of this older Rome when he intervened personally amid the strife of factions in order to determine "what sort of worship should be rendered to the Godhead, and what cultus is well pleasing to him."[2] State control of religion, which offends us, seemed quite appropriate in that period. The sharp reproach of the emperor against those who "impede the worship due to the highest God" derives from this sense of responsibility for the maintenance of the true cultus.

Of course, when the Christian worship replaced the pagan, more than the name was changed. Still the cultus was not demoted from first place. Only Constantine's persuasion that the cultus must follow precise rules, that it did not depend on the inner attitude of the participant, that it must be celebrated with rigorous exactitude by the priests in a sacred place, and that it was indispensable to the world and not dependent on the world— these presuppositions alone explain what is otherwise inexplicable, namely, that Constantine, not having been baptized, never partook of the central Christian rite, the Lord's Supper. He was concerned that it should be celebrated with rich and stately

2. *Ibid.*, no. 23 (316).

liturgy. For himself, he was content with reading the Scripture in his palace, with prayer, and with making addresses to his entourage.

The cultic view Constantine always retained. It is very evident in his letter concerning the holy sites in Mambre, Palestine.[3] From his mother-in-law Eutropia he learned that pagan rites were unabashedly celebrated at the very spot where the deity in the form of three angels visited Abraham, so that the locality chosen by God Himself was being befouled. Constantine commissioned a subordinate to burn the idols and wipe out any trace of the abomination. In its place the emperor had a church erected. At the point where in the old covenant the services of the holy law had commenced, only the All-Sovereign One and Savior should be honored. The bishops were reproved for not having reported this offense at which the pious Eutropia had taken umbrage. This was not a case of supplying a congregation with a place of holy worship, but rather of establishing suitable worship for a holy place. Anything less would have been a profanation.

It is from the same cultic perspective that one must understand Constantine's deep concern for intercession. His letter to the bishops at Arles closes with the plea that they should continually pray for him. He was not the first emperor to attach efficacy to Christian prayers; Galerius in his Edict of Toleration exhorted the Christians to pray for him and for the empire. Was Galerius' point that those whose loyalty had been questionable should now commit themselves unreservedly to good wishes on behalf of the emperor and the state? Not so much this as that the proper procedure should be observed. Galerius had no doubt about the efficacy of the cultus, even if he did not accept the faith of those whose help he requested. We find the same attitude in Licinius, who, when he suspected that the Christians were praying not for him but for his rival, began to suppress them. Constantine was on the side of the Christians and for that reason he might all the more expect help from their prayers, which would ascend directly

3. *VC*, III, 51ff.

to that power on whom depended his destiny and that of the empire.

Hence the essence of what Christianity introduced—and Constantine's request proves this—was "a new teaching about worship." But if in this expression the whole of Christianity seems to be confined to worship and cultus, we must not forget that alongside worship Constantine also mentioned faith and truth. The words "unanimity, faith, and truth" show the direction in which the emperor's cultic understanding of religion was expanded and deepened.

The extensive influence of the cultus was manifest in the moral sphere, especially in relation to the clergy. The emperor did oblige the clergy to fulfill their liturgical duties to the letter; this service was what justified their exemption from other duties. But it was not enough to say Mass correctly. They must also exemplify "holiness of life." For the Church this meant that the higher clergy should be unmarried. The emperor went along with this understanding to the degree that he rescinded the law which penalized bachelors and the childless. But a later law shows how much more was meant by "holiness of life." The clergy, most of whom still worked at some trade, were exempted from the tax laid on the crafts because "it is certain that their profit will be given to the poor."[4] The grounds for the special treatment accorded the clergy this time were not cultic—though such a basis would have satisfied that age—but rather, social. The lauding of the clergy at this point, to be convincing, must have been true.

The bishops whom the emperor sent from Gaul to Rome to settle a Church dispute were men "reputable in life and in the discharge of official duties." The letter[5] addressed by the emperor to the Council of Arles showed in its bestowal of praise what was expected of the bishops. Constantine assumed that they, trained in the school of Christ, would observe brotherly unity and patience with those in error. "Their verdict"—so reads the famous

4. Theodosianus, XVI, 2, 10 (353, May 26); Dö., no 146, pp. 205ff.
5. Donatismusurkunden, no. 18 (314).

passage—"must be received as if the Lord Himself sat on the seat of judgment."

Like Constantine himself the bishops were servants of God, "the leaders of the common weal," called to be co-workers with the emperor for the attainment of his goal. This obligated them to put themselves above reproach, though for his part the emperor was not quick to listen to reproaches against them. Constantine wanted as bishops "men of transparent goodness, orthodoxy and humanity." "Mercifulness" is ever and again their title to praise. The emperor hoped that his recognition of their courts would enable them to reconcile those at strife. The highest degree of confidence he shows in them is that their own testimony before a court is decisive evidence.

The second great characteristic of the Christian Church in Constantine's view, after appropriate worship and a worthy priesthood, was that the Christians were, as he said, "the people of the pacific law."[6] Earlier emperors justified their aversion to the Christians on the ground that they were disobedient, refractory, uncooperative with respect to the state. Constantine also appraised the Christians from a political angle, claiming pointedly that their influence was beneficial to the state. When he urged the Persian king to strengthen his throne by protecting the Christians, he pointed out that the Church fostered those qualities of which the state stands in need: the great should display justice and modesty; the subordinates compliance and patience.

Constantine was, therefore, not content to incorporate the Christians into the empire in the same way in which the Jews were permitted to live apart according to their own law. The Christian law was profitable for the empire itself because it supplemented the civil order. Constantine had an eye for the limits of state power and for the indispensability of that which the state cannot compel.

He saw in the Church a moral force. The martyrs had taught him that. He respected their composure, integrity, and stead-

6. *Ibid.*, no. 31, line 24 (321?).

fastness. The Christian life came to his attention primarily as it was lived by the clergy. The virtues which the emperor held up to them included self-discipline, fraternal peace, tranquility, and patience. The clergy should set the pattern of these qualities for the congregation and the congregation should exemplify them before the world. The clergy should arrest disintegration by setting tranquility against disturbance, friendliness against brutality, reasonableness against prejudice, and patience against animosity. That which is needful for the state is also that which God has ordained. Religion upholds morals. God evaluates deeds in terms of attitudes, according to whether they show "the right mind," "the untainted soul." When one is called upon to acknowledge justice on the other side in a dispute and to forgive injustice, the way is better paved for peace. If one is convinced that God "loves the meek" and gives "to the just and patient their due," ruthless self-seeking and sheer selfishness are more effectively curbed than by the emperor's command and exhortation. Religious obedience, moral responsibility, and political concern together produce the attitude needful for human communities.

Nothing was so important for the emperor as to find the Christians in the Church of one mind. Concord and harmony had been key words long before Constantine. A pagan author dedicated a book to *concordia* and the Senate an altar. Coins over and over again invoked the legend *concordia,* referring to the harmony of the emperors among themselves, with the Senate, and, not the least, with the armies. At times when the empire was falling apart the word often expressed more a hope than a reality. Afterwards, when there was only one emperor, the word could be dropped from the coins, but this does not mean that Constantine was any the less concerned for concord.

In letters sent to the bishops, to the councils, and to the congregations, he was forever urging them to be of one mind with each other. Peace and agreement are the very essence of the Church and every schism cuts at the root. Therefore Constantine was all the more aghast when he discovered that the Church was not immune to dissension. "I will and wish for all of you peace and unanimity," he said. The emperor, in line with the concern of the Church "for our peace and unanimity," showed how much this concord meant to him by his untiring effort to preserve it. "God works through revelation of the doctrine toward a consonance of unity." When the emperor summoned the Church to be of one mind, he did not think he was imposing on her something alien to her nature. All this had been written in the book committed to the Church. "The admonitions of the law, alike in the Old Testament and the New Testament," said Constantine, "bind the entire Church to unanimity."

Concordia, for Constantine, had not lost its ancient ring, even after the unity of the empire had been secured. Rather, the word took on a new significance. Harmony now had come to mean something more than agreement between the general and the army; all the inhabitants of the empire were to be included. To this end, which the civil order could not fulfill, the emperor turned for help to the Church. Although he appealed to the biblical law of love, his retention of the old Roman word *concordia* shows what he expected Christian love to accomplish.

In all this the Church had not become a department of state, but still it was seen from the angle of the empire. To refer to the Christians as "the people of the pacific law" shows what the emperor saw and sought in the Church and also what he found. He grasped the genius of Christianity and explained what it meant to him. Precisely because Christian love and Roman concord were conjoined, his phrase about the pacific law expressed a genuine relationship, equally worthy of the man who coined the expression and of those to whom it applied.

The cultus, in order to fulfill its meaning, must be authorized by God. The law which ruled the Christians must bespeak a higher name. So faith itself must be conjoined with truth. Together, root and fruit constitute a third ingredient, along with the worship of God and the Christian life. Only then could one say, "We possess the shining house of Thy truth."[7]

7. *VC,* II, 56.

What truth meant for Constantine is made plain by its opposite, error. By taking the measure of error we can see the scope of his truth. Error, for Constantine, was not simply a pardonable mistake, arising from the limitations of human understanding. It was rather faction, illusion, disorder, chaos, corruption—all these were comprised within the word "error." It cut deeply into human behavior and the life of the state. Its origin he believed to be religious and its deepest meaning lay in the denial of God. The state also suffers from ungodliness, said Constantine, "as from a grievous illness." Similarly, the way of truth passes through all human domains but ends in the knowledge of God. Private meditation and philosophical converse do not suffice to dispel all uncertainty. For these Constantine turned, rather, to the council of the bishops. The "great body of men distinguished by self-discipline and intelligence" stand under divine guidance in their quest for truth. They report the mind of God. Here the fullest authority decides what is dubious and establishes a norm in accord with the divine law, which allows of no uncertainty. Dissension, division, tumult, and the deadly poison of disunity will be dispelled in accordance with God's will by the light of truth. We can see how fully persuaded Constantine was that truth had its seat in the Church when we look at his directive to heretics that if they desired the truth they should address themselves to the Church universal.

In all the turmoil of the time, confidence in truth never deserted Constantine. The conflicts all resolved themselves into the one great battle of the age. Over against "the house of truth" stood "the temple of error"; over against the house of the true God, the altars of the many gods. Now was the time for a decision of faith and will. The adversaries were not simply opinions but powers in the heavenly places, the godly conferring blessing, the ungodly working corruption. To the very end of his life the emperor saw the cause of the fall of whole peoples in pagan sacrifice and the denial of the one God. Not only when repudiating paganism did he emphasize belief in the one God as the essential; when he came to express the essence of his own conviction this was again at the center. When it came to faith versus error, Constantine summed it up in one sentence. "We all honor one God and believe that He is One."[8] In professing this faith he knew that he was in accord with the Church.

The "worship commanded by God," "the people of the pacific law," "the shining house of truth," these were the expressions which summarized what the Church meant to Constantine. She assured him of heavenly protection. In her teaching and life she exemplifies those principles which bind men together beyond the civil order; she mediates the knowledge of God, which gives to every man the answer and at the same time opens the eyes of all to the decision demanded by the time.

Constantine was not indulging simply in a wishful dream. Despite exaggerations, there were some facts to substantiate his appraisal of the Church. The fidelity of the martyrs was altogether worthy of the respect he gave them. But still this esteem did not rule out dark shadows. And there were shadows. Peccadillos could be overlooked and many a shortcoming speedily corrected, but Constantine was not prepared to discover that severe crises could rock the very Church herself. Twice he had to witness the Church beset by disturbances, inner conflicts, and, eventually, schisms which shattered all his expectations.

Dissension in the West

The scene of the first conflict was Africa.[9] A disputed election arose over the bishopric of Carthage: a party of dissidents challenged the election of Cecilian. Although personal grudges were

8. Constantine to the Catholic Church of the Alexandrians (June, 325). Cf. *Dö.*, pp. 68ff.

9. W. H. C. Frend, *The Donatist Church* (Oxford, 1952) and his article in the *RAC*, IV, 128–147. Compare B. H. Warmington, *The North African Provinces from Diocletian to the Vandal Conquest* (1954). In his seventh chapter he objects to a derivation of Donatism from exclusively political and social factors. The same is true of the recent studies, among which may be mentioned those of Brisson, Tengström, Diesner, and Grasmück, who stress congregational independence over against the Christian state in addition to ethnic, social, and primitive Christian elements.

a factor, the fundamental question had to do with the treatment of those who had lapsed in the persecution of Diocletian, or, at any rate, had not been utterly intransigent in refusing any sort of collaboration with the government. Following the earlier persecution of Decius, the principle had been established that apostates, after due penance, could be restored to communion. But now the question affected the clergy, some of whom had complied with the order to turn over to the government copies of the Scripture to be burned. Could such "traitors" resume their office and should their official acts, performed after their lapse, be regarded as valid? The rigorists, who answered every question with a negative, took their name from their leader Donatus and were called Donatists. They believed that the Church must be a community of saints. Her primary mark is the suffering of martyrdom and they were unable to dispel the mentality of martyrdom after the persecution was all over.

The controversy rent the African Church. Cecilian, because lenient toward the lapsed, was unacceptable to the rigorists. Constantine did not remain a mere spectator. At the request of the Donatists he referred the case to some bishops from Gaul, meeting in Rome under the presidency of the bishop of Rome, the leading see in the west.[10] The ruling was unfavorable to the Donatists and they refused to accept it. Constantine then summoned representatives of all the western churches to meet at Arles, in southern Gaul, by this means opening up a new way for the determination of controverted issues in the Church. Constantine hoped that the bishops, true to their pacific role, would be able to compose the controversy and restore peace. He was therefore deeply upset when the Donatists again refused to abide by a second negative decision. Plainly they were false to the law of the Church and in their litigation as bad as the heathen. Still he did not refuse them a personal audience. Though of no mind to treat the council as a mere tool, he found himself driven to render a decision. The emperor, in his judicial capacity, then

10. H. U. Instinsky, *Bischofsstuhl und Kaiserthron* (1955), pp. 59–82.

listened to the case against Cecilian, deemed it unfounded, and again rejected the plea of the plaintiffs. Returning to Africa, the Donatists had recourse to violence. Constantine thereupon banished their guilty bishops.

But the Donatists felt that they had not been refuted. They insisted that an apostate had cut himself off from the life-giving stream of the Church and in consequence his ecclesiastical acts were invalid. The two parties had not come adequately to grips as to their theories of the Church. The Council of Arles was content to vindicate certain persons accused of apostasy, but one ruling did strike at the heart of the question. Proved apostates were to be deposed from office but their acts, while in office, were not to be considered invalid, which was to say that the rites of the church do not depend upon the personal character of the ministrant. The underlying concept of the Church, as embracing not only saints but sinners, was not squarely faced and the controversy as it continued became entangled in private grudges and social cleavages. The rival claims were taken before the civil courts because questions of property were involved. To which party should the government restore the churches? The Donatists objected to having the state make the decision. "What has the Emperor to do with the Church?" Their plea lost its force when they forsook the way of suffering in favor of violence. This was the first time the "martyrs" had defended themselves. Then their opponents went a step further in the same direction. Cecilian, convinced of the justice of his case, appealed to the state. Since in Carthage some of the church buildings promised to the Catholics were in the hands of the Donatists, he turned to the civil authorities. Pagan soldiers invaded the churches and struck down whatever stood in their way. A Donatist bishop was shot with an arrow. The shedding of blood did more than anything else to cause a schism.

When the emperor decided to intervene, the Donatists did nothing to alter his firm persuasion that they were rebellious, godless men. As a matter of fact, political and social disaffections had attached themselves to their movement. In many places the Berbers rose against the Roman overlords. Fanatical warrior groups called Circumcellions roved the country, plundering the land, burning villas and Catholic churches. The emperor was moved to take action, not only for the sake of public order but also to restore the united worship of God. This was in line with the Roman tradition that the ruler should exercise the office of high priest. But armed intervention did not last long. After a few years Constantine permitted the banished to return.[11]

What was the reason for this retreat? Constantine explained that the obstinacy of the Donatists had foiled his intention.[12] To be sure, it was politically expedient to permit the banished to return, but Constantine could not justify this freedom of religion unless it were allowed by God. Since, then, the state could not bring the Donatists to a better mind, there was nothing for it but to leave to God either their conversion or chastisement. Frequently Constantine quoted the verse, "Vengeance is mine, saith the Lord," which he interpreted as meaning that man should not leap ahead of God but should wait in patience for His intervention.[13] Constantine had been taught by the Donatist controversy to recognize limits to the responsibility of the Roman emperors for the true worship of God. The Christian faith required that these limits be respected.

---

11. *Donatismusurkunden*, no. 30 (May 5, 321).
12. *Ibid.*, no. 31 (321?).
13. The extent of this tolerance is evidenced by the occurrence at Cirta where, when the Donatists appropriated a church built by the emperor, he built another for the Catholics. Constantine to the Eleven Numidian Bishops (330), cf. *Dö.*, pp. 40ff.

XIII. *Dissension in the East: The Arian Controversy*

The east also, to an even greater degree, demonstrated to the emperor that the Church was by no means a sure haven of peace. In Alexandria, the chief city of the Hellenistic east and at that time the spiritual capital of the Greek Church, a doctrinal controversy had arisen which soon began to involve extended areas. What Constantine heard and thought about the beginnings of the Arian controversy is shown in a letter[1] which he addressed to the two champions, the bishop Alexander and the presbyter Arius.

It all started, so Constantine assumed, because Bishop Alexander asked his presbyter about the meaning of a passage in the Bible and Arius gave an unsatisfactory answer. The question need not have been asked, thought Constantine, and the answer might better not have been given. No law, he said, calls for the public discussion of such unimportant and, at the same time, such difficult questions. To do so leads to unprofitable, idle verbal contention, divides the Church, and confuses the faith. The philosophical schools do debate particular questions, Constantine admitted, but are quickly of one mind about the fundamentals. So, also, Christian fellowship should not be rent by idle quibbling

---

1. Constantine to Alexander and Arius (324); VC, II, 64–72. Cf. *Dö.*, pp. 55ff.

over words. If men want to debate minor matters let them at any rate not involve the populace. Better to keep silent. In the case of non-essentials like these there can be diverse opinions without a breach of unity, but for God and His providence, there can be only one faith.

The emperor offered to mediate the dispute, which seemed to him trivial and fraught with drastic consequences. Let both parties in good will reflect on what they had in common. Constantine's closing words show that he took this to heart. His letter affords an assured expression of those ideas that dominated the work and faith of his life. In view of the mighty truths and the noble mission of Christianity such squabbling over words, he continued, was pitiable. Let the Church be true to herself, let her be mindful of her grave responsibility. She imperiled the life's work of the emperor, shook the empire, and brought her own claims into jeopardy when she forsook the law of God and delivered herself up to the spirit of dissension.

How appealing the summons to abstain from a more precise formulation of faith might be to Constantine's generation may be guessed when a nineteenth-century historian (Heinichen) renders the same judgment. He thought Constantine's words golden when he said, "It were better not to have asked, nor to have answered such questions." "How regrettable that the Christian Church did not adopt these words for good and that Constantine did not adhere to them to the end!"[2]

Constantine wanted to curb divisiveness but he would not admit a pluralism of religious opinions for reasons of state, as if it did not matter what anyone believed so long as the peace was maintained. The welfare of the state itself required unanimity of conviction. The appeal to good will assumed a kernel of faith which alone could maintain that peace.

Constantine's first pronouncement in the great doctrinal controversy was easily understandable, but he could not stop with en-

2. F. A. Heinichen, *Commentarii in Eusebii Pamphil. Historiam Eccl.* (Leipzig, 1870), III, 780.

joining silence upon the parties. The aid of the Church was indispensable for the achievement of his ultimate aim of welding the empire into a cohesive whole. At that very moment the Church was faithless to her vocation and his exhortation did not allay the strife. The differences could not be glossed over. The emperor then had recourse to the device already used in the west of assembling a council, this time for bishops from all over the world. The meeting place was Nicaea, near his residence in Nicomedia. This council has ever since been known as the first ecumenical, meaning the first universal council, embracing both the east and the west. This time the emperor himself took part in the proceedings and tried to understand the issues.

We have an account of the opening of the session from the eyewitness Eusebius.[3] On the appointed day, the bishops assembled from near and far—the west too was represented, he noted —and gathered in the great hall of the imperial palace. To the left and right they took their seats. Then came members of the court, while the imperial guard remained outside. At the sign that the monarch was approaching, the entire assembly rose and he entered "as an angel from heaven," towering, robed in glittering purple decorated with gold and jewels, "his soul clearly adorned with piety and the fear of God, full of mildness and benevolence." In the midst of the hall a golden chair awaited him. Only after a sign from the bishops was he seated and then they, too, took their places. After a short greeting from the bishop on the right, the emperor himself took up the words in a calm voice, speaking in Latin which an interpreter translated into Greek.

Eusebius tells us that the emperor in person discussed the issues, approving, exhorting, blaming. Constantine himself, after the close of the council, related that as one among them he conferred with the bishops, with them sought the truth and participated in the decision. This does not mean that he attended all the sessions, but it shows that neither he nor they had any objection to his presence. As to the extent of his influence, there

3. *VC*, III, 6ff.

are only conjectures. Some hints give an idea of the limits of his collaboration.[4] When a bishop, suspected of heresy, produced his confession as a vindication of his orthodoxy, Constantine wanted to have this statement adopted by the council but the members objected that it did not touch on the points at issue.

What was the problem? At an earlier time champions of the Christian faith, in order to make it intelligible to pagans, had borrowed from philosophical terminology the concept of the *Logos*, as the mediator between man and God. This Logos (meaning either the reason immanent in God or the Word expressing God) revealed to man God's essence and will. Christians took over the expression and had then to decide how this Logos was related to God, because the Christian faith could scarcely speak seriously of a mediating essence between the Creator and the created. Arius voiced a prevalent opinion when he emphasized the transcendence of God, who was without beginning. And Arius looked upon the Logos as a creature, although the first and the most perfect of all creation, yet not of the essence of God. This Logos was nevertheless the instrument in the creation of the world, but only in a metaphorical sense could he be called God or the Son of God. He it was who appeared on earth in the fashion of a man. He lived in Jesus in place of the human soul. In answer to the fundamental question of the Christian faith, "Whom do we confront in Christ?" Arius answered, neither God nor man but a spiritual being. He rose higher than any man but whether he can lead us to God no one can say because the Logos himself did not attain sure knowledge of God.

The opposite side found its best representative in Athanasius. He, too, was a student of the Greeks and he, too, made use of Hellenistic modes of thought and concepts. He did not arrive

4. The lack of protocol might be interpreted as deliberate glossing on the part of a synod of the imperial Church with respect to inordinate imperial interference. But now we realize that on the contrary the subordination of the Church to the state had not yet begun. The Church was primarily impressed by the inspired outcome rather than by the preliminary negotiations, and the conflict of the parties was not yet worthy of note.

quickly at a firm expression of his position, but he was clear from the outset that for him the teaching of Arius was not acceptable. When Athanasius talked about the Logos it was to place him (or it) on the side of God; and the Logos was of God's essence, eternal and uncreated, in truth God's Son and very God. He it is who became flesh to save men from the destiny of death. He became man in order that we might partake of God. In Christ we confront God as He is and He encounters us as a man. Arius appeared to Athanasius to be close to paganism because he talked about an uncreated and a created God, just as the pagans talked about an unbegotten god and many begotten gods.

"The Logos cannot perfectly see and know his Father," said Arius. To which Athanasius replied, "He assumed a body and walked as a man among men that men might see his works and, through them, recognize the Father." The two statements reveal the contrast. In the one the highest spiritual power, embodied in Christ, must confess its inability to know God. The other talks about a sure knowledge. The rational concept of God on the part of Arius stopped short of full revelation. The eternal God cannot be embodied in the ephemeral. The being of God cannot be degraded by such a limitation. But for Athanasius self-disclosure was a part of God's nature. Athanasius was not troubled by the untouchability of God. His concept of God can only be grasped if it is seen to be one with God's action upon the world. Nor was he content with the knowledge of God, however important. The truth of which he spoke is not one which, in response to questions and quest, sometimes half discloses, sometimes half withdraws itself more remotely, but rather one which comes to us, summons us, enables us to participate in its nature. The biblical understanding is set over against that of the Greeks. Truth does not repose in itself, but meets us in the form of a man. Not by accident did Athanasius lay all the emphasis upon the work of Christ, who came in order to make us sons of God. The biblical concept, variously interpreted in the course of subsequent history, was related by Athanasius to immortality. "He revealed Himself through a body that we might receive the knowledge of the invisible Father. He assumed shame from men that we might inherit immortality." God himself entered into death and destruction, which man, of his own power, cannot overcome. This is the point at which Athanasius brought his meaning to full expression. Unlike Arius he did not think of God as utterly removed from the world, behind a veil, which Christ himself could not penetrate. God is close to us. The same God it is who brings us into life and delivers us from death. God is able not only to create and reveal but also to redeem. He does not come to us as "a stranger." Because Arius appeared to bring all this into question Athanasius must oppose him.

The language and the concepts of Athanasius belonged to his period and profoundly affected his statement about the faith, particularly in the way in which he used the Greek concept of substance and envisaged the final destiny of man as incorruptibility. But although he clothed his thoughts in words taken from Greek philosophy, he was nevertheless dealing with the biblical witness. This was what he set against the position of Arius. Although Athanasius' thought was cast in the mold of his age and cannot be revived in the same terms, still he had a right to believe that the Christian faith itself was at stake and not just some trivial details.

The question was both great and simple, the answer decisive. But the way to a sure understanding was even then not easy. Behind the discussion lay already a long history marked by spiritual wrestling, definitions with divisions and subdivisions, approaches from various angles, entanglements in formulae and distinctions, all leaving the problem still unsolved. One must have had a sense of personal involvement to do justice to a question which after all was not a matter of scholarship but must be grasped by the spirit.

Constantine came to the problem from another world. He was no stranger to the realm of mind and spirit and was not addicted to the anti-intellectualism of the military emperors before him, yet he lacked the presuppositions to grasp what it was all about. But he tried to find out and soon regarded himself as entitled to a judgment of his own. When Arius was not reconciled with Alexander, as Constantine a year before had confidently expected, the emperor came then to look upon him as an "abandoned servant of the Devil, who, with godless intent, has sowed this evil." What a year before had been a tolerable private opinion now came to be regarded as a pernicious public error. The responsibility for rending the Church, for which earlier both disputants had been blamed, was now cast solely upon Arius. Constantine, having studied the views of Arius, had come to see how they diverged from his own.[5] Arius divided the Son from the Father, whereas everything depended on the fact that the power manifest in the world and the will operating through history should not be separated from God. "Is not God everywhere, for we see that He is always present? . . . Does not the well-being of all things depend on His power, without division and separation?" Constantine believed that his own mission depended upon his faith and would be uncertain if God were not with him. The remonstrance of the emperor came out of his own experience and really cut to the core of Arius' position, for while Arius was afraid of losing God through contamination with the world, Constantine feared loss by putting God out of the world.

The sessions of the Great Council—this honorable designation persisted throughout subsequent history—were not smooth. So stormy were the debates raised by the reading of Arius' confession that the bishop who presented it was not allowed to read to the end. The parchment was ripped out of his hand.

We do not know who was the author of the draft finally accepted. On June 19, 325, the council proclaimed the new statement of faith. As to the rejection of Arius, all the members were agreed. The words which combined the traditional and the po-

5. Constantine to the Catholic Church of Nicomedia (Nov./Dec., 325). Cf. *Dö.*, pp. 70ff.

lemical traits definitely excluded his position. Above all else the point was emphasized that the Son belonged with the Father and was not a creature. The report of Eusebius[6] that the emperor himself proposed to the council the highly controverted word *"homoousios"* is not at all impossible. The word meant "of one substance," or essence, or being, and was applied to the Son in his relation to the Father. This word, which had behind it a long history and had been used previously in many senses, was to become the slogan of the Nicene position.

The council contained three parties: the adamant adherents of the Athanasian position; the ultra Arians; and a middle party, who had not yet fully made up their own minds. Because they agreed that Arius was wrong they were ready to that extent to concede that his opponents were right. Their goal was peace, an objective surely not simply imposed on the Church by the emperor. Nicaea undoubtedly set up, in the words of one participant, a sign against error. But this does not mean that the peace achieved removed all tensions. Nicaea was not the end but the beginning of doctrinal controversies which rent the Church throughout the century.

At the conclusion of the council, Constantine informed the local congregations of the result.[7] The preservation of unity and the rejection of the Arian error had been accomplished. God Himself, through the three hundred bishops assembled, had declared His will. The content of the newly formulated faith meant for the emperor that "we all worship one God and believe that He is One." Thus we see how Constantine related the

6. Eusebius to his congregation with respect to the Nicene Creed (June, 325). Cf. *Dö.*, pp. 74ff.

7. Constantine to the Catholic Church of the Alexandrians (June, 325). Cf. *Dö.*, pp. 68ff. For an analysis of the Nicene vote cf. Henry Chadwick, "Faith and Order at the Council of Nicaea: A note on the Background of the Sixth Canon," *Harvard Theol. Rev.* LIII (1960), pp. 171–195. For Arius, Athanasius and the formula of Nicaea compare especially J. N. D. Kelly, *Early Christian Doctrines* (London, 1958), pp. 226ff, together with Kelly's earlier book *Early Christian Creeds* (London, 1950), and G. L. Prestige, *God in Patristic Thought* (London, 1936).

homoousios of the Nicene Creed to the great contrast between the One and the many gods which he pointed up for his generation when he said, "Let no one hesitate. Let all go forward on the true way!"

But however easy the road that led out of Nicaea seemed at first, before long it ran into deep trouble under the sons of Constantine, although at the beginning the Church was well pleased with his endeavors to extend the peace and recall those who had been excluded. Eusebius of Nicomedia, the court bishop, was one of their number. He had been unwilling to repudiate his old companion Arius, but now he confessed his loyalty to the word *"homoousios"* and to the "peace,"[8] thereby winning the confidence of the Church and gaining the favor of the emperor. Reconciliation was not so easily effected with the Meletians—a party of opposition in Egypt, left over from the period of persecution, who would not give up their peculiar tenets. A mixture of rigor and compromise finally brought a number of them over. But the supreme test of the imperial policy was Arius, whose banishment Constantine was inclined to revoke. The emperor in his own person undertook to bring Arius to a better mind and invited the onetime "servant of the Devil" to his court. Arius agreed to an explanation which, without formal recantation, avoided the expressions that Nicaea had condemned.[9] This satisfied the emperor, particularly because the "separation" (that is, between the Son and the Father) which he found so objectionable in the position of Arius, was omitted from this statement. Constantine therefore called upon Alexander to restore Arius, if he were satisfied that Arius had accepted the Nicene

8. Communication of the banned bishops Eusebius of Nicomedia and Theognios of Nicaea to the second Synod of Nicaea (end of 327) and Constantine to Alexander of Alexandria (beginning of 328). From now on, Eusebius of Nicomedia was regarded by the emperor as of the Nicene party and no longer as an Arian. Consequently we must no longer see an Arian tendency in the baptism of Constantine at the hands of the "court bishop." Constantine to the end was of the Nicene party in the same sense as at the time of the council.

9. Arius and Euzoios to Constantine (end of 327). Cf. *Dö.*, pp. 78ff.

formula. "Thus harmony would dispel hate." But now came an unexpected resistance. Athanasius, who in 328 had succeeded Alexander as the bishop of Alexandria, would have none of it. He could not discover that Arius had renounced his error. Constantine withdrew his recommendation but without giving up his intent, as the sequel proves.

In subsequent years, the young patriarch at Alexandria, who was building up a position of great power in the Church, met nevertheless with opposition in his own land and even more so outside Egypt. The unity achieved at Nicaea proved to be brittle. The majority of the Greek bishops were in favor of mediating positions and did not agree with the inflexible intransigence of the young Athanasius. The growing bitterness of the conflict, in which base and lofty motives were entangled, is made evident in that the Meletians actually charged Athanasius with having murdered one of their leaders. When this priest was discovered concealed in a cloister the affair redounded to the credit of Athanasius.

The judgment of the emperor with respect to Athanasius had undergone a marked change. The utter intransigence with which Athanasius had repulsed the express order to restore the Arians could not but inspire respect and the emperor may well have discerned in the unyielding bishop a spirit akin to his own. When, then, new complaints continually arose from Egypt about the ruthlessness of his régime—rumors duly enlarged by the court circle—Constantine summoned the bishop to his presence. But Athanasius was able to silence all recriminations. The impression of his person was so great that Constantine recognized in him "a man of God." A message was sent by the emperor to Alexandria[10] giving vigorous expression to his displeasure over the ungrounded complaints and vicious slander against the bishop. Athanasius was praised for his zeal for the true doctrine and "his energizing spirit." But when Constantine declared Athanasius

10. Constantine to the Alexandrians (331/2). Cf. *Dö.*, pp. 96ff. To Athanasius, cf. F. L. Cross, *The Study of St. Athanasius* (1945).

to be "not unworthy of his own peace-loving faith," there was undoubtedly at the same time a gentle tone of admonition.

Peace proved to be elusive. The charges against Athanasius did not die down. The disorders knew no end. The emperor therefore called for a council at Caesarea (334), the city nearest Egypt. The council should investigate the charges and Athanasius should appear. He refused. A council meeting in the area dominated by his opponents was certain to condemn him. But, understandable as his action might be, Constantine could not view his rejection of the invitation as anything less than disobedience, indeed rejection of the decision of a council, behavior no different from that of the Donatists. No wonder that his view of the bishop deteriorated. He then called a new council at Tyre (335).[11] What he thought of Athanasius is plain from his reference to "those who disturb the unity of the Church." "A diseased contentiousness" seeks to bring everything into confusion, while "arrogance" endangers the harmony of the provinces. Let the bishops judge without regard to favor or disfavor. They should uphold the apostolic justice. Constantine solemnly reminded them of their obligation to Christian peaceableness. For him this was the hallmark of the faith; otherwise they were free.

The council was controlled by the opponents of Athanasius. They raked up everything that could be said against him, especially his contempt for the meeting of the previous year. The doctrinal question was forgotten. This time Athanasius was present but contrived to escape before his condemnation, made his way to Constantinople, and addressed himself directly to the emperor, who described the scene in person. As he was riding back to the palace he was confronted by a beggar in shabby rags. A courtier informed him that this was Athanasius. At first he was unwilling to hear him but then felt that he should not gainsay the plea of justice. Athanasius demanded that his detractors present their charges in the presence of the emperor.

11. Constantine to the Synod at Tyre (335). *VC*, IV, 42. Cf. *Dö.*, pp. 114ff.

Constantine's utter disillusionment with the bishops was voiced in the last document addressed to them.[12] Whereas, under the emperor's influence, the Church had spread beyond the frontiers of the empire and the world that stood so sorely in need of her, now she was violating her nature and vitiating her claims. "We do nothing," he said, "but feed dissension and hate whatever tends to the corruption of mankind." The reproach addressed to Athanasius in the first letter to Tyre was addressed now to his judges as well. "You would like to have your wrangling go on forever." Let them come at once to him and show that they were able to pass judgment without favor or enmity and without perversion of justice.

The accusers of Athanasius this time did not refer to the charge of murder or the breaking of the chalice.[13] Athanasius relates only a political charge.[14] He was alleged to have threatened to hold back the grain ships which sailed from Alexandria to supply Constantinople. The emperor, incensed, banished him to Trèves. The main reason no doubt was the growing conviction that Athanasius was the one who impeded the peace of the Church. This was not a critique of the doctrine of Athanasius. To Constantine's mind a faith which did not issue in peace and unanimity but served rather to gratify ambition was inconsistent with the constant injunction of the Lord laid upon all, and especially upon bishops. One might almost say that by this time the roles were reversed and that Arius enjoyed the aura of Nicaea, whereas Athanasius was regarded as the epitome of factionalism.

Constantine himself explained his procedure. On the one hand the plea of the Alexandrians for their bishop was sharply re-

12. Constantine to the bishops assembled at Tyre (between October 30 and November 7, 335). Gelasius, *HE*, III, 18, 1–3. Cf. *Dö.*, pp. 119ff.

13. A presbyter of Athanasius was alleged to have disturbed the worship of the Meletians, to have overturned the communion table, and in so doing to have broken a chalice. Athanasius himself was held responsible for the murder of a leader of the Meletians. Athanasius succeeded in uncovering the "murdered" man and presented him to the council.

14. Cf. *Dö.*, p. 123.

buffed. They shared the blame for the disturbances which had required military intervention. The case was different when a plea came from Anthony, the desert saint, remote from worldly concerns and ecclesiastical ambitions. Constantine sent him a courteous explanation.[15] Granted that some at Tyre may not have had the loftiest motives, nevertheless, wrote the emperor, one should not disregard the judgment of so many honorable and able bishops. Athanasius is arrogant, intemperate, and a fomenter of faction and disorder. The most obvious example is his refusal to reinstate Arius after the fulfillment of all reasonable demands—so it seemed to Constantine. The emperor thought of himself as the advocate of the Church, whose doors must always remain open. He had taken action against Athanasius, not because he was a nuisance, but because he had misused his office. Constantine hoped that when the young patriarch was removed from the factional bitterness at Alexandria he would cool his heels. For that reason he had not been deposed. The implication was that after he had grown more temperate, he might be restored. Constantine's son—also named Constantine, then the Caesar in the West, in whose residence the banished Athanasius resided—later appealed to his deceased father's intent, when he allowed Athanasius to return to Alexandria, referring to him as "the proclaimer of the holy law."[16]

The banishment of Athanasius made possible the realization of the emperor's original plan. The spokesmen of the Arians were sent to the council which had condemned Athanasius and which had now transferred from Tyre to Jerusalem in order to dedicate the newly completed Church of the Holy Sepulchre. The emperor's question whether the teaching of Arius conserved the

---

15. Letter to Antonius. Sozomen, *HE*, II, 31, 3. For a discussion of Constantine's relation to Athanasius see the posthumous essay of Henric Nordberg, "Athanasius and the Emperor," *Commentationes Humanarum Literarum* XXX. 3, Helsinki 1963, which is worthwhile reading though Nordberg could not accomplish a full, detailed study.

16. Letter of Constantine II to the Church of Alexandria. Cf. *Dö.*, p. 124.

apostolic teaching received now an affirmative answer.[17] Arius died just before his solemn reinstatement, but his followers were returned to their churches. In the east, though not in the west, the emperor's goal of peace seemed to have been realized.

Constantine viewed the Church from the vantage point of his own mission, in which she, too, was involved. If he had been a statesman only he might simply have suppressed the controversy which threatened unity; so long as mere trivialities were in question that procedure would have been appropriate. Squabbles over words should not be allowed to endanger public tranquility. But suppression of controversy would become highly dubious if the ruler undertook to determine what was trivial. Then keeping the peace might have been the criterion of what was important, as if truth were to be sacrificed to the civil order.

Constantine did not take this course. Neither, in his disillusionment, did he leave the Church to go to the Devil. Just as in the west he had done his best to bring the Church to a decision of her own on the controverted points, so also in the east. When the controversy assumed larger proportions he did not suppress it, but tried to promote a joint decision on the part of the Church after a full airing, and himself participated in the discussion and the conclusions. Because of his mission he had the right and the duty to do this.[18] Neither he nor the bishops regarded it as an unwarranted intrusion. Sharp misgivings over imperial participation

17. Constantine to the bishops at Jerusalem (Sept., 335), Sozomen, *HE*, II, 27, 13–14. Missive of the Synod at Jerusalem to the Egyptians and the Church universal (Sept., 335), Athanasius, *De Synodis*, XXI, 2–7. Cf. *Dö.*, pp. 118ff.

18. Constantine's remark that he is "a bishop of the extern(al)" is ambiguous; it either means bishop of the external affairs of the Church or bishop of the people outside the Church. This statement of the emperor has been much discussed. Does Constantine regard himself as the bishop who has to care for the wordly existence of the Church? Does he—as *Pontifex Maximus*—want to perpetuate the pagan cults or is his intention to proselyte the pagans? Despite all the scrutiny spent on these questions certainty cannot be attained. Any answer will depend on the general view one takes of Constantine. Cf. J. A. Straub in: *Dumbarton Oaks Papers* XXI (1967), pp. 37–55.

belonged to the next period; imperial pretension and episcopal rejection were to create tension, but not yet. From the Council of Nicaea the path could lead to the Council of Milan (A.D. 355) at which Constantine's son, Constantius, made the declaration, "What I will should be the law of the Church." Still, there was a larger danger implicit in the greatness of the Nicene achievement, namely, that the pronouncement of a council, removed from the context of the discussions out of which it arose, should be ossified into law. Constantine did not press the Nicene Creed as a legal enactment, to be read according to the letter rather than its original intent; but this possibility was not remote and later generations in Church and state did not avoid it.

For Constantine the doctrinal controversy was ended at Nicaea. Now a valid norm existed. There should be no more dispute about it. Something on which everyone agreed should not be given a private twist. Of course, the creed having been adopted must be understood. But how quickly controversy could arise over this understanding! Strife must be quelled, but how easy then to impede understanding! This second danger was the one into which a ruler, responsible for the public order, was most likely to fall. But Constantine was not motivated simply by political considerations, however important they might be. Unity, for him, was part of the very essence of the Christian faith itself. Consequently the power of true teaching to promote social unity must be assisted. Love is not secondary to faith; both spring from the same source. A truth which has become the monopoly of a party belies its essence. So Constantine said to the congregation at Antioch:[19] "I wonder whether I should say that, for you, truth is the source of salvation or of hatred," implying, of course, that it could not be the second. These words of Constantine point toward a suggestion by Augustine: "Truth is not the affair of individuals but belongs to all those who through her are called into community. From him who tries to appropriate truth for

19. *VC*, III, 60.

himself it is taken away, because he turns from community to self-seeking, from truth to error."[20]

Constantine's action is intelligible and above reproach. It matched his faith and the demands of the time. But still we cannot rest content with such a judgment. Did not the next generation bring to light the dangers lurking in his answers? And was he not responsible for the harm which grew out of his work? Was not the last council under his reign an ominous fruit of his ecclesiastical policy? And did not his son make manifest what was implicit in the father's course?

The attitude of the Council of Tyre was brought more fully to light later on. Five years after the death of Constantine the representatives of the Greek Church justified the deposition of Athanasius in these words: "Even if he were innocent of the charges brought against him at Tyre he should be condemned because his fanaticism and ambition have rent the Church. If he had a spark of piety he would have sacrificed himself like Jonah and suffered himself to be thrown into the sea in order to save the crew and the passengers from the storm which he alone had raised."[21]

The demand for supreme sacrifice on behalf of fellowship is here shown in a revealing light. If fellowship had been the only consideration one need not ask whether the bishops were right in demanding this sacrifice of Athanasius. But they compared him to Jonah running away from his duty and bringing a storm upon the Church, which he should allay by sacrificing himself. Suppose, however, that Athanasius were standing for the truth, without which the fellowship would be dissolved? The council was evidently not totally unaware of this when it flung at Athanasius the reproach of fanaticism and tried to suppress the

20. Cf. H. v. Soden, *Was ist Wahrheit?* (1927), reprinted in "Urchristentum und Geschichte," *Gesammelte Aufsätze und Vorträge,* I (1951), 22.

21. Synoda letter of the Eastern council of Philippopel, the countercouncil to Serdica, a. 343," *CSEL,* LXV, 62ff. *Dö.,* p. 117, note 2.

creed of Nicaea. This council was trying to get rid of the most formidable opponent to what it believed to be the true teaching. But if then the controversy was about the creed, its plea that discussion should be dropped for the sake of peace lost its cogency. Rather, the command of love was to witness to the truth which would restore the fellowship. In that case the hope for the recovery of harmony rested with him who had been cast out. Constantine too condemned inordinate ambition, saw in orderliness and patience the chief duties of the episcopal office, and pleaded for like-mindedness in the Church. But he approved of Athanasius' zeal and did not permit the Nicene Creed to be touched. He did not propose to sacrifice the unyielding Athanasius to the peace of the Church, but wanted to make him realize what a concern for fellowship required of him.

Constantine's interest in the unity of the Church was carried on by his son. But did the latter faithfully adhere to the course set by his father? Constantius also tried to restore the unity of the Church and found himself impeded by Athanasius. He, too, called a council and it also condemned Athanasius without inquiring into the doctrinal issues. Constantius went beyond his father when he imposed his will on the bishops, banished all the dissidents, and, having constrained the Church, altered the creed. Now the threat was not only to the freedom of the Church but also to her teaching.

The route taken by the Council of Tyre and by Constantius was not that of Constantine, and yet they could not have done what they did had he not done what he did. But he contrived to hold together procedures which in their hands fell apart and thereby lost their relevance. We may doubt whether he could have done any better, and, given the pattern which he had established, perhaps his successors enjoyed no freedom. But if his policies entailed dangers for the empire, no less perilous was the policy of the Church. Once a doctrine becomes the slogan in a partisan quarrel, no matter how correct, it cannot be a true teaching. It degenerates into a verbal wrangle; then to put a stop to this becomes not only a political but also a Christian duty.

Questions have to be answered in the context in which they are posed; one cannot assume that their possible implications will necessarily be worked out. That is why Constantine cannot be held responsible for what others did with his work. And yet we cannot let the matter rest here. We have to go back to Athanasius. The emperor did not see, and others did not see, that the whole Nicene cause would go down with Athanasius. Constantine banished him in the interests of peace but this very attempt to ensure the peace in fact wrecked the peace. To spell this out let us return to the point when the peace seemed to be assured. As a symbol of the one Church in the one empire a celebration in honor of the twentieth anniversary of Constantine's reign was arranged, for which Constantine invited the bishops to Nicomedia. The peace of the Church had just been restored by the Council of Nicaea. Eusebius describes the scene; how the invited guests passed through the ranks of the imperial bodyguards who, with naked swords, surrounded the palace; how the guests were conducted into the imperial chambers and there sat down to dine with the emperor. After a repast they were showered with costly presents. Eusebius reports that when the bishops fearlessly passed through the files of the armed guards into the very same palace from which the decree of persecution had been issued by Diocletian, there to be seated at the very same table with the emperor, they wondered whether it was all a dream. Some of the guests still bore the marks of the persecution. The emperor kissed the empty socket of one of the confessors, whose eye had been gouged out in the persecution under Diocletian. Who would not have been moved to believe that the impossible had happened? The emperor was a Christian. Could it be "that the kingdom of Christ had come"?[22]

22. *VC*, III, 15.

XIV. The Church's New Structure

Now the Church was an established component of the empire. The bishops had their place in the public life, with the same rank as the highest officials. Yet they did not lose their distinctiveness. This point was later expressed in the ritual of the court; the bishop was not obligated, like others, to kneel in the presence of the emperor. Though Constantine did not enact this particular feature he gave evidence of particular trust in the bishops. To this a widely circulated story bears witness: at Nicaea he had declared that if a bishop sinned he would throw over him the imperial purple. When denunciations of bishops were presented to him he had a fire kindled and flung them into the flames. He protected the honor of the episcopal office although at the same time reminding the bishops of their responsibility.

In addition to other favors and exemption of the clergy from taxation, a law permitted bequests to the Church, whereby she acquired the resources for an extensive social role. Constantine realized the latent capacity of the Church in this regard and laid upon her new duties while supplying the means for their discharge. The state itself in antiquity did not assume welfare functions, except that Constantine continued the earlier practice of feeding the populace of Rome and extended it to Constantinople. But he did not shut his eyes to the need and demand and committed to the Church the care of the poor and the sick. He was not making a new assignment. The Church had long been devoted to such tasks and had developed a special ministry for the purpose. Now she rose to her new duties. How she did so is described by Lactantius, who had come to be, for Constantine, one of the most important spokesmen of the Church. While the chief objects of such care were the widows and orphans mentioned so frequently in the Old Testament, the Church directed herself also to strangers and even to those unknown, from whom no help or return could be expected. To tend the sick who had none to look after them was the supreme example of *Humanitas*. This term, for Lactantius, gathered up all the commands of love. He borrowed the word from Cicero, who inherited it from the circle of Scipio Africanus, who, having conquered Greece, was surrounded by Greek philosophers. In this circle the concept of *Humanitas* was elaborated. It was a code for gentlemen characterized by gentleness and magnanimity. For the Christian humanity was the command of God directed toward the destitute and the outcast. It reached to the very lowest levels and gave help which could not be requited. This is nowhere more evident than in the ultimate "work of piety," the burial of strangers and the poor. "We do not leave the image and likeness of God to be the prey of beasts and birds but we give it back to the earth from which it came. The place of kinsmen is taken by mankind. Wherever a human being is needed, that is where we belong."[1]

Eusebius relates[2] how during the great plague in the area controlled by Maximinus Daza, the Christians were the only ones who, in the midst of calamity, showed their love for mankind. There were some who day by day nursed the sick and buried the dead, for whom no one cared. Others assembled the hungry from the entire city and distributed bread.

The emperor Julian the Apostate paid a grudging tribute to the measure and significance of this Christian service. Writing to Arsacius,[3] the chief priest in Galatia, he urged the pagans to

1. Lactantius, *Institutiones*, VI, 12, 30.
2. *HE*, IX, 8.
3. *Epist.*, 84a (ed. Bidez).

compete with the Church: "the growth of this godlessness [Christianity] was especially due to philanthropy to strangers, burial of the dead and seeming purity of life. . . . The godless Galileans [the Christians] feed not only their own poor but ours as well." Julian attempted to construct a pagan church modeled in every detail on that of the Christians. The pagan priests should stay away from the public houses and theaters, should take on no demeaning business occupation—just like the Christian clergy. In the temples, as in the churches, there should be a seemly divine worship. The writings of the ancients should be read, teachers should address the people on the subjects of faith in the gods and moral duties. Just as the bishops gave letters of introduction to traveling Christians, so also should the pagan laity on their journeys be commended to the new congregations that they might be more closely bound to each other. Not the least of Julian's concerns was the exercise of philanthropy. For him, also, humanity had come to mean care for the strangers and the poor. At the same time pagan philanthropy should be used as a device to advance the cause of the gods. "In every city numerous hostels should be established that strangers, whether or not of our faith, may experience our philanthropy whenever they need it." The emperor made extensive resources available: thirty thousand scheffels of wheat and sixty thousand measures of wine annually. "Teach," he proclaimed, "the adherents of our religion to add voluntary contributions and accustom them to philanthropy. It is shameful when our poor lack assistance." Almost as significant as this tribute to the Christians was the way in which Julian proposed to restore paganism. His prescriptions for the cultus and the clergy were taken from the Church. This alone—although it had no root in paganism—warranted hope that the old faith could be restored. In all of this Julian, unwittingly and unwillingly, was the heir of the first Christian emperor.

But to return to Constantine's reign. The exemption of the clergy from civil duties was in part predicated upon the assumption that all their time and knowledge would be consumed in caring for the multitude of parishioners who would flock into the churches, for, "Now that the divine Power has been made manifest to all," thought Constantine, "many who hitherto held back through fear or unbelief will come to knowledge and a right mind" to such a degree that the churches will not be able to hold them. Hence the bishops, with state aid, should enlarge existing churches and construct new ones. The emperor himself led the way. Immediately after his entry into Nicomedia he began there the construction of a great church as thanksgiving for the victory over "his enemies and God's enemies." The same was done in the other great cities of the east. Eusebius particularly praised the stately edifice at Antioch, not only for its incredibly high octagonal dome but also for its rich decoration.[4]

Constantine's concern for the equipment of the churches is evident in his instruction to the most learned of the bishops, Eusebius of Caesarea,[5] which says: "Let fifty well-written parchment manuscripts of the Bible be made ready for use in the churches." As speedily as possible a deacon should bring the copies by the imperial post to the capital and present them to the Emperor. The Bible meant much to Constantine; the dignity of God's house called for the use of costly parchment; but practical usability was not to be sacrificed.

Constantine gave particular attention to the holy places in Palestine. The most holy for the Christians was the Sepulchre of Jesus, long inaccessible to them because the emperor Hadrian had deliberately erected a temple to Venus on the site. First of all the temple must come down and the sepulchre be uncovered. The emperor ordered that the stone, the wood, and the very earth with which the grave had been filled should be carried away because contaminated by demons. In a special letter he told the bishop of Jerusalem what the site meant to him and how it was to be treated:[6] The relic of the Holy Passion, so long buried, is

4. VC, III, 50.
5. Ibid., IV, 36.
6. Ibid., III, 30.

now by an indescribable miracle brought again to light. In the providence of God the holy place has been purified from shameful idolatry and now should be glorified by the building of a church more majestic than any other. "The most wonderful site in all the world must in proper glory shine." The emperor goes into details. Not only must the highest officials take on the work, but one of the architects of the capital will be released for this assignment. Artists and craftsmen will be engaged. The bishop should at once inform the emperor what will be needed in the way of pillars, costly marble, and gold for the wainscotted roof.

Eusebius describes the final construction.[7] The portico which led in from the street gave a foretaste of the beauty within. The visitor would go through an anteroom sustained by pillars with corridors on the sides. He would then enter the basilica, with five aisles formed by plain square columns. If he entered through one of the three doors, he emerged into a wide space partitioned by rows of pillars. The middle section, that is, the nave, probably was of great height. The ceiling, bedecked with gold, shimmered "like a great sea." The beauty of the colored marble on the walls added an impression of solemnity. At the end of the nave was the semicircle in which stood twelve pillars, crowned by silver vessels, one each for the twelve Apostles. These were a present from the emperor. Left and right at the end of the aisles a door led to a paved court whose columns surrounded the center of the entire structure, the sepulchre itself. The grave cavity, from which the rubbish, dirt, and the stone roof had been removed, was richly adorned. "More powerfully than any words the tomb witnessed to the Resurrection," after it had itself experienced a resurrection through restoration. The spot defiled by enemies must itself participate in the work of God being brought to fulfillment by the emperor. Ancient Jerusalem had had to expiate the murder of the Lord by complete devastation and had even lost its very name [after the destruction by Hadrian the name of the site was

7. *Ibid.*, III, 33ff. Cf. K. J. Conant, "The Original Buildings at the Holy Sepulchre in Jerusalem" (1956).

Aelia Capitolina]. But now another city by that name was arising. Eusebius even dared suggest, with but slight qualification, that this was the New Jerusalem promised in the Book of Revelation (Rev. 21:2). In the meantime the church and the bishopric received the name *Anastasis,* meaning the Resurrection.

On two other holy sites churches were erected; one at the cave where the Nativity occurred at Bethlehem and the second on the Mount of Olives from which Christ ascended to heaven.[8] These churches were also memorials to Helena, the mother of Constantine. She was always close to him, especially in the period of his loneliness. She was converted to Christianity by her son and then committed herself so completely that he felt she had always been a Christian. Now she made a pilgrimage to the Holy Land in order that, as Eusebius said, she might honor the "foot-prints of the Redeemer" and present thank-offerings for her son and grandson. One may well believe that she was prompted by the tragedy in Constantine's own domestic circle, even though this is not expressly attested. As empress dowager she gave largesse to the soldiers, bestowed pardon upon prisoners and those banished, and distributed bread and clothing to the poor. In the churches she appeared dressed with "taste and modesty," seated in the midst of the congregation. In both the Church of the Nativity at Bethlehem and the Church of the Assumption on the Mount of Olives her piety created an enduring memorial.

"Not the place but the assembly of the elect constitutes the church." This statement made by Clement of Alexandria[9] would have been scarcely intelligible to Constantine. He might more readily have said just the opposite—that the place makes the church. It was Constantine who started the vogue for holy places, although of course the graves of the martyrs had long been commemorated by chapels.[10] To be sure, it was quite natural for Helena to revere places associated with the story of

8. *VC,* III, 41ff.
9. Clement of Alexandria, *Stromata,* VII, 29.
10. Cf. A. Grabar, *Martyrium,* 2 vols. (1946).

redemption, but the attachment of holiness or unholiness to something tangible was not inherent in Christianity. Yet it was the concept behind Constantine's anger when he found heathen cults at the spot where the three angels appeared to Abraham; and it was on this account that he arranged for the earth, which bore the temple of Venus and was therefore defiled by demons, to be removed.[11]

In the west, as in the east, the emperor began to build churches after his decisive victory. What Constantine added to the lordly structures reared by his predecessors in honor of themselves and the mistress of the world were not palaces or halls of justice. The basilicas which he built were churches.[12] The model was not the pagan temple, for this would not accommodate great congregations. Besides, the Christians did not wish to evoke memories of the abandoned cult. The churches were modeled after the secular hall, its meaning now altered. A beginning was made with the cathedral church, the residence of the Roman bishop. The Lateran Cathedral Church, "Head and Mother of all the churches," first realized the concept of a Christian ecclesiastical edifice. It had a rectangular center nave, which rose above the two side aisles by means of windowed chambers. The nave opened up through a high triumphal arch into the transept. This is where the altar was located. Behind it was the apse, with the bishop's throne between the priests' seats. This was more than a place of assembly for the congregation; it was itself a holy place, an image and likeness on earth of the world above—the spot, indeed, where both were conjoined.

The Lateran basilica was the first and for a long time the only Christian church within the walls of Rome. Alongside this bishop's church stood the oldest baptistry known to us, where a legend of the fifth century claimed Constantine to have been baptized at the hand of Bishop Sylvester. It was a round structure,

11. *VC*, III, 27.
12. Cf. F. W. Deichmann, *Frühchristliche Kirchen in Rom* (1948).

modeled on the Roman baths. Both the bishop's church and the baptistry were richly endowed with land in Italy and Sicily.

These were not the only examples. Ten Roman churches go back to the time of Constantine and his family. At the spot dedicated to the memory of the Apostles on the Appian Way, where in the second half of the third century cultic meals were celebrated in honor of Peter and Paul, the emperor erected the Church of the Apostles, with room for numerous graves. Early Roman tradition tells us that Constantine transferred the remains of the Apostles from this site to their original tombs, those of Peter to the Vatican and those of Paul to the road leading to Ostia.[13] A modest church was constructed over the remains of Paul, to be replaced under Constantine's successor by an impressive basilica of the dimensions of the Lateran Church. Constantine erected also a church in honor of two Roman martyrs, Marcellinus and Peter, with tombs attached for the imperial family. Here Helena was to be interred. In her palace in the Lateran area the piety of a grandson dedicated the large hall as a Church of the Holy Cross. In so doing Constantine was reverting to the practice common in the third century of using part of a private house as a church. In the very beginning the Christians had assembled in the house of a well-to-do fellow believer who placed his parlor, shall we say, at their disposal; the room was not thereby withdrawn from secular use. There was no need to build special churches. The congregations were small and in any case the early Church knew no such thing as a sacred spot, for nothing earthly is holy, neither man nor the work of man. But when an edifice was consecrated solely to the worship of God it would inevitably be regarded as sacred. Constantine did not start this development, which was already under way in the third century, as we can see from some theological protests

13. Cf. T. Klauser, *Die römische Petrustradition im Lichte der neuen Ausgrabungen unter der Peterskirche* (1956), and A. M. Schneider, "Die Memoria Apostolorum an der Via Appia" (1953).

against the practice. We may add that it is human and fitting to prepare a dignified place for God's service and Word—a place corresponding to the worshippers' mood and enhanced for that purpose by the arts.

The Lateran Church was intended for the bishop and the congregation. St. Peter's became the great basilica of the martyrs. Richly endowed like the Lateran, it was also given endowments in the east. As a foundation of the universal monarchy it should not belong exclusively to the west. In size and shape St. Peter's resembled the Lateran Church but its pre-eminence was that it enshrined the *"memoria Petri."*[14]

In the midst of a pagan cemetery on the side of the Vatican Hill sloping down toward the Tiber, there was already in the second half of the second century a modest memorial. About the turn of the century it was called the *tropaeum,* that is, "the monument of victory." Was this set up by a single venerator of Peter? Was his memory to be kept alive at the very spot where he was executed? We can be certain only of this, that by Constantine's time the bones of the Apostle were firmly believed to lie under the *tropaeum.* Above this little stone the mighty structure of St. Peter's was reared. The exact spot was at the center of the square located between the Triumphal Arch and the apse. The holy place was enclosed by a sepulchre surmounted by a baldachin upheld by four fluted marble posts. In the sixth century Pope Gregory the First raised the level in this part of the church in order to introduce an altar, as was commonly done above the graves of martyrs. Beneath the altar was a space that could be reached only by bending down. This was called the *confessio Petri.* From this a shaft led down to what was assumed to be the grave proper. Into this *"confessio"* gifts and petitions were laid, directed to the Apostle. It was to this tomb of St. Peter, the

---

14. Cf. *Esplorazioni sotta la Confessione di San Pietro in Vaticano,* 2 vols., (Città del Vaticano, Rome, 1951). For the older literature see H. Lietzmann, *Petrus und Paulus in Rom* (1927[2]). Also T. Klauser (see fn 13), and E. Schäfer, *Das Petrusgrab und die neuen Grabungen* (1950/51).

chief relic of Rome, and no longer to the *tropaeum,* that the piety of the Middle Ages was directed.

What the erection of this impressive structure meant to Constantine is evident in the inscription plainly carved in the semicircle of the apse[15]:

> *Quod duce te mundus surrexit in astra triumphans*
> *Hanc Constantinus Victor tibi condidit aulam.*
> (Because under Thy leadership the world has
> risen triumphant to the stars
> Constantine the Victor, has dedicated to
> Thee this structure.)

The address is to Christ, who had given Constantine victory, with the result that now the world which had been abased could raise its head in triumph. A legend of the Middle Ages—and a very influential one!—translated this inscription differently. It assumed that the person addressed was not Christ but Pope Sylvester and took the Latin word *"mundus"* to be not the noun meaning "the world" but the adjective meaning "pure." The word *"aula"* was taken not as structure in the sense of this church but rather as symbolizing the whole empire. The reference was to the tale that Constantine, having been cured of the leprosy by this pope, conferred upon him temporal sovereignty over the western portion of the empire and, so as not to interfere, betook himself to Constantinople. With this in mind the inscription was understood as being addressed to Pope Sylvester:

> Because under thy leadership he [Constantine] rose purified
> [of the leprosy] triumphant to the stars
> Therefore Constantine, the victor, has conferred upon
> thee the empire.

The legendmaker was evidently not bothered by the shift in person. The medieval German poet, Walther von der Vogelweide,

15. E. Diehl, *Inscriptiones Latinae Christianae veteres,* vol. 1 (Berlin, 1961), No. 1752.

mindful of all the evils which ensued when the Church was invested with temporal power, said that poison had then fallen from heaven.

The original meaning of the inscription is no less far-reaching since it sums up the significance of the Constantinian transformation. St. Peter's Basilica is a memorial to the thanksgiving of the Christian world. The inscription in St. Peter's rises to a higher level than the one on the statue in the basilica of Maxentius. That was the saying of a general who had overcome the tyrant. Now we hear the words of a ruler who speaks for the entire world. Here, too, he is the victor. It is his only title, and as such he lays his laurel at the feet of Him by whom he has been lifted to this eminence. The world to which he had proclaimed his faith and which then rose from decay and disintegration stands now beside him. Whereas once the victorious general addressed the populace in the hall of his rival, now the people, united and healed, join in his word and confess in thankfulness what they have experienced. And all this took place not in the basilica of Maxentius but in that of St. Peter.

The words of the inscription belonged properly to Rome, even if this senatorial city could not understand it. With these words, as well as by the churches of his construction, Constantine reached into the future. Of the seven churches which in the Middle Ages crowned the seven hills of Rome, five go back to Constantine.

Why did Constantine build churches? Gratitude for divine help prompted memorials of victory to the Helper. The emperor's duty of caring for stately worship led him to erect impressive edifices, worthy of himself and of the Church. The confident assurance that the logic of history and his own exhortation would bring more people into the Church led him to enlarge old structures and build new ones. His missionary zeal did all that could be done to stimulate further growth, and desire to call attention to his own faith led him to go beyond unobtrusive meeting places in private homes or in the suburbs to build monumental struc-

tures vying with those of ancient Rome. If in the Middle Ages
the churches towered over the cities, Constantine was responsible
for initiating the movement. He put the Church into the midst
of the life of the people.

These monumental churches show where the emperor looked
for the support of the empire. More personal yet is the setting
up of crosses both inside and outside the churches. This is the
point at which the cross became a token of victory. A century
earlier a Christian writer had said, "We neither honor nor do we
need crosses";[16] a century after Constantine another Christian
complained of a horde of crosses (the writer who said this would
allow only one in the apse[17]). The change was due to the first
Christian emperor and was intimately connected with his own
experience. A Church historian of the fifth century wrote: "He
held the divine Cross in great reverence because it had enabled
him to subdue his enemies and because it appeared to him in a
heavenly vision."[18]

The vision of the cross and the magical power of the *labarum*
point to the Cross of Golgotha. The mosaic in the baptismal
church of the Lateran shows the Lamb of God with the cross
on his head. Friday, the day of the Crucifixion, was given a
special place in the week. An early legend brings the very Cross
on which Christ was crucified into direct connection with Constantine. Ambrose relates[19] that when Helena made a pilgrimage
to the Holy Land, she stood on the site of the Crucifixion and
cried out, "Here is the place of the battle, where is the victory?
I am looking for the standard of salvation." A miracle of healing
proved the authenticity of a log lying near the Holy Sepulchre;
it became the chief relic of Jerusalem. In the seventh century the
Persians carried it away. The emperor Heraclius brought it back
in triumph. A piece of the Cross served as a relic in the church

---

16. Minucius Felix, *Octavius*, XXIX, 6. Cf. A. Grillmeier, *Der Logos am
Kreuz* (1956); and Erich Dinkler, see Bibliography.
17. Nilus, *Ep.*, IV, 61. Migne, *PG*, LXXIX, 577ff.
18. Sozomen, *HE*, I, 8.
19. *De Obitu Theodosii*, XLIIIff. Cf. J. Vogt, *RAC*, III, 372ff.

built in the palace of Helena, to this day called the Santa Croce.
Splinters of the Cross found their way to all lands. Helena gave
Constantine two nails from the Cross, so Ambrose relates. One he
placed in his diadem, the other in the bridle of his war horse.[20]
Constantine kept the memory of the Passion alive even while he
abolished another frightful reminder. Crucifixion as a mode of
execution was abolished by law.[21] It trespassed too closely on
the uniqueness of the Cross. That was why the emperor Julian in
turn abrogated this law.

Perhaps we can find another clue to Constantine's understanding of the cross in the early Christian practice of beating the cross
and of its use as an amulet to dispel demons. This is the simplest
explanation of the representation on the gable of the palace in
Constantinople where the cross displays its conquering power by
cutting through the dragon. The Cross of Golgotha overcame its
demonic assailants. The more the enemy was seen to be demonic,
the more important became the heavenly standard which put the
demons to rout. Whereas previously the Cross had been associated with shame, now it was indissolubly linked with victory.
The confession which Eusebius saw in the Roman statue of "the
victory-bringing Cross" received full expression on the gable of
the palace. Constantine believed that his course was entirely
compatible with that of Jesus. He said, "God chose a worthy body
to reveal faith and virtue, to dispel error, to bring a new
teaching of worship, to display an example of purity, to overcome
the sting of death and to proclaim the victory of immortality."
The very attempt of Jesus' enemies to destroy Him served to
demonstrate His power. The Cross to which godlessness nailed
Him became the triumphal arch of victory.

The cross in battle! How was that compatible with the word
of Jesus to Peter, "Put up thy sword"? Constantine did not treat
the incident after the manner of the *Heliand,* the first Christian

20. Socrates, *HE,* I, 17, testifies to the spread of the story.
21. Cf, fn 9, ch. VIII, Sozomenos, *HE,* I, 8, 13.

poem in the German language, where the doughty Peter was lauded for drawing his broadsword in defense of his liege Lord. Constantine, closer to the text, reproved the disciple's lack of confidence, not because the Christian should never take the sword and should suffer injustice rather than commit it, but because Peter was foolhardy to start a fight of uncertain outcome, when assured help lay to hand.[22] Having seen so many miracles, Peter should not have doubted what God could do were He so minded. Said Constantine, "This is a marvelous ground of assurance when such wonderful and incredible things happen through Him who is the Lord of history." The emperor's own faith had been confirmed by his miraculous victory; surely it would be a lack of faith to disdain the power of the Cross so marvelously proffered.

The Cross, a mighty sign of the power of God! As Constantine's course had begun under this standard, so the present time stood under its protection. The Cross is the goal determining the beginning, continuance, and duty of the empire. The Cross demands reverence and proves its power. It belongs in churches as well as in battle. According to the *Liber Pontificalis*, a heavy gold cross was to decorate the grave of the Apostle in St. Peter's.[23] It was not the only one. Before long the Cross took its place in all the churches. The unquestioned pre-eminence of the Cross henceforth in liturgy and art is another legacy from the first Christian emperor.

The sign of the Cross went beyond the confines of the Church. To this day one finds it on the flags of nations. A nail from the holy Cross gave its name to the iron crown of Lombardy. Another nail accounted for the sacred character of the holy lance, one of the imperial German treasures. And the Church took no umbrage when the Cross was used on banners in battle. Ambrose again is our witness: "With the Cross of Christ and in the name of Jesus

22. Eusebius, *Oratio*, XV, 3 and 4. Cf. *Dö.*, p. 301.
23. *Liber pontificalis in Silv.*, ed. Duchesne, I, 176.

we go into battle, brave through this sign, through this banner unflinching."[24] The Persian king was so informed in the letter sent by Constantine toward the end of his life, and the Goths too began to feel the bite of the Cross in a defeat which both sides attributed to the Christian banner.[25] It was then that the Goths began to embrace the faith which had given Constantine success. The Christian Germans adopted the Cross and went to battle under the King of Heaven. Another version of the same attitude appears in the Ottonian period, which also conjoined the Cross and victory, though this time the host was led by St. Michael, "the angel who gives victory."

However, we must not leave the impression that this was the final word of the Church. There were Christians who still felt the incongruity of cross fighting against cross. And throughout Christian history there have been continued protests. Nevertheless, the contrast between the days when Celsus could level the charge that no Christian would serve in the army and those when Christian armies on both sides used the cross as if it were a club with which to batter out each others' brains is indeed striking.

A Hymn of the Cross,[26] popular in the fourth century, shows us the attitude of the period. The poet sees in the Cross a "secret." It "reaches to heaven to reveal the *Logos*. The arms extend to the right and to the left to dispel the fearful might of the foe, and to hold together the cosmos. The Cross is planted in the earth in order to bind together the heaven above, the earth beneath and that which is under the earth. The Cross is the instrument of salvation, the cement of the world, the scourge of polytheism, able to repel its champions and, in all respects, the mark of the victory of Christ over his enemies." The hymn understands the Cross as a cosmic symbol, pointing above and below and con-

---

24. Ambrose, De Abraham, II, 7, 42. Migne, *PL*, XIV, 498.
25. Socrates, *HE*, I, 18, 4.
26. Acts of Andrew: *Martyrium Andreae*, I, 14, ed. Bonnet (1898), p. 54.

joining all. The Cross is a universal monument of victory and, in this sense only, is referred to as the Cross of Christ. All in all we have here a faith which we may assume to have been widely prevalent in the churches. In accord with tradition, Gregory of Nyssa gives this interpretation of the Cross which, he says, joins the four arms and thus shows the great mystery of how all is united and the varied natures brought into harmony.[27] Here we see the divine power which, as an inner bond, runs through the cosmos and holds it together. In another passage he refers to the verse in Ephesians 3:18 about the height, length, and breadth of the Cross and again sees it as the archetype of the great mystery of the union—through the power of God—of the heavenly, the earthly, and that which is under the earth. Although the significance of the Cross of Jesus in the economy of salvation is not overlooked, the Cross has come to be a universal symbol of the divine operation in the cosmos.

It is not the same thought, but the two are not unrelated, when the Cross becomes the sign of the victory of Christ over Satanic powers. The Hymn of the Cross has the tone of a song of victory. The great preacher of the Greek Church, John Chrysostom, takes up the strain of the Cross as the sign of victory.[28] At the same time it is a weapon—a bold figure—with which Christ overcomes the power of the Devil and the demons and cuts off the head of the dragon.

Constantine was not alone in regarding the Cross as a mighty sign in which he could place his trust. Admittedly he went beyond the usual Christian view. The Cross, confirmed by a miracle from heaven, was taken by him into battle, set up for adoration in the churches, and erected over the empire. But although the Cross was assigned a new function the Church did not think that its nature had been thereby violated. The Church could come to the new by way of the old. Of course, it is a big

27. Gregory of Nyssa, *Oratio de Resurr.* Migne, *PG*, XLVI, 621–625. *Catechesis magna, PG*, XLV, 81C.
28. Chrysostom, *In Matth. Hom.*, LIV, 4. Migne, *PG*, LVIII, 537.

jump from Paul's words about the Cross in Corinthians I to Constantine's understanding. But was the cosmic speculation any closer? Constantine's view will not do for us; the cosmic interpretation is perhaps more acceptable. But every age must be judged by its own standards before it is brought to the test of the Gospel. And which then can survive?

On the street called the Philadelphion in Constantinople, from which the Avenue of the Apostles leads out, the emperor set up a column surmounted by a golden cross beneath which stood his own statue, together with that of his mother and those of his sons. He placed himself and his family beneath the protection of the Cross. In the days to come the Roman Empire stood beneath the Cross and so likewise did all Europe.

XV. Paganism

To affirm Christianity was to deny paganism.

Constantine's opinion of the religion he had abandoned did not change, although his expressions became somewhat sharper in the course of time. The suspicion on our part that such consistency has been imposed by the Christian tradition is quickly dispelled. The codified laws say nothing other than what we find in the emperor's letters and edicts transcribed in Church documents; nor do the writings directed specifically toward pagans. If the letter to the Persian king was decisive, though not meant to be offensive, surely Constantine would have had no reserve in speaking to his own subjects. Hence we have no reason to lament the loss of a parallel pagan tradition.

Constantine intended a sharp reproof when he told the Donatists they had sold out to the heathen. He branded rites connected with the lustral offerings as "foreign superstition."[1] No one, in fact, should be required to participate. When pagan rites were celebrated on holy sites, such as Jerusalem and Mambre, he talked about the "outrage . . . of shameless men," desecrating the holy places with "damnable images" and "unholy sacrifices."

How far and how deeply did this flat repudiation go? Were there not some areas unaffected? The ancient rite of augury, going back to Roman antiquity, associated religion with prediction of the future. An examination of the entrails of the sacrificial

1. Lustral sacrifice: Theodosianus, XVI, 2, 5 (323, May 25).

animals preceded the persecution of Diocletian. Maxentius, to his undoing, had accepted their prophecy. Constantine disregarded its warning and was not penalized by heaven. In the year 319 two ordinances undertook to suppress private *haruspices*.[2] They could easily be subverted to political ends when malcontents circulated the prediction of the oracle that an unpopular régime was about to totter. There had been such prohibitions earlier. Although Constantine did not renew them, he was as cool toward augury as toward the entire pagan cultus, saying, "Those who think it will do them any good may go to the public altars and shrines to present their sacrifices. We do not forbid the ancient rites if practiced in full daylight." But the emperor made it quite evident that he set no store by them. "Those addicted to superstition may have their rites in the open." This order had a political intention. The new feature is that the disapproval now extended also to the permissible public sacrifices.

A directive of the following year also had political significance.[3] When lightning struck the imperial palace, the *haruspices* were at once to be asked what it portended; this move crushed any private suspicions of an evil omen. The order says nothing about Constantine's private attitude but he certainly was not a man of the enlightenment. There were mantic rites at the dedication of Constantinople and a law on magic forbade anything detrimental to health and reputation,[4] but allowed whatever would ward off sickness or rain and hail from the vine crop. Black magic, with its potions for hurt or love, was not allowed, whereas white magic to improve health or weather was permissible.

We return now to the problem of the Arch of Constantine. What can one say of the continuance of the cult of the sun god evident on the arch? Constantine was not the only one to be

---

2. Theodosianus, IX, 16, 1 (319, February 1 or Sept. ?); Theodosianus, IX, 16, 2 (319, May 15 or after Sept.?).
3. Theodosianus, XVI, 10, 1 (320/1, December 17).
4. Theodosianus, IX, 16, 3 (321/4, May 23).

involved, assuredly, for the Church looked upon King Sun as a demonic power irreconcilable with her own confession. A Church order decreed[5] that "severe and remorseless judgment would be passed on Christians who worshipped or swore by the sun." The denunciations of the cult of the sun in the Prophets were reiterated (Jeremiah 10:2 and Ezekiel 8:16–18). The sharpness of tone indicates that belief in the sun was still vigorous and that its appeal invaded Christian congregations. The sun god of Emesa, identified with the Persian Mithras, assembled devotees into the city which bore his name, the Phoenician Heliopolis. This god was able to serve the philosophers also as the manifestation of the transcendent deity. Since the cult of the sun was universal the emperor Aurelian, only a generation before Constantine, had made it the religion of the empire. Aurelian built a beautiful temple to the sun in the capital and popularized the cult by making December 25, the birthday of the Unconquerable Sun, a public holiday.

The content of this faith was not so rigid that it could not be interpreted in a variety of ways. That was why many Christians could understand the sun as being Christ, "the Sun of Righteousness" (Malachi 4:2). Under Diocletian some Christian sculptors did not scruple to carve an image of the sun. But when it came to a statue of Asclepius they refused and were martyred.[6] Evidently their faith, which forbade them to make a pagan idol, took no offense at an image of the sun.[7] Even in the fifth century there were Christians who did not regard a reverent glance toward the great luminary as offensive; Pope Leo the Great had to re-

---

5. *Didascalia*, ch. XXI. On the cult of the sun compare P. Schmitt, "Sol invictus. Betrachtungen zu spätrömischer Religion und Politik" (1944).

6. *Acta Sanctorum*, November 3, pp. 748ff.

7. A ceiling mosaic of a sepulchre found under St. Peter's shows Christ as the sun god with his car. Alfons Maria Schneider thinks it is to be dated in the period when the line between Christianity and the sun cult was so ill-defined that coins could be minted showing the cross alongside the sun. This would then be another illustration of the attitude of the sculptors under Diocletian, who did not regard carving an image of the sun as incompatible with their faith.

press the custom on entering St. Peter's of genuflection toward the sun.

Hence Constantine's course was not unparalleled, when for a time he retained his faith in the sun alongside that in Christ. But after a decade he must have realized the inconsistency. Not only did the sun god disappear from the coins,[8] but the word "unconquerable," always associated in the imperial title with the sun, was replaced by the words "the Conqueror." This referred back, of course, to the great victory but it did not deify the emperor by giving him the title of a god. The sun was demoted from the status of a god to that of a work of God.[9] Like the moon and the stars the sun kept his appointed course and obeyed the will of the Creator. In the same vein we may cite a repudiation of the highest significance. In the second of the great addresses of the year 324 Constantine attributed to his "Apollo" a decided share in the disorder of the times. How different from the speech of the orator in 310 who caused the god in his temple in Gaul to predict Constantine's rule over the world. Now Constantine, in reviewing the past, lays on Apollo the blame for the misfortunes of the empire. Diocletian was misled by his "base oracle" into starting the persecution. Apollo was the only pagan deity thus expressly rejected by name. The very god longest revered of the ancient Pantheon was now declared to be a force making for corruption. The emperor Julian was right when he reproached his hated uncle with having been untrue to the sun god.[10] Julian, when he restored this cult, brought out the signifi-

8. That such a coin could be minted even after the victory over Licinius is shown by Maria R. Alföldi, "Die Sol-Comes-Münze vom Jahre 325" (1964).

9. VC, II, 158.

10. This testimony of Julian disposes of the assumption that the pillar of Constantine in Constantinople is a proof that he worshipped the sun (cf. ch. VII, fn 7). Even if the tradition is correct that Constantine erected a pillar topped by a statue of the sun for which he substituted his own head, it need not be so interpreted. He may simply have utilized an earlier masterpiece, as on the arch at Rome, and he may have wished to display the powerlessness of the god whose statue he decapitated. A different view is taken by Altheim, Der unbesiegte Gott (1957), pp. 105ff.

cance of Constantine's rejection and at the same time showed that the sun cult was the core of paganism. Julian's "Hymn to the Sun" is the fullest expression of his faith and the last great confession of the conquered god.

The monument of the victory of Christ over the sun is Christmas. Constantine himself did not institute it, but the Church did in his time. This happened appropriately at Rome, where Aurelian had built a temple to the sun god and had ordered the entire empire to honor the day of his birth. The Roman Church was now ready to take over the Roman holiday. Christmas, the second great Christian festival, of later origin than Easter, may have had its start in Alexandria as the feast of Epiphany, when the "dayspring from on high" began to shine. At the end of Constantine's reign this celebration became attached to the twenty-fifth of December. The day dedicated to the *sol invictus* was now consecrated to Christ. In deliberate contrast, reference was made not to the sun but to "the true Sun." In the eastern Church the observance did not become general until the close of the doctrinal controversy. It was there regarded as the festival of the confession of the Incarnation of the Son of God. This marked the final triumph of the Nicene Creed. Subsequently the Christmas festival, carrying with it also such reminders, has endeared itself more than any other to Christian folk.

A new faith can afford to allow the old one to die of its own weakness without direct confrontation, but the new one does better to set forth clearly wherein the difference lies. This Constantine did when he explained to King Shapur why sacrifices were rejected and with what they were replaced: "I shun all abhorrent blood, all noxious odors. The taint of this lawless, shameful error has brought many nations to ruin."[11] In striking contrast to their former use the sacral expressions are inverted: what had once purified now defiles; what had dispelled, now attracts evil; what was commanded is now proscribed. This is

11. *VC*, IV, 10.

not just a matter of words. The letter gives a special reason for the prohibition of sacrifice: "What Divine Providence has bestowed on men for their needs, that is not placed at their arbitrary disposal." Whereas formerly men sacrificed something valuable and perhaps necessary to the gods, in order thereby to win their favor, Constantine now warns against this affront to Providence by abusing its gifts. To try to upset the ordering of the heavenly Lord is impious capriciousness. Such words would have sounded blasphemous to a pious pagan. Did not man hallow the best he had by bringing it as an offering to the temple? But, said Constantine, "God requires only a pure heart and an unblemished soul." This statement changed not simply words but the understanding of religion itself. The change was one of practical and political nature but its origin was Christian. This was a mature judgment which gave considered reasons for the earlier rejection of the cult of sacrifice.

How did all this affect the emperor's behavior? Since the old cultus had ceased to be official there was no longer any need for the high officials to perform the sacrifices to gods and emperors. The imperial cult had come to an end. We are not the first, then, to be astonished when Constantine conceded the request of the Umbrian town Hispellum to put up a temple to him and to his house and to install a priest.[12] The town wanted the honor of a building constructed under imperial favor for the celebration of annual games. The emperor furthered the project with the provision that "the building dedicated to us is not to be blemished by the imposture of superstitions." There should be no sacrifice to the emperor. The games were thus divested of cultic significance. The temple was not called a temple but a public building, and the priest became a director of the games. With the sacral element removed the games were unobjectionable. Later on Constantius, the son of Constantine, who forbade all sacrifices and wanted to close all pagan temples, was

12. For the inscription compare *Dö.*, pp. 209ff and 339.

not averse to retaining some Roman temples as recreation centers where games could be held.[13]

Constantine did not close the pagan temples. If he destroyed two Phoenician temples and the temple of Venus at Jerusalem[14] it was because of immoral rites in the one case and the desecration of the Holy Sepulchre in the other. The confiscation of the silver and gold with which images were adorned, together with other temple treasures, was a financial measure not without precedent in pagan days. The transfer of statues and votive offerings to Constantinople was intended to adorn that city and at the same time to show the impotence of the old gods and exhibit the triumph of the new faith. There is one exception, the destruction of the great temple of Asclepius at Aegae, in southern Asia Minor. Was this because Asclepius appeared as the primary rival of Christ? Was it because serpents were here worshipped and the serpent, for Constantine, was a symbol of the demonic powers?[15] We do not know.

Another peculiar and difficult problem had to do with the army. To ensure its correct religious disposition, Diocletian and Galerius had dismissed the Christians from the forces. Constantine also regulated worship in the army. The Christians had their own service. The pagans were to assemble every Sunday in the open that they might petition the Lord of Heaven to be gracious toward the emperor and the empire. The emperor himself composed the prayer for them to use:

We know that Thou alone art God. We acknowledge Thee as king. We implore Thee as the helper. To Thee we owe victory. Through Thee we were stronger than the enemy. We thank Thee for gifts re-

---

13. Theodosianus, XVI, 10, 3 (346 or 342, November 1). Campare also Jacques Gascon, "Le Rescrit d'Hispellum," *Mélanges d'Archéologie et d'Histoire* LXXIX (1967) pp. 609–659.

14. VC, III, 54ff; IV, 39.

15. Correspondingly, Julian in deliberate contrast regarded the serpent on the banners as the guarantee of victory. Libanius (*Oratio pro templis*, LIX, ch. 39) thought that Constantine's memory was besmirched through the closing of the temple of Asclepius.

ceived and hope for those to come. We beseech Thee fervently that Thou wilt favor Constantine, our ruler, and his sons, by Thee held dear. Preserve them for us in health, in length of days and victory.[16]

We can the better understand this prayer if we compare it with the one Licinius gave his soldiers before the battle with Maximinus.[17] Some have regarded this as the model for Constantine's prayer. Others, on the contrary, think Licinius to have been dependent on Constantine. But much more important than the literary dependence, which cannot be demonstrated either way, is the difference of application. Licinius' prayer was to be spoken by pagans and Christians alike but that of Constantine only by the pagans. They were not called upon to say what they did not believe, but their prayer could expect to be heard only because it was addressed to the one God. Although they were not compelled to enter the church they were invited to the outer court. There in the light streaming out from the true worship, they became in a sense participants and thus they shared in the support which the Church gave the state, but they were not forbidden to go to the pagan sacrifices, and the army, including its Germanic contingents, long remained prevailingly pagan.

Constantine did not lump Christians and pagans in one all-embracing formula. His prayer contained what the Christian deemed necessary, the pagan possible, a legacy of the old Roman belief in the victory-bringing cultus of the army. The edict of Galerius, which committed the protection of the empire to the old gods, expected from the Christian God at least some additional help. The Edict of Milan did not deny to any cult access to the godhead, even though divine favor rested especially on the Christians. Constantine's army prayer no longer expects anything from the old religion. A non-Christian prayer for the emperor would do no good unless directed to the right God.

When a ruler realizes that his age is confronted by a religious decision and that he is divinely commissioned to take the lead,

16. *VC*, IV, 20.
17. *DMP*, XLVI; cf. p. 50.

must he not regard the continuance of past tradition perilous? Since Constantine believed that the worship of the many gods was responsible for the calamities of the empire and that the establishment of Christianity had brought good fortune, was it not necessary for the welfare of the state that the one should be forbidden and the other alone recognized? Later emperors did indeed think so. If Constantine did not take this course did he not contradict his own persuasions? The integrity of his faith was surely questionable if at the first opportunity he could leave it out of account. Did Constantine talk one way and behave another? Did he follow politics rather than religion? The conclusion would be inescapable were it not for another assumption on his part, which we have not mentioned before, that of the voluntary character of his faith.

This new note was already struck at Milan. The edict spoke of "free adherence" in the service of the deity both on the part of the emperor and his subjects. There is no denial that both cults can reach the ear of God, even though unmistakably the Christian religion elicits greater favor. Each man should decide freely. Both have their rights in heaven and on earth. This statement bespoke freedom for both and a period of toleration. It was a tentative solution, necessarily so, because all was in flux, a solution necessary for the state and in accordance with the ambiguity of the religious situation. It did justice to the immediate task confronting Constantine but at the same time conformed to his basic principles by insisting that emperor and subjects have the same freedom to decide. Because the edict did what was called for it deserves its subsequent reputation as the classic document of Constantine's tolerance. But it could not last.

Would the same policy obtain if the weaker party, which had just attained toleration, became the stronger? The political outlook would then be altered; might there not be discrimination against those who had now become the weaker party? In the interim, Licinius, who at Milan had been allied with the victor at Rome, had come to be Constantine's enemy and had been defeated. The victory over him, as at the Milvian Bridge, occurred under Christian auspices. But the thanksgiving for the victory was, as before, an Edict of Toleration. The freedom of choice which the Edict of Milan gave to the Christians was now extended to the pagans.

The conclusion of this great document, issued at the time, proclaims toleration. The form is remarkable—the emperor addresses himself not to his subjects but to God. "In the interests of all men on earth I desire that Thy people may live in peace. Those in error should enjoy peace just as fully as the faithful. This will bring them to a right mind. None shall endanger another. Let each live according to his own persuasion. . . . The orthodox must know that they alone live a pure and holy life whom Thou hast called to labor in accord with Thy commandments. But those who disregard them may keep the temples of error. We have the luminous house of Thy truth. . . . He who will not be saved, let him not blame anyone else, for the power of the means of salvation is manifest to all. . . . But no one should impose his conviction on another. What anyone has experienced and known he should use, whenever possible, to help his neighbor, but if that cannot be, then let the neighbor go his way. The struggle for deathlessness [immortality] can be undertaken only voluntarily. In this area one gets nowhere with coercion."[18]

The emperor, confirmed in his mission by his victory, called upon his subjects to follow him on his way, but he restrained himself from issuing a command. He could teach, advise, and exhort, but where faith was involved he might not wield the ruler's sword. He was not content simply to grant religious freedom to the pagans or to make tolerance incumbent upon Christians. He went further and committed the accounting to God. The reason he did not close the temples or interdict paganism was not political expedience; the ground on which he would have to answer to God was his conviction that in the realm of faith only freedom

18. VC, II, 56–60. Compare chaps. V, VI.

mattered. This was his justification before God. He left no doubt
about his own conviction. He spoke of "abominable error" and
of "the temple of deceit," but the way must be left open. The
erring are to be won through the witness of their neighbor, the
influence of the community, and the testimony of events.

Here we see why the victorious ruler allowed the pagan cult
to continue. Not that he was satisfied to have the present situation perpetuated indefinitely. This was, rather, a proselytizing
tolerance. His goal was unity of worship, but because of the very
nature of faith he felt not merely warranted, but under obligation
to permit the service of the gods. This is the more remarkable
because Constantine personally felt no remaining tie with the old
religion[19] and, indeed, considered it a menace, "rebellion," and
"abominable error."[20]

The persuasion that faith cannot be constrained was not alien
to the Church. Any reflection on the essence of Christianity must
lead to this conclusion. The missionary realizes it when he
reaches the limits of his efforts. Any defender of the Church
against pressure from the state has always to revert to this point.
Lactantius put it well during the persecution of Diocletian: "Religion is the only place where freedom can erect her citadel."[21]
"There is nothing which so rests on freedom as religion. No one
can be compelled to worship what he will not." Torture may

19. A. H. M. Jones (*Atti del X Congresso Internazionale di Scienze
Storiche* [Rome, 1955], pp. 267–71) maintains that Constantine with his
"syncretic beliefs" throughout almost his entire reign showed no hostility
to the pagans, and Grégoire and his school talk of secret pagan sympathies
and point to the continuance of the sun cult. But already in 219 Constantine
spoke of paganism as superannuated. Sunday for him took its significance
from Christianity. In 324 Apollo was sharply rejected. The Helios statue is
a legend. The pagan sanctuaries became for him temples of error. Julian
reproached Constantine for abandoning the sun (cf. J. Vogt, "Kaiser Julian
über seinen Oheim Konstantin den Grossen"). These few facts are sufficient
to exclude syncretism and paganism.

20. There is no real inconsistency between Constantine's toleration of
paganism and suppression of heresy, because the latter threatened to pervert
the faith. Compare H. Dörries, *Constantine and Religious Liberty* (1960),
pp. 98ff.

21. Lactantius, *Div. Instit. Epitome*, XLIX, 1, 2; V, 19, 11, 23.

force one to sacrifice but it cannot generate devotion. This was the voice of the persecuted. Now the victor took it up and gave it a new, full tone. Only he who has the power to suppress is in a position to accord toleration. The final proof of genuine tolerance comes when he who has the power and is convinced that his position alone is true, nevertheless renounces constraint. Only in this case is the Christian understanding of faith conserved.

Constantine observed toleration, though many Christians did not agree with him. "I am told that some are saying the worship of the temple and the powers of darkness are broken." They are consequently looking for an imperial edict to put an end to the public worship of the gods, otherwise, they think, the great turn of events is being disregarded and the powers of darkness may once more gain the upper hand. Constantine understood these wishes and he, too, perceived the damage which might overtake the empire should the pagan cult continue. But he was thinking not so much of the cultus as of those pagans who took part in it. He pointed out how deeply entrenched was their faith in the old gods. No prohibition would change this. Constantine was thinking as a Christian when he had an eye to the inner response. Christians who criticized him were thinking as Romans when they regarded the external cultus of paganism as more important than the inner attitude of the pagan.[22]

Constantine took the considerations adduced in favor of suppressing paganism seriously and was ready to answer to God for disregarding advice which had many influential sponsors. This is apparent from the comments of Bishop Eusebius, who has preserved for us the emperor's statement. The bishop praises it as a confession of Constantine's faith and as a missionary appeal to the new provinces. But when it comes to the refutation of paganism, Eusebius overlooks the limits set by Constantine.

22. Gibbon regarded the Edict of Toleration as a façade behind which paganism was to be suppressed (ch. XXI, II, 414). A. H. M. Jones, on the other hand, thinks it witnesses to a secret sympathy for paganism. One does better to stick to the words of the document. For a broader discussion of this question see: H. Dörries, *Constantine and Religious Liberty* (Yale, 1960).

Eusebius says nothing about the toleration extended to the pagans. On the contrary, he exults in the noble deeds of the emperor when he closes a temple or removes idols, whereas actually the suppression was merely a matter of civic morality requiring police action. Eusebius sees in this a sign of the impotence of the gods. The removal of the golden images disposes of an obstacle and will help to convince the old believers of their error. The bishop is the one who first lets the emperor go beyond the limits he had set for himself. For that is what was done by Constantine's son, Constantius, who undertook to close the temples and prohibit the sacrifices.[23] Admittedly, he was not too successful. Even the renewal of the measure against sacrifice by Jovian and Valens left the temples open. The unmitigated expression of the policy of constraint found its fulfillment only under Theodosius the First who, in his famous Edict of 380, made Christianity the state religion with the words, "We wish that all people ruled by our clemency should live in the religion given by the Apostle Peter to the Roman people and taught to this day, as the faith declares."[24]

This law was the basis for the future legislation. Although directed primarily against the unbeliever within, the principle could not but affect the unbelievers without; prohibition of any

23. The claim of Constantius II that his prohibition of pagan sacrifice (*Cod. Theod.*, XVI, 10, 2) was a carrying out of a final law of his father breaks down in view of the silence of Julian and the *Codex Theodosianus*, and Libanius said the opposite.

The judgment of N. H. Baynes that Constantine at the end made "a frontal attack on paganism" (p. 357) simply does not hold up. On the other hand, one is not to infer pagan sympathies because of the retention of the title *"Pontifex Maximus."* (F. Stähelin, *Zeitschrift für Schweizerische Geschichte,* XVII [1937], 410, and Burckhardt.) All it meant was that the pagan cult was assured of his protection from interference. Theodosius, who abandoned the tolerance of Constantine, was the first to drop the title. See also the competent essay of Joseph Vogt, "Toleranz und Intoleranz im constantinischen Zeitalter: der Weg der lateinischen Apologetik," *Saeculum* XIX (1968) pp. 344–361.

24. Theodosianus, XVI, 1, 2, W. Ensslin, "Die Religionspolitik des Kaisers Theodosius des Grossen"; consult also his essay, "Staat und Kirche von Konstantin dem Grossen bis Theodosius dem Grossen." N. Q. King, *The Emperor Theodosius and the Establishment of Christianity* (1961).

pagan worship was simply the consequence. And the outcome was that in those Christians whose demands Constantine had refused to heed now gained their wish. To be sure, the development was slow in reaching its ultimate conclusion and the voice of protest against constraint was not altogether silenced. Chrysostom warned, at any rate against shedding blood, but that the Christian confession was obligatory on all subjects of the empire was taken for granted. Theodosius II would have only Christians in his army because the presence of heathens would cause the withdrawal of divine favor and jeopardize victory. The emperor could not longer bear to look upon the sacrifices, which were not yet extinct. "Can we any longer suffer the very course of the seasons to be disrupted because heaven is alienated by pagan faithlessness? Why has spring lost its grace? Why has summer by scanty yields deprived the farmer of his hopes of harvest? Why has the raging winter made the rich earth barren in the bond of unbroken frost? Is it not because nature has overstepped her bounds in order to punish godlessness? If we are not to suffer this any longer divine majesty must be appeased by adequate expiation"—that is, by the speedy execution of the laws against pagans and heretics. This is the concept of the classical world in Christian dress.[25] In almost the same words the pagan orator Libanius addressed the emperor Theodosius I on behalf of the old temples, which were threatened in the country particularly by hordes of monks. "The temples," he said, "are the very soul of the fields. . . . The farmers believe that they labor in vain if they are deprived of the gods who reward their labor. . . . All hopes of children, of flocks and of ears are vain."[26] The plea addressed by Symmachus to the Roman Senate for the restoration of the Altar of Victory in 384—no less worthy a testimony to the old religion—refers to a famine in connection with the cutting off of the vestal virgins' stipend: "We must not blame the earth, we

25. Law of Theodosius II, 438 Jan. 31 (Leges novellae ad Theodosianum pertinentes, ed. Th. Mommsen et Paulus M. Meyer II, pp. 10, 75).

26. *Oratio pro Templis,* IX and X.

should not accuse the sirocco, we cannot say that fire has destroyed the seed or that weeds have choked the fruit. The year has been withered by sacrilege. For, of necessity, the whole harvest will fail if the first fruits are not consecrated to the divine service."[27]

The position taken by Theodosius I corresponded in reverse to that of Diocletian. On the very spot where the temple had stood the church replaced it. But the religious demands of the state now cut deeper. The old Roman understanding of religion called for public observance, but the Christian demanded personal adherence. The Church envisaged a congregation of men participating devoutly in the worship of God rather than simply watching a sacrifice. The result was that the state now entered the domain of inward attitudes. The Christian appeal addressed to all men now had become a command of the state, binding upon all citizens. Theodosius, not Constantine, was the creator of the state Church.

The distinction between the two emperors might escape the Christians, but the heathen perceived what it meant. In his plea for the temple, Libanius set Constantine over against Theodosius. He complained, indeed, that the first Christian emperor had supposed another god would help him and for himself had discontinued the sacrifices; though he did confiscate temple treasures to build his new city, in other respects the temples were undisturbed, the cultus continued unimpeded.[28] The spokesman for the opposition showed genuine insight into Constantine's policy: his own clear-cut decision and at the same time his self-imposed limits. Libanius could also appeal to Constantine in setting Christian principles over against Christian behavior. "In the law itself of the Christians," he said, "persuasion is recognized as right and force is reproved. . . . Why do you rage against temples and transgress your own laws? . . . In such matters one

27. Symmachus, *Relatio*, III, 16 (*Mon. Germ. Hist. Auct. Antiq.*, VI, I [1883], pp. 283, 7-9).
28. *Oratio pro Templis*, VI.

must convince, not compel. He who cannot do the first and leaps to the second will accomplish nothing and deceives himself if he thinks he can."[29]

Constantine's successors did not understand him as his opponents had. What a reversal—Constantine versus the Constantinian era. Modern tolerance has had to struggle painfully against that era of the intolerant state Church. Its basic source was the Edict of Theodosius. In the sixteenth century this still provided the legal basis for the execution of Anabaptists in the Zürich of Ulrich Zwingli's time. They were drowned *nach römischem Recht,* "in accord with the Roman Law," and that meant the Code of Theodosius. Zwingli saw in Theodosius the very model of a devout prince. If, then, even the humanist of the Protestant Reformation could accept Theodosius so unquestioningly, certainly for the Middle Ages Constantine and Theodosius were indistinguishable. The beginning of the fusion was made in the days of Theodosius himself by Ambrose, bishop of Milan, the emperor's spiritual counselor. Ambrose held that Constantine had set the course for all who came after him. When Theodosius died his remains were interred in Constantine's city and Ambrose, in his funeral oration, pictured Theodosius in heaven in the company of his great forerunner.[30] Thus Christians saw the unity between Constantine and Theodosius, the heathen the differences—and the documents are on the side of the heathen. How can we explain the contradiction between the two emperors?

For Libanius as for Lactantius the only way of dealing with unbelievers was either by persuasion or force. This was clear and simple. But was it realistic? Constantine repudiated force and thought to win the unconvinced through the testimony of their neighbors, through the Word. To this was added the (to him) inescapable lesson of recent, freshly experienced historical

29. *Ibid.,* XX. As Richard Klein, *Symmachus,* Darmstadt 1971, pp. 92ff, has shown, Symmachus too, in his famous *Relatio,* connects his demand for tolerance with Constantine.

30. *De Obitu Theodosii,* XL.

events and, allied to them, the imperial peace extending its favors impartially to all. These were not to his mind notions alien to the faith, as it were proselytizing afterthoughts. No, the experience of divine power for victory was as much a part of his faith as the conviction of Christianity's power to cement the community. The dangers lurking in these convictions were hidden from him. He himself at any rate never thought of propagating Christianity by appeal to the rights of success or of popularity.

The pagans were now in a difficult position because Constantine believed that the very unity of the empire depended upon their acceptance of the true faith. Consequently, to say *No* to Christianity was not so easy as it once had been and the temptation to say *Yes* for the wrong reasons was strong. Persecution had served to guard the purity of the faith, but now power was on its side. Could the faith accept such assistance? This was a new question for the Christians and one not easy to answer. Even when the emperor merely confessed his faith—and what else could he do?—weak characters were tempted to follow suit. Other more responsible persons observed that the new order was opening the way for the healing of society and they were prepared to help, but they embraced not so much the Gospel itself as the force for social regeneration which it evidenced. Such considerations could induce men to join the Church without really embracing the faith and all of this could happen without any direct intervention on the part of the emperor. Yet such intervention, too, was not lacking. The church built by him in a pagan city attracted followers through the rich largesses he enabled it to dispense; this was preaching not with a tongue of iron but of silver.[31] A town in Asia Minor received back its forfeited municipal status because its inhabitants were Christians.[32] Aid gladly given, but how dubious! Constantine emphatically did his best to commend Christianity. He talked, exhorted, warned, reproved, and opened the door of the Church just as widely as the hinges

31. *VC*, III, 58.
32. Cf. *Dö.*, pp. 212ff.

would permit. He wanted his subjects to say *Yes*, but he would not compel them. That is what kept his faith still Christian. This was the first time in history that power was being tested to see whether it would respect faith. Constantine stood the test.

At the same time the movement from the emperor's wishes to state requirements appeared very slight. And when that happened the transition had been made from respect for religious liberty to the intolerance of the Theodosian Code. The way was paved, as we have noted, by the old Roman attitude that the welfare of the state depended upon true worship. This was, however, compatible with a degree of tolerance because polytheism could be comparatively tolerant, inasmuch as it could take in many gods and, since Rome demanded only cultic conformity, inner conviction could be left untouched. But a faith which witnesses to the saving truth must fight error. It cannot conceal the unconditional quality of the word proclaimed; it cannot let the erring perish even though he resists. Intolerance is therefore a peculiarly Christian temptation, and if power become conjoined with faith, then force may be sanctified. The more seriously an emperor took his responsibility, the more did he feel compelled to care for the faith of his subjects. Precisely because he was devout, Theodosius was tempted to be intolerant. Must not men be protected against themselves? Augustine put it sharply when he said, "Is there any more dangerous murder of souls than freedom to be wrong?" This text for centuries gave good conscience to those who, in the name of the true faith, sought to eradicate the false by fire and the sword.

But Christian faith, which even in chains asserted its freedom, must see to it that others, also, enjoy the same. Only he who is convinced of this can observe tolerance toward an opponent. Religious liberty depends upon something deeper than doubt as to whether one is right or mere indifference. Where there is no basic respect for conviction, a state without religion—if it discovers that religion impinges upon its life—turns quickly to suppression, and tolerance ends in an intolerant tyranny. Constantine was persuaded that he was right, the pagans wrong. Yet the very sharpness of his judgment, because based on conviction, enabled him to maintain his tolerance. He experienced no disappointed expectations which might have provoked him into a revocation of his edict. He knew to whom he accorded tolerance and he knew why.

The Bronze Head[33]

The bronze head from the last years of the emperor's life shows clearly the marks of his fatigue. His tremendous energy was spent. He who, until now, had enjoyed splendid health was stricken with a sickness in the spring of 337 which soon proved to be critical. He tried in vain to recover by visiting the hot baths at Helenopolis on the Asiatic coast across from the capital. There in the chapel of the martyr Lucian he expressed his desire to be baptized. Confession of sin, renunciation of the Devil, and an affirmation of faith, this was the customary sequence in preparation for baptism. The postponement of baptism to the deathbed was also not unusual. Not a few Church fathers, and some from old Christian families, were baptized only in their latter years and many, like Ambrose, only shortly before being inducted into the episcopal office. Constantine's biographer says that he delayed in the hope of being baptized in the Jordan River. The main reason for the postponement was certainly that he wished to die in albis, in the white baptismal robe, symbolic of innocence.[34]

After his death at Pentecost in the year 337 Constantine's remains were taken to the capital and, awaiting the arrival of his son, were on view in the Great Hall of the palace. There, as he lay in a golden sarcophagus in the midst of imperial splendor, he was adored as in life. An edict was even issued still in his name.

33. Cf. H. Kähler, p. 23, note 67.
34. VC, IV, 61ff.

After the solemn procession to the Church of the Apostles he was laid in a porphyry sarcophagus in the mausoleum, surrounded by steles of the twelve Apostles. He himself had arranged that services in honor of the Apostles should regularly be conducted at this spot for the benefit of his soul.[35] His son then amassed relics of Luke and Timothy so that from now on the emperors should repose under the protection of the greatest saints. In a very brief time Constantine and his mother were declared to be "equal to the Apostles" and were themselves numbered among the saints of the Church. Their portraits adorned the great wall of the Greek churches.

35. *VC*, IV, 60 and 70ff. Cf. *Dö.*, pp. 413ff. Constantine's only thought was that the steles of the Apostles would ensure prayers on his behalf, not that he was to be rated above the Apostles as O. Weinreich implies when he adduces the concept of the 13th god to interpret the arrangement; nevertheless this idea has found many followers. An analogy to the emperor's arrangement for his burial can be seen in the custom of burying the dead "ad sanctos," i.e., near to the graves of the saints. A striking example for this practice, which spread in these days, is reported by Theodoret in his *Historia religiosa*. The famous Syrian eremite, Jacob, assembled in a sarcophagus made for him relics of Apostles, prophets and martyrs, and had himself buried next to the coffin. He would, so he hoped, rise again together with them and would be made worthy of the vision of God. Migne, *PG*, 82, 1449 A/B.

XVI. The Impact of the Church on the Empire

The Christian contemporaries of Constantine were overpowered by what they experienced. "God who caused light to shine in the darkness has, with an outstretched arm, led his servant Constantine as a savior." Amid the shadows had appeared a figure of light, who inaugurated a new era. The great Church History of Eusebius, which begins with the appearance of Christ on earth, ends with another redeeming act of God, who led forth His people from the oppression of persecution.

What were the traits of this figure? Eusebius, in his oration in the presence of the emperor, described not only what he was but what he ought to be.[1] The picture painted, so to speak, before the emperor's very eyes showed what his era saw in him and what he had a right and duty to see in himself. The introduction to the address before the ruler on the occasion of his greatest celebration is astonishing: the true emperor—declared the speaker —is in heaven and to sing his praises the whole assembly, and Constantine with them, are summoned; God's Logos rules the entire world; His image, the earthly monarch, serves under His command and assists in His work but only as a man; called and equipped by God he must first learn to master himself; he must bear in mind—and this is astonishing in a political oration—that the shepherd of the people differs from a goatherd or a cowherd

1. Oration of Eusebius on the thirtieth anniversary, *Opera*, I, ed. Heikel, 195–223.

only in his rank; the magnificence which surrounds him and the
wealth which he distributes to his subjects should mean no more
to him than stones and worthless metal, since against sickness
and death they are useless; only as an exemplar of piety can "the
friend of God" be true to his commission; his rule is modeled
after the heavenly pattern; through him God realizes His plan
for history: in the repulsing of the barbarians, in the victory
over the demons, in the elevation of the Cross, and in the herald-
ing of the true God. For this reason God extends His hand from
heaven to his servant and mortals join in the songs of angels.
Together they celebrate the one God, the Lord of all, the one
Savior, the Giver of every good thing, and also the one emperor,
who, together with his sons, beloved by God brings order upon
earth.

Here, almost at the end of Constantine's life's work—he died
only two years later—the old Roman concept of the ruler was
applied to him, but with a fundamental modification. From beyond the memory of man the ruler had been regarded as the
image and imitator of the divine model. But now we hear that
the true Emperor is above and His lieutenant is only a man. And
if the majesty of the emperor is exalted above all earthly comparison, nevertheless only his rank marks him off from a goatherd.
If before he had been made into a god, now he should laugh at
those who make such silly pretensions. Eusebius keeps the picture
of the image of the heavenly monarch, but at the same time retains
the distinction between the Creator and the creature; even the
purple is not holy of itself. One can take all these expressions in
one of two ways. Either the orator is toning down the classical
concept of the emperor or else he is inflating with courtly rhetoric
the modesty already achieved. Actually both elements are present
—imperial power and genuine humanity. The diadem is not degraded but the light is focused on the sign Constantine saw in
the vision which led him on his way and to which he dedicated
the empire, the sign of the Cross. Eusebius in formulating the
Christian concept of the emperor grasped the reality and en-

sured its continuance. The conclusion is reminiscent of the acclamation of the emperor: "One God, one Logos, one emperor." The perversions implicit in this formulation became manifest in the words of Louis XIV, "*Un roi, une loi, une foi,*" and in the vastly more sinister slogan of the Nazis, "*Ein Volk, ein Reich, ein Führer.*"

The concept of the ruler shone through the figure of Constantine and gave it universal significance. Nevertheless, he did not lose his personal characteristics. They were too marked to be resolved into a type. He remained the conqueror who had saved the state from corruption and dissolution and had renewed it from within by overcoming the godless powers. In his *Life of Constantine* Eusebius undertook to display for future generations the figure of the ideal ruler. From then on in the East the image of the emperor carried unmistakable reference to Constantine, just as in the West that of Charlemagne was the great prototype. The Byzantine ruler was glorified by calling him "a new Constantine," not a new Augustus.

When the impossible happened and the emperor had become a Christian, the Church was confronted unexpectedly with a new responsibility. She was unready. Since she lived in the midst of reality, how could she be ready for that which was extremely remote from the real? But when the remote became actual could she refuse to take part? She would in that case reject her commission "to go into all the world" (Matthew 28:19), but if she hearkened, her form would be changed. Spiritual unity and unanimity were in accord with her nature, but her structure would have to be modified if she were to take her place as the universal Church in the universal empire. What Constantine saw and desired in the Church was not alien to her essence, but the emperor helped her to adapt herself to the new role. He did not bestow his favor because the Church already had the requisite traits, as if hoping to find here a pillar for his empire. This happened within the new situation.

Centralization ensued. The network of alliances between local congregations in the various districts, with particular rights and duties for the oldest among them and special honor for certain bishoprics, was dissolved at Nicaea and supplanted by an overall structure. The ecclesiastical provinces were now to correspond to the political. Only Rome, Alexandria, and Ephesus retained their old status. The political importance of the state determined also the relative rank of the churches. This principle led to sharp conflicts when Constantinople, the new Rome, took an equal place with old Rome. The claim of the bishop of Constantinople to be the ecumenical patriarch was the mark of the emergent state Church. The trend in that direction began under Constantine. The Church accommodated herself to the new situation precisely as at Arles she had modified her position over military service and the holding of civil office. This freed her from outmoded ordinances which would only have held her back from the discharge of her new responsibilities; but at the same time there was loss with respect to ancient usage and valid tradition. And was it safe that the center of political power should be also the focus of the Church's life? Whether the Church was doing too much or too little in meeting the new circumstances the future alone would disclose.

Undoubtedly the emperor wanted the Church to adopt the pattern of the empire, but he did not force the issue. Yet at Nicaea he did intervene to bring about uniformity in the matter of the cultus. Without a doubt the emperor envisaged the participation of the Church in the life of the empire, but he did not demand it. The case was different, however, when the Council of Nicaea took up the question of when to observe Easter. The united empire could not have one section celebrating one day and another another, and the Church acquiesced.

The emperor helped to give definitive shape to the Church's structure by vesting authority in ecumenical councils to settle disputes about doctrine and life. The unifying of the Church's structure, the conferring of authority upon her courts, and the universal representation in councils were all first conferred on the Church in the period of Constantine.

But although the emperor achieved all this, the changes were not alien to the essential nature of the Church. The later councils of the imperial period, though in all details modeled after those of the state, conceived themselves as Church assemblies. They sat in the presence of the open Bible and believed their decisions to be imparted by the Holy Spirit. The primitive concept of the council (Acts 15:28) survived even into the time of the imperial Church of Justinian.

The Church in confrontation with the state assumed the form in which she was fitted to operate. Constantine filled her hands and furthered her work. The goods of the Church were the goods of the poor. The great philanthropic work of the Church, with which she attempted to alleviate grinding poverty, was made possible through the resources supplied by the state. But she also gave of her own. Ambrose and Augustine melted down Church silver. The great and beautiful churches now arising by the score provided room for the growing congregations, while giving to God honor upon earth. When the bishops were accepted on a par with the foremost men in the empire they were in a better position to speak a word in high places. Of course, there was a danger here, too. As Jerome said, "The Church grew through persecution and was crowned through martyrdom. But since the emperors have become Christian she has become greater in riches and poorer in virtues."[2] He was thinking obviously of the increasing worldliness of the Church of his day. Where temptation lies men may succumb. Property is compromising; it makes more difficult that carefree attitude which the Gospel enjoins. Even the building of churches involves one in the cares of the world. That is why Augustine would allow it only in the case of specific need. And because a bishop occupied so high a position in the social scale, the factors determining his

2. Preface to the *Vita Malchi*.

election were no longer solely his fitness for the Church but also his pedigree and social rank.

The Church was now called upon to give her message to crowds streaming in through her doors. Whatever their reason for coming they were not to be neglected. All had lived through the same years and the approach must be made through what they had experienced in common. The hour of victory allowed the Church to address the masses in solemn assembly. She found a hearing because men realized that the old world from which they came was disintegrating. The declining order of public life demanded a new support and the imperiled public morality called for a surer grounding than the old faith could supply. Outward good fortune and inner need determined the hour of the Constantinian Church.

She now confronted the common life of the secular world. There was a community of feeling which sustained individuals and gave them guidance as to what to do and what to leave undone, an impetus ordering and protecting life but an opening also for pernicious illusion which, like an infectious disease, laid hold upon all.

In this new situation a new sort of preaching was in order, with its own rights and its own dangers. The Church could not now simply draw individuals into her fold. She had a responsibility for the entire culture in which these individuals were placed. There was more to be done than help the pure and the good. Now city and town were to be made healthy. Everyday life in house and workroom, on the street and in the forum, must be brought under the light of the divine. Inevitably the emphasis had to be on moral commandment. "Righteousness exalteth a people." This was the kernel of Constantine's piety and that of his age.

Who can gauge what this meant for the life of the people? Often enough it meant religious complacency and the blessing of very unholy weapons. Yet how much strength for daily living, how much comfort in calamity did men owe to the Constantinian Church of the people!

New questions confronted the Church. What was the meaning of the Ten Commandments and what the meaning of the Gospel for the common life of the people? Would the former be properly observed and the latter not cut short? He who tried to do justice to both might miss the right answer and find himself in the position of the impeccable elder brother rather than the prodigal son. The Church would have to think through what these questions entailed. Was she equal to the task morally and spiritually, or would she merely take answers from outside? In that case, without knowing it, she might stumble into alien territory or simply succumb to pressure. This is a danger in every time and place, sometimes glaringly evident, sometimes eluding the most careful scrutiny. The line is often a fine one between becoming all things to all men and simply becoming like them. When the organization of society, when the economic norms, when the constitution of the state are all regarded as divinely ordained and unchangeable, then the frontier beyond which the Christian world can go has already been passed.

The ancient world looked to the ruler as the sustaining power. This assumption the Church found already fully established, for just as during the period of the imperial cult all Christians had been excluded from the common life of the empire, so now that the cult had been abolished they could, like other citizens, accept the emperor without reserve. They had no political philosophy of their own to prevent it. Still, the first of the Ten Commandments was at all times valid: "Thou shalt have no other gods before me." Neither men nor anything on earth should be deified. This basic conviction governed the Church's attitude to all the pretensions of the age; but a mere outward formulation could not set rules for particular cases. Some Christians made the sphere of the permitted larger, some smaller. Augustine, though with some misgivings, allowed genuflection before a human being.[3] Many Christians questioned whether this was not going too far, but others were so unreserved in their adoration of the emperor that a legal decree of 425 called a halt; public adoration, it said, is due only to God.[4] The abuse which Honorius sought to check, even though there was no sacrifice, was evidently a survival of the ancient imperial cult. Although the taproot of the cult, the sacrifice, had been severed, this did not prevent the sprouting of the lesser roots so that the past was perpetuated without even being noticed.

At this point we encounter popular superstition. But even in the classical form of the idea of the Christian emperor as delineated by Eusebius we sense a certain pre-Christian legacy. The fulsome flattery with which he loaded the emperor seems to exceed Christian limits. On the other hand, the reminder to the emperor that he was human and the disdain for the purple and the diadem show that the first commandment had not been forgotten.[5] Although the fulsomeness is not to our taste, theological judgment remains, nevertheless, intact. Were it not for these qualifications Eusebius would have given a handle to the misunderstanding and would have been false to the Church. But a good many of those who later took over his Christian picture of the emperor did not perceive the force of his basic theological interpretation.

At one point the contact of Church with state was fateful, however friendly in appearance. When Constantine forbade the assemblies of the heretics, confiscated their books, turned their houses of prayer over to the Catholics, and told them to join the Orthodox Church,[6] then the Christians greeted his orders as not only permissible but laudatory. With astonishing rapidity

3. Augustine, *De Civ.*, X, 4.
4. Theodosianus, XV, 4, 1.
5. This is commonly not recognized. W. den Boer, 'Some Remarks on the Beginnings of Christian Historiography," *Studia Patristica*, IV (1961), 348–362, still says that "the Christian emperor worship" begins with this oration of Eusebius as an enlarged legacy of the pagan concept of "divine kingship" (p. 360).
6. *VC*, III, 64–66.

the Church forgot the lessons of the persecution, that only genuine converts should be received. She did harm thereby not only to those committed to her by the state but also to herself, no matter how she soothed her conscience by insisting on examination before admission. All too readily she permitted her claim to be the only custodian of the truth to be enforced by the state. It was not long before she herself called for such constraint. Through the mouth of her great doctor, Augustine, she applied the words in the parable about the great banquet, "Compel them to come in," to the coercion of heretics by the state. If Constantine is reproached because he denied to the heretics the freedom which he granted to the pagans, a vastly greater blame rests on the Church. She not only gave in to state policy at this point but made it her own.

The modern observer is repelled because the Church in the course of her history has been able to endorse so many different, even contrasting forms of political and social life. But there is no Christian constitution as such. It will not do to treat the past as an iron law for the future; but it is no less pretentious to assault the present in the name of some exclusive ideal state. Different constitutions may meet the needs of particular times, but in and of themselves they may not be any more Christian than the constitution of Constantine. The Church had no cause to work for a change in the political structure, cutting down the emperor's throne and perhaps his head too. Similarly the Constantinian Church did not undertake to alter the whole structure of society, not even at the point which to us is so insufferable, the retention of slavery. The Church succumbed to the world only when she surrendered her value judgment. Denial of the slave as brother would have been denial of the faith. When the old or the new order is bedecked in holy robes, when it is not merely tolerated as that which is but revered as that which ought to be, then the Church has gone over to alien territory.

Along with the subtle infiltration of a foreign spirit we have noticed in the Arian controversy how the state applied pressure over the teaching of the Church and the Church did not invariably resist. This was in the period after Constantine. But even when the emperor regarded himself as a Christian the Church might clash with the wishes of the state, as in the case of the emperor Phocas, who desired that his soldiers fallen in battle be treated as martyrs. The persecutions did not end with Diocletian; indeed they assumed perhaps a more menacing mien. No favor from the emperor could outweigh the damage done when Christian teachers were forced to submit to extraneous pressure. This was to put the Church in chains, albeit chains of gold.

The question keeps coming up whether the Church of the fourth century was aware of the danger inherent in imperial favors. Did she not notice that she was about to sell her freedom? The question makes sense in view of the Church's most recent experiences with state connections. But does Constantine deserve blame? Did he restrict the freedom of the Church? He did take it upon himself to communicate the decisions of the Council of Nicaea to the people, but the Church could hardly take umbrage at having her decisions widely disseminated. Her preaching was meant to reach everybody. Constantine instructed his officials not to interfere with the new regulations of the Church's life. This protected her polity. Constantine in the end took part in the deliberations of the council and participated in the decisions. The Church accepted his policy gratefully and without protest. This could be taken to mean that the state always had the right to participate. Later emperors deemed it to be their right not only to call councils, but to influence their decisions, to confirm them, and to make them into law. The state Church had come to take this for granted. Constantius thought he was following his father when he gave directives to a council. All the more significant then that Athanasius, in opposing Constantius, appealed to the example of his father. Constantine did not name bishops, did not occupy churches with soldiers, did not exercise rule within the Church, and did not even confirm the decrees of councils.

How astounding that, a generation after Constantine, two such opposite interpretations could be voiced! The son who succeeded Constantine has the right to be heard. He wanted to carry on the work of his father—to imitate him even to the point of postponing baptism to his deathbed. But of no less weight is the testimony of the bishop, incumbent of the most important see in the east. Banned by both father and son, Athanasius, while condemning the son, excused and praised the father. How are we to explain the discrepancy between witnesses of such eminence? Constantius could claim considerable support from Constantine's policy. Both wanted the unification of the Church under a common and obligatory creed. But there was a difference, not only over the teaching but also over the manner in which it was to be carried out. Constantius forfeited rapport with the bishops. Constantine had enjoyed their confidence. What claim had anyone, he thought, to encroach upon their rights? That could only happen when confidence was gone. Exact repetition of the past may violate the spirit of that past. Athanasius sensed this and set himself sharply against the measures of Constantius which, in form only, followed the procedures of his father. Athanasius had retained confidence in Constantine despite severe treatment and had appealed to him against the decision of the Council of Tyre. But when Constantius followed his father slavishly, Athanasius resisted. The testimony of Athanasius is confirmed by that of another champion of the Church. Ambrose of Milan asserted that Constantine did not give orders to the bishops but left their judgment free.[7] We have, then, the word of two leaders of the Church that her freedom was not threatened under Constantine. It was the same story as that of the toleration of the pagans. Successors went far beyond Constantine.

A new age dawned for the Church. The emperor no longer opposed her. He gave the Church freedom and scope and associated her with himself in his task. But a great opportunity is also a great temptation. Should the Church then renounce such

7. *Ep.* XX, 15, Migne, *PL*, XVI, 1048b.

opportunity? It would have been a lack of faith to go to the desert or the catacombs. This did not mean that the Church had to forget the days of penury and suffering, but there was no point or right in stirring up persecution for the sake of being persecuted. The Church would not have been true to herself, if in self-righteousness she had refused to go through the open door. She must heed the call to what looked easier but what was, in many respects, a harder route. The Christians took it with some joy. Why not? And, stumbling and rising on their way—sometimes complacent when it was smooth, sometimes complaining when it was rough—they accepted riches and honors not always with full awareness of the responsibility entailed. Yet when they were clear-eyed they were aware that their loyalty was to the Church and not to the emperor and the world. To be sure, they could not be entirely clear in their own consciences in Constantine's period any more than earlier or today. Yet for the sake of the Lord who led them, this stretch of their way had also its meaning and its justification.

XVII. The Impact of the Empire on the Church

What did Constantine and his work mean to the empire? If the Christian authors are the best men to tell what he meant for the Church, his opponents are better in the case of the empire. Said one of them, "He was a mighty man who brought to pass whatever he attempted. He strove for mastery over the entire world."[1] This is the judgment of Eutropius in his brief *History of Rome*. All pagan authors, no matter how much they belittled the emperor, saw as his greatest contribution the restoration of the unity of the empire. He remained for them the liberator of Rome, who had also overthrown the second tyrant. It is very significant that those who looked upon Constantine as the great destroyer nevertheless declined to justify his rivals. They regarded Maxentius and Licinius as enemies within the empire who deserved their fate. The second great achievement of the emperor was the repelling of the Germans. The conquest of the Franks and the Goths gave him a title to fame which no one begrudged. If Eutropius spoke slightingly of Constantine's craving for the victor's laurel, he gave credit more to his energy than to his luck. There was less unanimity over his wisdom in taking the conquered into his service. Julian reproached his uncle with admitting the Germans into the highest offices. The reply to this charge on the part of a less prejudiced writer was that Constantine had always elevated strangers worthier than those

1. Eutropius, *Breviarium Historiae Romanae*, X, 4.

advanced by his reproachful nephew.[2] Others saw it as praise-worthy in a statesman and a general that as victor he should win over the vanquished.

And of course no one could overlook the founding of the new capital. Constantinople was soon not simply the bulwark but the very heart of the empire. Among the critics Julian was enough of a ruler to appreciate the strategic quality of the site. Some objected to the outlay or blamed the hasty construction. Libanius thought the city a monument to Constantine's ambition and reproached him with robbing temples to meet the expense; this sin was sorely expiated by the fall of his dynasty.[3] Possibly the numerous churches blinded the pagan rhetorician from seeing the political and strategic advantages. But precisely because of its churches Augustine may have regarded Constantinople as the culmination of the emperor's achievements.

The attitude of Julian, the last pagan emperor, toward his predecessor was in general that of his fellow pagans. "He was the destroyer of the old laws, as well as of the usages once established by the gods." This comment referred primarily to the religious enactment but was meant to include Constantine's entire administration. An historian of the fifth century, for whom Julian was a hero, criticized especially the reform of the army under Constantine and the system of taxation; and indeed the pagan authors were very far from seeing in Constantine's consolidation of the empire a continuation of the reform of Diocletian. Rather, for them, the shadow of the religious laws extended over Constantine's entire work. In his treatise entitled *The Banquet* Julian[4] invited all the Roman emperors to dine with the gods, there to be received or rejected according to their merits. This device gave him a chance, in a sort of Judgment Day, to assess the earlier rulers. Although the style is somewhat stiff and

2. Ammianus Marcellinus, XXI, 10, 8; 12, 25.
3. *Or. pro templis*, XXXVII.
4. *Convivium (Caesares) Juliani Opera.*, ed. Hertlein, I (1875) 393–432. Cf. J. Vogt, "Kaiser Julian über seinen Oheim Konstantin den Grossen" (1955).

pedantic, this was a bold and intriguing venture. Alexander and Trajan are given the highest rating, as one would expect. At the end Constantine is brought in to justify himself. In the presence of such illustrious company his cocky manner wilts. He must see that his achievements do not equal those of the great emperors. Since he did not pattern his life after the gods, but served the lowest of all the Olympians, the goddess Indulgence, he is dismissed from the table and has to take his place with Jesus, about whom all the guilty are gathered. To assess Constantine's measure, gods and heroes are summoned, but they only reduce his stature.

The pagans saw Constantine through dark glasses, thus proving the strength of the colors that do come through. Their judgments confirm Constantine's own view, which subordinated all else to the great contrast between the religions. Pagans and Christians were agreed that this was the crux.

The unification of the empire, the safeguarding of the frontiers, the founding of the capital, the reform of the administration—Constantine could point to all these as resting upon the new foundation. But Julian saw it all as an earthquake and its author as the wrecker of law and morals. And, indeed, had not something essential to security been shaken? What good were these innovations to the empire? The question applies first of all to the position of the monarch. When his authority vanished the state itself was in danger. There was no sacrifice to the emperor, no images in the temples. Did not all this give Julian the right to cast reproaches? Constantine, too, was occupied with the problem of his authority and gave it an ever loftier grounding. The clinching argument was his victorious course and his commission. The role of servant in which he was cast did not prevent him from taking over all the appurtenances of the traditional imperial dignity. The new element in his policy replaced the old not by negating but by integrating it. What he lost by ceasing to be a god he gained under the protection and direction of the Lord whom he served. His successors could not appeal in the same way to a personal mission and therefore placed the stress increasingly on the Christian injunction, "to obey the powers that be" (Romans 13). "He who assails your authority contradicts the ordinance of God." So spoke Ossius of Cordova, the ecclesiastical adviser of Constantine. He said this to Constantine's son at the very moment when he was telling him not to overstep the bounds of his office.[5] This was the basis of authority for the Byzantine emperors and came to be deeply embedded in the conscience of the people.

When the authority of the emperor was given this new base would the empire be rejuvenated? Constantine invited the congregations, so long aloof from political life, to share with him and support him. The empire should be their home. But what, then, of the pagans who hitherto had ruled the state? If we look at the example of Diocletian, who excluded the Christians, and of Theodosius, who excluded the pagans, we would expect them all to have been dismissed. In modern times there have been those who, weary of wars of religion, have taken a third course and have allowed two opposing religious parties to participate in political life. This was the solution of Henry IV of France in the Edict of Nantes. But Constantine was not weary. His own experience of free decision, his very faith, enabled him to take his stand without constraining others and therefore to make use of them in civil administration. The independent spirit in which he carried forward the work of Diocletian, whose religious policy he opposed, enabled him to work with those who still adhered to paganism. This freedom facilitated a transition in the empire without a sharp break. Thus at the very beginning of the Constantinian era, the Christian faith disclosed a possibility which is worthy of note, even if it was subsequently set aside.

When the state enlisted the Christians, what powers were given room to expand? Would they work weal or woe? We know what Constantine looked for: a power of integration, loyalty to law, faith in truth, courage to live. For the public life it meant a

5. Cf. *Dö.*, p. 115, note 1.

great deal that men should look upon their labors as ordained by God and to be discharged "under the great Taskmaster's eye." For the common weal it was healthy that a belief had taken hold which claimed work from every member. Disdain of this principle had debilitated the ancient world. No less important was the current set in motion against the widespread sexual irresponsibility of the age. Belief that whatever happened happened by Divine Providence enabled one to endure more steadfastly under pressing circumstances, indeed to see in them a more profound meaning than in unclouded good fortune. At the same time this deeper faith sharpened sensitivity to one's neighbor's need. The Christian could not wink at injustice but became instead the mentor of the mighty. When Diocletian looked to old Roman virtues he was trying to revive the forgotten. Now emerged a movement whose drive was constantly alert and attuned to the realities of the present. The impetus of the new beginning swept away obstacles and the critical gaze of observers kept it in tension. The Christian must show that his faith would interpenetrate every area of life. Sensitive to the demands of time and place, he should take seriously the world of men and serve them with all that he possessed.

But this demand to serve one's neighbor seemed incompatible with the quest for the fulfillment of the life beyond. The Christian was not to immerse himself in the world, as if his salvation lay in the world and in the fashion of that world. A measure of detachment might restrain the Christian from revolutionary fanaticism and to that degree would be welcome to the state, which can no more suffer anarchic fervor than stark conservatism. What Christianity, if taken seriously, could mean for the state was put well by Augustine. "Let him who claims that Christianity is incompatible with the state," wrote the great African father, "let him recruit an army of genuine Christians; let him display subjects, husbands, wives, parents, children; let him exhibit kings, judges and tax gatherers who live according to Christian standards; then let him dare to say that Christianity is incompatible with the state. Indeed, let him hesitate for a single moment to confess that this teaching, if followed, is the very salvation of the state."[6]

The objection to which Augustine was replying did not originate in his day and was directed earlier against the work of Constantine. That was why Augustine was able to lend his testimony to the emperor. In fact, Augustine's reply was almost more appropriate in the mouth of Constantine than on the lips of the eloquent advocate of the *City of God*, who actually had less concern for the state.

Whereas the state, now so intimately bound up with the Church, benefited from her virtues, so also, it suffered from the Church's defects. The religious controversies which rent the Church affected the state too. If the Church was split, the state was torn. The co-incidence of doctrinal quarrels with rifts in the social structure made them even more ominous for the state and the frequent intervention in the succeeding centuries of emperors in the doctrinal disputes was ominous for the Church. The result was that general unrest and national conflicts assumed a religious garb. This led to the secession of the Syrian and Coptic national churches and finally to the loss of extensive territories to Islam. But could the unity of the Byzantine Empire have been maintained had there been no doctrinal controversies? Could the Church have remained unified if Byzantine mismanagement and national clashes had not been injected? Who can say?

How can we best describe the relationship of Church and state brought about by Constantine? Should it be called "a community of fate," "a marriage," "a covenant"? No phrase really sums it up. They served each other and ruled each other. They determined

---

6. *Ep.*, 138, 15. This comment of Augustine has to be taken into account when the question is reconsidered how far Christianity can be held responsible for the decline of the Roman empire. Once, Gibbon had been quick to assert Christian responsibility, and now again the question is raised by A. Momigliano, "Christianity and the Decline of the Roman Empire" in: A. Momigliano (Ed.), *Conflict* (1963).

each other and were determined by each other. They helped each other and were under obligations to each other. They shared in each other's merits and defects. Who was the giver? Who the sufferer? Wherein lay the advantage? Where the loss? Much that catches the eye can be assessed. Much, no less important, can scarcely be divined. What does it all add up to?

The new forces at work in the empire began in silence. The most influential preacher in the first generation was unquestionably the emperor himself. In him was embodied that aspect of the new which spoke to his contemporaries. The cardinal point was an interpretation of history sustaining and in turn sustained by faith. Here was an integrated view of history which constituted also a summons to make history. The emperor evoked moral forces and strengthened them by heavenly expectations. His aspirations were not earthbound, yet the ideals of the other world did not exclude this world; they envisaged a future, breaking in a golden dawn over all humanity, embraced in the kingdom of peace. Overarched by the Providence of God Constantine felt that he was led by a mighty hand and shielded against all foes, whether on earth or in heaven. The law governing all that happens excluded both arbitrariness and resignation. Life became ordered and orderly. All of this adds up in no small measure and one can well believe that such a faith, proclaimed by such a victorious emperor, would not fail to make an impression. Such a faith was well suited to be that of an empire which, after great successes, looked to new horizons and considered nothing unattainable.

Constantine's understanding of history, even though basically his own, was not alien to the Christian thinking of his time. Lactantius and Eusebius, under the impact of the fall of the persecutors and the victory of the Church, saw their faith in the divine direction of history confirmed and to it they gave eloquent expression. The history of the Church long persecuted pointed to this culmination. God had vindicated His Church and showed that righteousness is the key to all that happens. Lactantius wrote a book on the *Deaths of the Persecutors,* not in order to wallow in their gore but to show forth the mighty acts of God, who "casts down the mighty from their seats and exalts those of low estate" (Luke 1:52). But was this not to forget that during the persecutions the martyrs had been sustained by nothing so trivial as earthly vindication? Theologians in their new day forgot this and did not combine the two experiences—that true faith risks persecution, while the crime of the persecutors will be avenged. One might say that the martyrs were being adored rather than heeded. One can understand why, if one examines the theological thinking of the period. Eusebius did not believe that the Church was called upon to bear witness like the martyrs by walking in the footsteps of the Lord. Rather, because she had not imitated the Lord she had been chastened. For him the periods of persecution and of vindication were not two opposites. The first was a cleansing penance to which the second properly succeeded. The vindication was a reward, although transcending all merit. Constantine's philosophy of history was never put to the test. After his victory neither his power nor his right was called in question. Only in the next generation was a question raised. One of the bishops banished by Constantius contested his right to interfere with the Church. Constantius answered in his father's vein, "If I have done wrong, I shall not last long." If God did not punish him that proved that he was right. The son took the word of his father, now formalized in another context, and used it instead of giving an answer of his own. And the churchmen were of the same mind. As if he were recalling the words of Constantius, Ambrose explained the death of Valens at the hands of the Goths on the grounds that God had punished him for favoring the Arian heresy. All the more confidently does he prophesy the orthodox Gratian's victory over the Goths.[7] But the future refused to be pinned down. Gratian was murdered. Ambrose had refuted the first objection to the Constantinian theory of history posed by the barbarian invasion when he

7. *De Fide,* II, 16.

pointed to the heresy of Valens. To be sure, his prediction as to Gratian was not fulfilled. Nevertheless, his point of view persisted and at the beginning of the next century received its highest expression. The ancient world had believed in the eternity of Rome. Now the Christians made this belief their own.[8] Peter and Paul, they believed, watched over their city. Here rested their bones as a foundation of eternal peace. Rome's great martyr St. Lawrence was portrayed in the toga of a Roman consul and gave protection to his earthly counterpart. The saying placed by Virgil in the mouth of Jupiter was now validated. "I have established an eternal kingdom." After Constantine had established an eternal empire, Rome had acquired an imperishable glory. She herself could now say, "No barbarian enemy now scales my walls. No foreign invader strides through the city to take my youths into slavery."

Shortly thereafter this arrogant belief collapsed. In the year 410 Alaric and his Goths broke into the "Eternal City." The pagans said, "Aha! This is the chastisement visited upon the Christian city by the pagan gods." Augustine, in his great work *The City of God*, had both to refute the pagans and sustain the Christians. As for the pagans, he gave up the old view shared by pagans and Christians that true religion ensures good fortune. Deeper insight shows that good fortune and misfortune are not neat contraries. Good fortune can be misfortune and misfortune can be salutary. He who believes that God is in His heaven can yield himself to His leading, even when it crosses his desires and goes beyond his understanding. "If what we wish does not come to pass, then something better will come." There is no such thing as a Christian claim upon success, either for Rome or for the emperor. The fate of Gratian is enough to show that. To be sure, the contrary is not true either, that the world has been committed to the Devil and his minions. To refute the contention of the pagans that goods and power depend on the favor of the old gods, Augustine replied, "God endowed the emperor Constantine

8. *Contra Symmachum*, I, 541ff.

with more gifts than anyone had ever ventured to desire. He allowed him to found a city, the daughter of Rome, without a temple or an image of the demons. He ruled long and as the sole emperor defended the entire Roman world. He was victorious in his wars and overthrew the tyrants. He died a natural death in high honor and left behind him sons as heirs of the empire."[9] But if this was enough to refute the pagans the Christians were not to use it in a pagan sense. "So that no emperor should become a Christian in order to attain the success of Constantine, God wiped out the Christian emperor Jovian faster than the pagan Julian and suffered Gratian to be struck down by a tyrant." Augustine had his eye not on the Christian empire but on its collapse and he pointed to its founder only as a particular example to help explain the riddle of the present disaster. Which does not mean that Augustine meant to leave the last word with those who completely denied Constantine's view of history. Augustine looked for an answer which would combine refutation and vindication.

Constantine did not live to see the collapse of the unity of the empire. His view of history was based on his own experience. He had seen the persecuted vindicated. His faith that God had vindicated them confirmed him in the religious interpretation of his own conquering course. The Lord of all the world held the hand of His servant. While this faith was neither a formula nor a claim, it was living and true. "The world rests on righteousness." Such a slogan is fitting for the beginning of a Christian empire. There is, however, the higher Christian Word of the Gospel that "the world rests on grace." But the higher is not without the lower and grace does not demolish righteousness when it cuts athwart "justice." There is a higher unity and though the kingdom of earth has its right and law, it must yield to a higher realm that in alien majesty abases the loftiest to abject lowliness.

Few generations are confronted by decisions of such signifi-

9. *De Civ.*, V, 25.

cance as those of Constantine's time. The occurrences evoked in contemporaries the feeling that they were living at a turning point in history. The universal cry found in the emperor its herald. The landscape was divided by a mountain range over which he would lead his people and all mankind.

Constantine realized that the question of decision was directed first of all to him. He carried it with him on his course, which was not that of a prophet but of an emperor. The Word which called him gave him power and that power was placed at the service of the Word, that the weak might become the mighty. Their destiny had drawn him and he now believed that they stood with him under the same obedience. At the same time the commission was his own, even if he could not discharge it alone. To this he committed himself and thereby was given his stature. In this way he closed one era and opened another.

We no longer come under the forces which affected contemporaries and can scarcely imagine the sense of the astounding which gripped the men of that day. But we are in a better position to reflect on something which still stands after fifteen hundred years.

In what measure shall we judge? We cannot apply the norms of other periods of efflorescence nor judge by the ideals of our own times. We have to judge an age first in terms of its own possibilities; only then can we see to what degree they were accomplished. An age ruled by the demonic is deplorable, no matter what it may have contributed in economics, art, and science. True greatness may lie where it is commonly denied. Yes—but who can measure history in these terms? If one focuses on that which has lasted, which has given form to human life, which has sufficed the centuries, one is warranted here, too, in speaking of greatness. And so one cannot reject the verdict of contemporaries and of posterity, which denies greatness to the hero of the day but grants the accolade to one who saw what was needed and did it.

Constantine faced the commission assigned by his time, needed by his time. He did not meet all of the needs—who could? But he did surmount the task laid upon him. His solution set the course for posterity without relieving it of responsibility to preserve, recast, and sift. His program was not messianic, exceeding the possible on earth, nor was it a closed system constricting the future.

Constantine's hour was one of new beginning, filled with all manner of hopes, threatened by all manner of temptations. It is easy enough to gaze at the fallen blossoms that have borne no fruit. The ground around the tree is white with all the petals and the burgeoning is long concealed before it comes to light. But is there then no fruit?

"Constantine the Great," "Athanasius the Great"—posterity has bestowed on both men the highest title it can. Both lived in the same age and left the stamp of their spirit upon it, the one so comprehensively that it is called the "Age of Constantine," the other in a narrower sphere, but with no less far-reaching influence. They jostled each other, though without genuine meeting.

It is not easy to define the relation of the great emperor to the great doctor. The contribution of each to his age is very different and even contrary. Constantine opened the door for the Church to take her place in society. She should become the educator of the peoples and by the power of her faith and her love should raise up a deeply endangered world. She must interpret the Word to the intellectuals and to the masses. The danger was implicit that in so doing she would accommodate the Word to her hearers. This is the danger which Athanasius saw and which he forfended. There were those who thought he stood in the way of work which the Church had assumed not unadvisedly and which demanded her best effort. The result was a bitter controversy at the very moment when unity was so important—this complaint could not be stilled. The task to which the emperor invited the Church was great and good and, at the same time, the bishop's protest was highly necessary. Who can decline the task in order to avoid the danger of a perversion of faith? But should one close one's eyes to the danger in order not to hinder the work?

The emperor banished Athanasius as an obstinate impediment to his policy of peace. But in the end the steadfast bishop was so identified with the cause that to affirm Nicaea was to affirm Athanasius. At first the correctness of his view was obscured by power struggles and his own intransigence. The emperor felt that he must step in. He had to silence that voice which was destined one day to give the purest expression to the very faith which undergirded the emperor's undertaking.

One is perplexed to see how Constantine in his effort to meet the momentary need should have done something which called his whole heritage into question, but it was this course which brought Athanasius to his stature. In banishment he worked out his position with the clarity that gave power to his witness. Only thus was he able to fulfill his spiritual office. One may well wish that Constantine could have looked beyond the immediate moment and that Athanasius had grasped the role of the Church in its fullness, but such wishes ask more of men than they can give. Athanasius threw no stone at Constantine, by whom he was banished. Shall we dare to cast the first?

The tension between the two men points to another historical insight. The doctrinal controversy concluded at Nicaea disclosed another mountain range to be surmounted with respect to the relation of the Church and the empire. The bond with the empire was seldom regarded by the Church as a fetter. In Constantinople especially the bond was deemed indissoluble. Shortly before the fall of the city the patriarch Antonius IV told the "king" at Moscow that Christians could not have a Church without the emperor. Moscow came to regard herself as the third Rome, following Constantinople, the second. Ivan the Terrible looked upon himself as the successor of Constantine, the first czar. Ivan had so high a view of his authority that resistance was "rebellion against God." A fugitive prince replied that he had the authority of God only so long as he was godly. Ivan demanded silence of the Church. Constantine called upon her for speech. And the Word must be spoken, whether by Ambrose the free to Theodosius the pious or by the patriarch in chains to Ivan the Terrible.

Constantine's mission carried him beyond the greatness of what he did to the greatness of that to which he aspired. A war hero, he looked beyond the bloody laurel and knew the limits of constraint. He respected the freedom which is the life-giving air of faith. His goal was exceedingly high and those who came after him sank back to the level of what they could attain. But the empire, which gave the Church a home and took the faith and the Word to itself, did not lose concern for mankind as a whole. Faith goes beyond the earthly and the Word cannot be intimate with power, even though its right be conceded. Yet there was greatness in Constantine's joining up with the Church's universal mission in the effort to achieve a universal goal, even while recognizing that such a task exceeded human powers.

Constantine's work endured. It looks now as if it is coming to an end. Will it cease to speak to us when what he did, what he wished, binds us no longer? Now that we can no longer appeal to his work perhaps for the first time the man behind the work will clearly emerge.

Who was this man? A man of ambition, he nevertheless pointed an ambitious courtier to the grave, "the end of all ambition." He delighted in display, and yet on the throne suffered himself to be reminded that he was a man and should not let himself be beguiled by the glory of the empire. He discerned beneath the impotent Word the higher power and he sensed in the cruelties of history meaning and judgment. In the midst of injustice and brutality he craved justice, amid passion he longed for quietude, and out of error looked for truth. He knew how to persuade and reconcile and, again, how to terrify and rebuff. He showed magnanimity, was not niggardly but allowed his wrath to drive him to wanton retribution. He was a ruler with a very high sense of his power and capacity, who nevertheless took as his highest title that of "Servant" and was devoted to his mission.

On this account, then, we cannot separate the man from his mission. He remains always the emperor. But as he was more than his impact, so he reaches out beyond it. He heard two demands—the one of the world, the other of faith; the one needed power, the other, rather, freedom. They were united and interpenetrated each other. We cannot blame him for the way he understood both demands, even though in altered circumstances we cannot repeat what he did. What was laid upon him is not laid upon us. If, in the light of later experience, we think to impose our concept upon the past, then we shall not grasp the significance of that earlier hour in history. How can anyone who is not prepared to listen confront history? There is still one final question that faced Constantine and cannot be overlooked. What has power to do with the Word? Can there be here only alienation, contrast, and strife? Or can there be proximity, service, and freedom? Any man seeking a new answer to this question should not overlook the one given in earlier times, whether he approves of it or seeks to find a better answer than that given by the first Christian emperor.

XVIII. Conclusion

In a work intended for a wider public one cannot leave a study of Constantine without inquiring into his significance for our time. However important he may have been for military history, jurisprudence, and the continuance of the Roman Empire, these achievements do not place him among the great in the world's history. The accomplishment with which his name is primarily associated reaches far beyond his century and even beyond the Byzantine Empire. Constantine was the ruler who inaugurated a system which has lasted for fifteen hundred years and still leaves its imprint, namely, the union of the Christian Church and the state. This is a duration few institutions ever attain. His decision set the pattern for ages to come and they have had to wrestle with the difficult problems inherent in his system.

But even if we approach Constantine from our own age we cannot detach him from his own. To assess Constantine and his period we must see what contemporaries said about him and even more what he said about himself. As for contemporaries, we have the two orations at Trèves, the one in 310 before the conquest of Rome, the other three years later after the battle of the Milvian Bridge. At the end of Constantine's career we have the evaluation of Eusebius. But we cannot simply repeat this. We must set the emperor in a much larger framework.

Historians have long debated whether Constantine was a Christian or a politician. To be sure, the historian is not a searcher of hearts, but it is indisputable that Constantine thought of himself as a Christian. We have no right to call his own utterances into question. Yet we must ask what kind of a Christian he was. How much of earlier Christianity did he retain? What meaning did it have for him and for his work? Only after answering these questions are we in a position to evaluate the man.

To ask whether he was primarily political or religious is anachronistic. Religion determined politics and politics determined religion. Nor will it do to say that Constantine was half Christian and half political. He was wholly political. How can one be a statesman, a doctor, a farmer, only halfway? And to say this is not to pass judgment on the integrity of his Christian faith. How can one know whether faith is genuine even in the case of a parson or a monk?

However important it is to look at the past from the viewpoint of the present, that viewpoint cannot be imposed upon the past. We must not forget that history has a quality of once-and-for-all. To apply modern categories to the past is to canalize history and make it flow always in the same course. But not even similar events have the same meaning in different periods. The fire in the imperial palace in 303 did not have the same meaning as the fire in the Reichstag in 1933 and what Hitler meant by "Providence" was not what Constantine meant.

But how are we to arrive at an understanding? We are skeptical of fulsome praises and distrustful of wholesale debunking. Motives are always mixed and we do not get a true picture by fastening onto the worst. Since the great work of Jacob Burckhardt we have had enough depictions of Constantine cast in the shadows. An historical figure ought to be appraised in terms of his strength; then we are in a position to diverge from his course. Precisely because the line of slavish repetition is cut we can confront the man.

The image of Constantine was set for many centuries by Eusebius' *Life of Constantine*. The biography was written shortly after the death of its hero in order to lay before the emperor's sons and successors the example of the godly prince. Eusebius felt that they needed it. He stated expressly that he had omitted all shadows which might dim the splendor.[1] In consequence the highest claim to fame possible to a Byzantine emperor was that he should be entitled a "new Constantine." Of course, the Latin Church did not, like the Byzantine, number Constantine among the saints. Nevertheless he was regarded along with Charlemagne throughout the Middle Ages as the ideal ruler. Only a few revivalist preachers and poets such as Dante lamented the "Donation of Constantine," which had brought the Church to the corruption of opulence.

Not until modern times was the place accorded to Constantine seriously contested and this from two opposite quarters. The main Protestant reformers certainly were not yet ready to raise a doubt, but the left wing of the Reformation and later the Pietists attacked the power vested in the Church and the reputation of the emperor who first brought this about. Gottfried Arnold, who in his *Kirchen- und Ketzerhistorie* (1699–1700) gave expression to the Pietist interpretation of Church history, held Constantine primarily responsible for the secularization of Christendom: "If Constantine be measured in terms of the first uncontaminated Christianity one will have to say that he was no true Christian and was baptized as a deceiver and seducer of the Church."[2] The Enlightenment, which sought to emancipate the state and society from the shackles of the Church, saw in Constantine the one who introduced the fetters and consequently drew his picture without halo or goldleaf. Voltaire set over against each other the Christian and the pagan witnesses and passed judgment, like Arnold, in moralistic terms. The verdict was based on the so-called "murders" of his relatives. "He had a father-in-law and made him hang himself; he had a brother-in-law and caused him to be strangled; he had a nephew of twelve or thirteen years and had him throttled; he had a first-born son

1. *VC* I, 11.
2. *Kirchen- und Ketzerhistorie* Teil I/II, IV 2 § 3.

and he had his head cut off; he had a wife and he caused her to be suffocated in the bath. A Gallic contemporary author said that 'he liked to clean out the house.'" Voltaire concluded that Constantine did as much harm to the empire as he conceivably could.[3] Edward Gibbon erased the Christian traits of the Roman *generalissimo* and presented a secular picture. The indisputably Christian characteristics were held to detract from his reputation. His chief mistake was that he suffered himself to be persuaded to come to terms with the Christian Church.[4] "The decline of the Roman empire was hastened by Constantine."[5]

In the nineteenth century Jacob Burckhardt, in his masterly presentation of the age of Constantine the Great, proceeded from the assumption that power is evil and portrayed the emperor as the personification of the demonic. "In a genius driven without surcease by ambition and lust for power there can be no question of Christianity and paganism, of conscious religiosity; such a man is essentially unreligious." Burckhardt charged Eusebius with endeavoring at any price to make the first great protector of the Church into an ideal prince. "Hence we have lost the picture of a genius in stature who knew no moral scruple in politics and regarded the religious question exclusively from the point of view of political expedience." At the same time Burckhardt, when he spoke of Constantine as "a murderous egotist," full of "fearful malignancy," did not deny his historical greatness: "The great

3. Oeuvres Complètes de Voltaire, Dictionnaire Philosophique II (Paris, 1878), p. 250. Il avait un beau-père, il l'obligea de se pendre; il avait un beau-frère, il le fit étrangler; il avait un neveu de douze à treize ans, il le fit égorger; il avait un fils aîné, il lui fit couper la tête; il avait une femme, il la fit étouffer dans un bain. Un vieil auteur gaulois dit qu'il aimait à faire maison nette (p. 247). The conversion of the image of Constantine is discussed by Werner Kaegi, "Vom Nachleben Konstantins," *Schweizerische Zeitschrift für Geschichte* VIII (1958), pp. 289–326.

4. Gibbon quotes according to a French poem: "He used the altars of the Church as a convenient footstool to the throne of the empire" and he adds that in the end Constantine himself might have taken the mask of the believer for real. *History of the Decline and Fall of the Roman Empire* (1776–88), ch. XX, vol. II, 324/25.

5. Ibid., ch. XXXVIII: General observations on the fall of the Roman empire in the west (p. 624).

man, frequently unconsciously, consummates higher decrees, and an epoch is expressed in his person, while he believes that he himself is ruling his age and determining its character." From this dreadful but politically great man the Christian Church had nothing to lose and paganism nothing to gain. In drawing this picture Burckhardt was thinking of the figure who dominated his own age, Napoleon Bonaparte.[6]

The modern picture of Constantine still shows the traces of these attacks on the thousand-year-old image given by Eusebius. Despite various shadings, the political interpretation has prevailed. As for Constantine's religious policy, some have held that he entertained open or secret inclinations to paganism, or that he was syncretistic, or that he was not interested in religion at all. Conscious or unconscious presuppositions determine the view. Some measure Constantine in terms of the early Christian ideal and find him wanting; some think of him as an unprincipled powerseeker with no morality save that which served his own ends. Some, mindful of the fact that "Truth is the first casualty in warfare," interpret the sayings of Constantine with respect to the Church (if genuine) simply as a device to win over the opposition and utilize the ecclesiastical organization developed under the pressure of persecution as a pillar of the state. At best Constantine's own religion was no more than a blending of pagan and Christian, without interest in religious controversies, and ready to leave their solution to power factors. Precisely because Constantine was so completely secular he was able out of disintegration to introduce a new era.

But such interpreters fail to see that Constantine interpreted his own behavior quite differently. According to their view his deeds and his words contradict each other. But the "realistic" interpretation must face up to its own presuppositions and subject them to scrutiny. To begin with, these historians are entirely mistaken in believing that Christianity constituted a power factor

6. Jacob Burckhardt, *The Age of Constantine the Great* (1853/1949), ch. 8 and 9.

to be reckoned with. In the west in particular, where Constantine began his political career, the Christians were a minority. And what is more, they held aloof from political life. Constantine was the one who first affiliated them with the state and gradually built them into a political factor. Moreover, the "realistic" interpreters are compelled to view the Christian references in the imperial proclamations either as sheer rhetoric or as interpolations inserted by Christian secretaries, or else to regard the edicts in their entirety as spurious. But this one cannot do after the discovery of an official papyrus of the controverted Edict of Restitution of 324 and one cannot suppose that so imperious a man as Constantine would turn over to secretaries questions about which he was greatly concerned, as he says in the Edict of Milan.

Constantinian scholarship has not stood still since the time of Burckhardt. Solid work has been rendered and sound results achieved. Anyone who works in this field is deeply indebted to his predecessors. But for all the verification of details, we are still far from having achieved a consensus on the broader questions.[7]

And we never shall, unless we respect a man's word as much as his deed. The word gives the deed a name. If the deed does not measure up to the word, the word at any rate sets forth that to which the man aspired. We must allow Constantine's utterances to speak to us. These documents leave no doubt that from

7. Only a few years ago one of the most competent scholars in the field, Joseph Vogt, remarked that almost all the books on Constantine published recently still "contradict each other in essential points." "Bemerkungen zum Gang der Constantinforschung" in: *Mullus,* Festschrift für Theodor Klauser (1964). Even the historical predicate "the Great" is not undisputed. For the history of this cognomen cf. Peter Spranger, "Der Grosse. Untersuchungen zur Entstehung des historischen Beinamens in der Antike," *Saeculum* IX (1958) pp. 22–58. According to Spranger this cognomen is used about fifty years after the death of Constantine. Ammiamus Marcellinus and Sozomenus are the first to testify to this usage. It neither originated from the exuberant praise of the Panegyrics nor was it taken from the emperor's self-evaluation in which "Maximus" stood beside the traditional titles as "Pius" and "Felix." "The Great" stems from the anonymous usage of those who later on looked back and tried to assess the person and the work of Constantine.

the time of the battle of the Milvian Bridge Constantine regarded himself as a Christian.

Still, we cannot stop simply with a refutation of the political interpretation of Constantine. As we saw before, to ask whether politics determined his religion or religion his politics is anachronistic. For him politics was a matter of religion and religion a matter of politics. The alternatives of Arnold and Burckhardt will not do. A convinced Christian faith and participation in the life of the world are not mutually exclusive. Admittedly, this observation does not settle the problem of the character of Constantine's Christianity: how much of the pre-Christian did he carry over and what did Christianity mean for him and his work? We cannot simply take over the Eusebian idealization, nor can we revere a gilded icon of St. Constantine. We can neither idealize nor denigrate. And we should not pass moral judgment, but rather attempt to achieve historical understanding.

The question is no longer whether Constantine was a secular politician, a mere pagan, a syncretist, or a convinced Christian. The question, on a new level, is how his Christianity took shape. He thought of Christ as the god of battle, of the Cross as the sign and giver of victory. He looked to a truer and more unified cultus as the basis for the security of the empire. This was the faith of the first Christian emperor. Plainly it had a distinctly Roman cast. This does not mean that the name alone was changed and not the faith. Nor does it mean that Constantine adhered to a heretical form of Christianity, Arianism. We have seen in what sense he adhered to Nicene orthodoxy. But the way in which the new was understood in terms of the old and the old in the process deepened rather than discarded, the way in which the Roman heritage gave a stamp to the Christian empire, this is where we must look for the peculiarity of Constantinian Christianity, the faith of a single ruler and of many centuries. On this level a vastly more important and intriguing task confronts us: that we should understand his personal character and his historical impact.

Chronology

* = Died
** = Executed

Maximian resumed the purple and married his daughter Fausta to Constantine

308 After the failure of Galerius to take Rome a conference of the rulers at Carnuntum

Maximian was again required to abdicate. Licinius made Augustus of the West

310 Maximian**

311 Galerian's Edict of Toleration. Galerius*

312 Constantine's march on Rome. Battle of the Milvian Bridge

313 The Edict of Milan. Constantine's campaign against the Germans. Licinius conquers Maximinus Daza.* Beginning of the Donatist controversy

314 Constantine in control of a large part of the Balkans through the first partitioning with Licinius. Imperial residences at Sirmium and Serdica instead of at Trèves: separation of east and west

Synod of Arles

315 Constantine's tenth anniversary. Dedication of the Triumphal Arch in his honor at Rome

321 The law with respect to Sunday

324 The second conflict between Constantine and Licinius

The battle at Chrysopolis

Licinius**

The universal monarchy: edicts of restitution and toleration

325 The Council of Nicaea: doctrinal solution of the Arian controversy. Constantine's twentieth anniversary celebrated in the midst of the bishops

326 Executions of Crispus and Fausta**

Constantine's last visit to Rome in connection with his twentieth anniversary

328 Athanasius elected bishop of Alexandria

330 Dedication of Constantinople

332 War with the Goths

335 Synod at Tyre; banishment of Athanasius

Dedication of the Church of the Holy Sepulchre at Jerusalem

337 Constantine*

List of Abbreviations

CSEL	Corpus scriptorum ecclesiasticorum lantinorum, Vienna 1866ff
DMP	Lactantius, De mortibus persecutorum
Dö	H. Dörries, Das Selbstzeugnis Kaiser Konstantins
HE	Historia ecclesiastica (if without further name: Eusebius, Hist. Eccl.; otherwise: Gelasius, HE; Sozomen, HE, etc.)
Migne, PG	Patrologia Graeca, ed. J. P. Migne, Paris 1864–1886
Migne, PL	Patrologia Latina, ed. J. P. Migne, Paris 1844–1864
Paneg	Panegyrici latini
Pauly-Wissowa	Paulys Realencyclopädie der Classischen Altertumswissenschaften, Stuttgart 1893ff
RAC	Reallexikon für Antike und Christentum, Stuttgart 1950ff
VC	Eusebius, Vita Constantini

Bibliography

I. On the Late Roman Empire

Andresen, C., "Die Kirchen der alten Christenheit," *Die Religionen der Menschheit*, XXIX 1/2 (Stuttgart, 1971).

The Cambridge Ancient History, vol. XII (Cambridge, 1939).

Gaudemet, J., "L'église dans l'empire romain," *Histoire du droit et des institutions de l'église* tom. III (Paris, 1958).

Gibbon, E., *The History of the Decline and Fall of the Roman Empire* (London, 1766–88); new edn., ed. J. B. Bury, vols. I–VII (London, 1909ff).

Jones, A. H. M., *The Later Roman Empire, 284–602 AD* (Oxford, 1964) 3 vols.

Lietzmann, Hans, *A History of the Early Church*, 4 vols. (New York, 1961).

Momigliano, A., ed., "The Conflict between Paganism and Christianity in the Fourth Century," *Essays* (Oxford, 1963).

Palanque, J. R., and others, "De la paix constantinienne à la mort de Théodose," in Fliche-Martin, *Histoire de l'Église III* (Paris, 1947).

Rostovtzeff, M., *Social and Economic History of the Roman Empire* (Oxford, 1926).

Seeck, O., *Geschichte des Untergangs der antiken Welt I–VI* (Stuttgart, 1895ff); vol. I (Stuttgart, 1921⁴).

Stein, E. *Geschichte des spätrömischen Reiches*, vol. I (Wien, 1928); French edn. ed. J. R. Palanque (Paris 1959).

Vogt, Joseph, *Der Niedergang Roms* (Zürich, 1965); English edn., *The Decline of Rome* (New York, 1968).

II. General Works on Constantine

Burckhardt, J., *The Age of Constantine the Great* (1853), trans. Moses Hadas (New York, 1949).

Dörries, Hermann, "Das Selbstzeugnis Kaiser Konstantins," *Abhandl. der Akademie der Wissenschaften Göttingen, Phil.-hist. Klasse,* 3.Folge Nr.34 (Göttingen, 1954).

Jones, A. H. M., *Constantine the Great and the Conversion of Europe* (London, 1948).

Koch, Hal, *Konstantin den Støre* (Copenhagen, 1952).

Piganiol, A., *L'empereur Constantin* (Paris, 1932).

Vogt, J., "Constantin der Grosse" in *Reallexikon für Antike und Christentum,* III (1957), col. 306–379.

———, *Constantin der Grosse und sein Jahrhundert* (Munich, 1960²).

III. Surveys of the Literature

Baynes, N. H., "Constantine the Great and the Christian Church," *Proceedings of the British Academy* (1929), pp. 341–442.

Delaruelle, E., "La Conversion de Constantin, état actuel de la question," *Bulletin de litt. ecclésiastique,* LIV (1953), 37–54, 84–100.

Gerland, E., "Konstantin der Grosse in Geschichte und Sage," *Texte und Forschungen z. byz.-neugr. Philol.,* XXIII (1937).

Karpp, H., *Theologische Rundschau, Neue Folge,* XIX (1951), 1–21 and XXIII (1955), 247–258.

Kretschmar, G., "Der Weg zur Reichskirche," *Verkündigung und Forschung,* XIII (1968), no. I, 3–44.

Piganiol, A., "L'État actuel de la question constantinienne," *Historia,* I (1950), 82–96.

Stroheker, K. F., "Das konstantinische Jahrhundert im Lichte der Neuerscheinungen 1940–1951," *Saeculum,* III (1951), 654–680.

IV. The Main Sources

"Codex Justinianus," *Corpus iuris civilis,* vol. II, ed. P. Krüger (Berlin, 1877).

Codex Theodosianus, bks. I–VIII, ed. P. Krüger (Berlin, 1923–26); bks. IX–XVI, ed. Th. Mommsen (Berlin, 1905). English translation with commentary by C. Pharr (Princeton, 1952).

Coleman-Norton, P. R., *Roman State and Christian Church. A Collection of Legal Documents to A.D. 535* (London, 1966), 3 vols.

Eusebius, "Vita Constantini" in *Eusebius' Works,* vol. I, ed. I. A. Heikel (Leipzig, 1902). On the text and the question of authenticity compare the work of Winkelmann. A full evaluation of the work is still a desideratum. New edition by Winkelmann is appearing English translation of Eusebius in *A Select Library of Nicene and Postnicene Fathers of the Christian Church*, ser. 2 vol. I (1890) by A. C. McGiffert and E. C. Richardson.

Eusebius, "Historia Ecclesiastica," in *Eusebius' Works*, vol. II, ed. E. Schwartz (Leipzig, 1903–09).

————, "Laus Constantini," *ibid.*

Lactantius, "De mortibus persecutorum," ed. with a French translation J. Moreau, vols. I and II (Paris, 1954), *Sources chrétiennes*, XXXIX. English translation in *Ante Nicene Fathers*, VII, pp. 301–322, by W. Fletcher.

Panegyrici latini, ed. with a French translation E. Galletier, vol. II (Paris, 1952).

The Roman Imperial Coinage, vol. VI.: "From Diocletian's Reform (A.D. 294) to the Death of Maximianus (A.D. 313)," by C. H. Sutherland (London, 1967), vol. VII.: "Constantine and Licinius A.D. 313–337," by P. M. Bruun (London, 1966).

"Urkunden zur Entstehungsgeschichte des Donatismus," ed. H. v. Soden and H. v. Campenhausen, *Kleine Texte*, CXXII (Berlin, 1950²).

"Urkunden zur Geschichte des Arianischen Streites" in *Athanasius Works*, vol. III, 1, ed. H. G. Opitz (Berlin, 1934ff).

Zosimus, *Historia Nova*, (6 bks with omissions), ed. L. Mendelssohn (Leipzig, 1887); the pagan criticism of Constantine. English translation by J. J. Buchanan and H. T. Davis (1967).

V. Alphabetical List

Aland, K., "Die religiöse Haltung Kaiser Konstantins," *Studia Patristica*, I, (Berlin, 1957) 549–600, reprinted in *Kirchengeschichtliche Entwürfe* (Gütersloh, 1960), pp. 202–239.

————, "Kirche und Staat in der alten Christenheit," in: *Kirche und Staat*. Festschrift für H. Kunst (Berlin 1967), pp. 19–49.

Alföldi, A., "Die Ausgestaltung des monarchischen Zeremoniells am römischen Kaiserhofe," *Mtlgen. d. Dt. Arch. Instituts Röm. Abt.*, XLIX (1934), 1–118.

————, "Insignien und Tracht der römischen Kaiser," *ibid.*, L (1935), 1–171. Both essays are reprinted in *Die monarchische Repräsentation im römischen Kaiserreiche* (Darmstadt, 1970).

————, "The Helmet of Constantine," *Journal of Roman Studies*, XXII (1932), 9–23.

Alföldi, A., "Hoc signo victor eris. Beiträge zur Geschichte der Bekehrung Konstantins des Großen," in: *Pisciculi*. Festschrift F. J. Dölger (Munich, 1939), pp. 1–18.

———, *The Conversion of Constantine and Pagan Rome* (Oxford, 1948).

———, "The Initials of Christ on the Helmet of Constantine," *Studies in Roman Economic and Social History in Honor of Allan Chester Johnson* (Princeton, N.J., 1951), pp. 303–311.

Alföldi, M. R., *Die Constantinische Goldprägung* (Mainz, 1963).

———, "Die Sol-Comes-Münze vom Jahre 325. Neues zur Bekehrung Constantins," *Jahrbuch für Antike und Christentum, Ergänzungsband*, I (Münster, 1964), 10–16.

Anastos, M. V., "The Edict of Milan," *Revue des Études Byzantines*, XXV (1967), 13–41.

Bainton, R. H., *The Travail of Religious Liberty* (Philadelphia, 1951).

———, *Christian Attitudes Toward War and Peace* (New York, 1960).

Bates, M. S., *Religious Liberty: An Inquiry* (New York, 1945).

Baynes, N. H., "Eusebius and the Christian Empire," *Byzantine Studies and other Essays* (London, 1955), pp. 168ff.

Beck, H. G., "Konstantinopel-das neue Rom," *Gymnasium*, LXXI (1964), 166–174.

Berchem, D. van, *L'Armée de Dioclétien et la réforme constantinienne* (Paris, 1952).

Berkhof, H., *Kirche und Kaiser* (Zürich, 1947).

Bidez, J., *La vie de l'empereur Julien* (Paris, 1930).

Brezzi, P., *La politica religiosa di Costantino* (Naples, 1964).

Brisson, J. P., *Autonomisme et christianisme dans l'Afrique romaine* (Paris, 1958).

Brown, P. R. L., "Religious Coercion in the later Roman Empire," *History*, XLVIII (1963), 283–305.

———, "St. Augustine's Attitude towards Religious Coercion," *Journal of Roman Studies*, LIV (1964), 107–116.

Bruck, G., "Die Verwendung christlicher Symbole auf Münzen von Constantin I bis Magnentius," *Numismatische Zeitschrift*, LXXVI (Vienna, 1955), 26–32.

Bruun, P., *The Constantinian Coinage of Arelate* (Helsinki, 1953).

———, "Studies in the Constantinian Chronology," *Numismatic Notes and Monographs*, CXLVI (New York, 1961).

Buckland, W. W., *The Roman Law of Slavery; the condition of the slave in private law from Augustus to Justinian* (Cambridge, 1908), reprinted London, 1970.

Cadoux, C. J., *The Early Christian Attitude to War* (London, 1919).

Calderone, S., *Costantino e il cattolicisimo*, vol. I (Florence, 1962).

Campenhausen, H. v., "Der Kriegsdienst der Christen in der Kirche des Altertums," *Offener Horizont. Festschrift für Karl Jaspers* (1953), pp. 255–264.

Cochrane, C. N., *Christianity and Classical Culture. A Study of Thought and Action from Augustus to Augustine* (Oxford, 1960).

Coleman, C. B., *Constantine the Great and Christianity* (New York, 1914).

Conant, K. J., "The Original Buildings at the Holy Sepulchre in Jerusalem," *Speculum*, XXXI (1956), 1–48.

Cross, F. L., *The Study of St. Athanasius* (Oxford, 1945).

Cumont, Franz, *Les Religions orientales dans le paganisme romain* (Paris, 1929⁴).

Daniele, J., "I documenti constantiniani della 'Vita Constantini' di Eusebio di Cesarea," *Analecta Gregoriana Ser. Fac. Hist. Eccles. Sect.*, vol. I (Rome, 1938).

Dawson, Christopher, *The Making of Europe* (London, 1936).

Deichmann, F. W., *Frühchristliche Kirchen in Rom* (Basel, 1948).

Diesner, H.-J., *Studien zur Gesellschaftslehre und sozialen Haltung Augustins* (Halle, 1954).

———, *Kirche und Staat im spätrömischen Reich* (Berlin, 1964²).

Dinkler, Erich, "Das Kreuz als Siegeszeichen," *Zeitschrift für Theologie und Kirche*, LXII (1965), 1–20.

———, *Signum Crucis. Aufsätze zum Neuen Testament und zur Christlichen Archäologie* (Tübingen, 1967).

———, and Dinkler-v. Schubert, Erika, "Kreuz," *Lexikon der christlichen Ikonographie*, II (1970), 562–590.

Dörries, Hermann, *Constantine and Religious Liberty* (New Haven, Conn., 1960).

Downey, G., "The Builder of the Original Church of the Apostles at Constantinople," *Dumbarton Oaks Papers*, VI (1951), 53–80.

Dumbarton Oaks Papers, XXI (1967), 11–249 (Dumbarton Oaks Symposium 1966 "The Age of Constantine: Tradition and Innovation").

Ehrhardt, A., "Constantin der Grosse. Religionspolitik und Gesetzgebung," *Zeitschr. d. Savignystiftung f. Rechtgesch. Romanist Abtlg.*, LXXII (1955), 127–190.

———, "The Adoption of Christianity in the Roman Empire," *Bulletin of the John Rylands Library* (1962), pp. 97–114.

Ensslin, W., "Gottkaiser und Kaiser von Gottes Gnaden," *Sitzungsber. d. Bayer. Akad. d. Wiss. Phil-hist. Kl.* (1943) vol. 6.

———, "Die Religionspolitik des Kaisers Theodosius des Grossen," *Sitzungsber. d. Bayer. Akad. d. Wiss. Phil.-hist. Kl.* (1953), vol. 2.

———, "Staat und Kirche von Konstantin dem Grossen bis Theodosius dem Grossen," *Akten des IX. Internat. Kongresses für byz. Studien,* II (Athens, 1956), 405–415.

Esplorazioni sotta la Confessione di San Pietro in Vaticano (Città del Vaticano, 1951) 2 vols.

Fabrini, F., "La manumissio in Ecclesia," *Università di Roma. Publicazioni dell'istituto di diritto Romano e dei diritti dell'oriente mediterraneo,* XL (Milano, 1965).

Franchi, P. de'Cavalieri, *Constantiniana* (Rome, 1953).

Frend, W. H. C., *The Donatist Church* (Oxford, 1952).

———, "The Failure of the Persecution in the Roman Empire," *Past and Present,* VIII (1959), 10–27.

Gascou, J., "Le rescrit d'Hispellum," *Mélanges d'Archéologie et d'Histoire,* LXXIX (1967), 609–659.

Gaudemet, J., "La Législation religieuse de Constantin," *Rev. Hist. Egl. de France,* XXXIII (1947), 25–61.

Grabar, A., *Martyrium. Recherches sur le culte des reliques et l'art chrétien antique,* 2 vols. (Paris, 1946).

———, *Die Kunst des frühen Christentums von den ersten Zeugnissen christlicher Kunst bis zur Zeit Theodosius' I.* (Munich, 1967).

Grasmück, E. L., "Coercitio. Staat und Kirche im Donatistenstreit," *Bonner historische Forschungen,* XXII (1964).

Greenslade, S. L., *Church and State from Constantine to Theodosius* (London, 1954).

Grégoire, Henri, "La conversion de Constantin," *Revue de l'Université de Bruxelles,* XXXVI (1930/31), 231–272.

———, "About Licinius' Fiscal and Religious Policy," *Byzantion,* XIII (1938), 551–560.

———, "Eusèbe n'est pas l'auteur de la 'Vita Constantini' dans sa forme actuelle et Constantin n'est pas 'converti' en 312," *Byzantion,* XIII (1938), 561–583.

———, "L'authenticité et l'historicité de la Vita Constantini attribuée à Eusèbe de Césarée," *Académie royale de Belgique. Bulletin de la classe des lettres et des sciences morales et politiques,* XXXIX (1953), 462–479.

Guarducci,M., *I graffiti sotto la Confessione di St. Pietro in Vaticano, I–III* (Città del Vaticano, 1958).

Gutermann, L., *Religious Toleration and Persecution in Ancient Rome* (London, 1951).

Habicht, C., "Zur Geschichte des Kaisers Konstantin," *Hermes,* LXXXVI (1958), 360–378.

Janin, R., "Constantinople byzantine," *Archives de l'Orient chrétien,* IV (Paris, 1950) (Paris, 1964²).

Jones, A. H. M., and Skeat, T. C., "Notes on the Genuineness of the Constantinian Documents in Eusebius' Life of Constantine," *Journal of Ecclesiastical History,* V (1954), 196–200, cf. Winkelmann, *Texte und Untersuchungen,* LXXXIV, pp. 66–70, 121–131.

Instinsky, H. U., *Bischofsstuhl und Kaiserthron* (Munich, 1955).

——, *Die alte Kirche und das Heil des Staates* (Munich, 1963).

Kähler, H. "Konstantin 313," *Jahrbuch d. Deutschen Arch. Instituts,* LXVII (1952), 1–30.

Karayannopulos, J., "Konstantin der Grosse und der Kaiserkult," *Historia,* V (1956), 341–357.

Karpp, H., "Die Stellung der Alten Kirche zu Kriegsdienst und Krieg," *Evang. Theologie,* XVII (1957), 496–515.

Kelly, J. N. D., *Early Christian Creeds* (London-New York-Toronto, 1950), (1960²).

——, *Early Christian Doctrines* (London, 1958), (1965³).

King, N. Q., *The Emperor Theodosius and the Establishment of Christianity* (London, 1961).

——, "The Theodosian Code as a Source for the Religious Policies of the First Byzantine Emperor," *Notthingham Mediaeval Studies,* VI (1962), 12–17.

Klauser, T., "Der Ursprung der bischöflichen Insignien und Ehrenrechte," *Bonner Akademische Reden,* I (1953²).

——, T., *Die römische Petrustradition im Lichte der neuen Ausgrabungen unter der Peterskirche* (Cologne, 1956).

Knipfing, J. R., "The Edict of Galerius (A.D. 311) Reconsidered," *Revue Belge de Philologie et d'Histoire,* I (1922), 693–705.

Koep, L., "Die Konsekrationsmünzen Kaiser Konstantins und ihre religionspolitische Bedeutung," *Jahrbuch für Antike und Christentum,* I (1958), 94–104.

Kraft, H., "Kaiser Konstantins religiöse Entwicklung," *Beiträge zur hist. Theologie,* XX (Tübingen, 1955).

Kraft, H., "Zur Taufe Kaiser Konstantins," *Studia Patristica*, I (*Texte und Untersuchungen*, LXIII, 1957), 642–648.

Kraft, K., "Das Silbermedaillon Constantins des Grossen mit dem Christusmonogramm auf dem Helm," *Jahrbuch für Numismatik und Geldgeschichte*, V and VI (1954/55), 151–178.

Lietzmann, H., "Der Glaube Konstantins des Großen," *Sitzungsber. d. Preußischen Akad. d. Wiss. Phil.-hist.* Kl. (1937), no. 29.

——, *Petrus und Paulus in Rom* (Bonn, 1927²).

L'Orange, H. P., and A. v. Gerkan, "Der spätantike Bildschmuck des Konstantinsbogens," *Studien zur spätantiken Kunstgeschichte*, X (1939).

MacMullen, R., *Constantine* (New York, 1969).

Mamboury, E., and T. Wiegand, *Die Kaiserpaläste von Konstantinopel* (Berlin-Leipzig, 1934).

Mario, A., "Alcune considerazioni sul cosidetto 'editto' di Milano," *Studi Romani*, XIII (1965), 424–432.

Moreau, J., *La Persécution du christianisme dans l'empire romain* (Paris, 1956) (Germany, 1961).

Mosna, C. S., "Storia della domenica dalle origini fino agli inizi del V secolo," *Analecta Gregoriana. Ser. Fac. Hist. Eccles, Sect.*, B, no. 28 (Rome, 1969).

Müller, K., "Konstantin der Grosse und die christliche Kirche," *Hist. Zeitschrift*, CXL (1929), 261–278.

Nesselhauf, N., "Das Toleranzedikt des Licinius," *Hist. Jahrbuch*, LXXIV (1955), 44ff.

Nock, Arthur D., *Conversion. The Old and the New in Religion from Alexander the Great to Augustine of Hippo.* (Oxford, 1933).

——, "The Roman Army and the Roman Religious Year," *The Harvard Theological Review*, XLV (1952), 187–252.

Nordberg, H., "Athanasius and the Emperor," *Societas Scientiarum Fennica Commentationes Humanarum Litterarum*, XXX, 3 (Helsinki, 1963).

Overbeck, F., "Über das Verhältnis der alten Kirche zur Sklaverei im römischen Reiche," in his *Studien zur Geschichte der alten Kirche*, I (Schloß-Chemnitz 1875), 158–230.

Peterson, E., *Der Monotheismus als politisches Problem* (Leipzig, 1935), reprinted in *Theologische Traktate* (Munich, 1951).

Piganiol, A., "Dates Constantiniennes," *Revue d'histoire et de philosophie religieuses*, XII (1932), 360–372.

Preger, T., "Konstantinos Helios," *Hermes*, XXX (1901), 457–469.

Quasten, J., *Patrology,* vol. I–III (1950–1960).

Schäfer, E., "Das Petrusgrab und die neuen Grabungen unter St. Peter in Rom, *"Evangelische Theologie,* X (1950/51), 459–479.

Schmitt, P., "Sol invictus. Betrachtungen zu spätrömischer Religion und Politik," *Eranos Jahrbuch,* X (Zürich, 1944), 169–252.

Schneider, A. M., "Byzanz," *Istanbuler Forschungen,* VIII (1936).

————, "Die Memoria Apostolorum an der Via Appia," *Nachr. d. Akad. Göttingen* (1951), vol. III.

————, *Konstantinopel, Gesicht und Gestalt einer geschichtlichen Weltmetropole* (Mainz, 1956).

Schoenebeck, H. v., "Beiträge zur Religionspolitik des Maxentius und Constantin," *Klio,* suppl. XLIII (1939).

Schwartz, E., *Kaiser Constantin und die christliche Kirche* (Leipzig 1936[2]).

Seeck, Otto, "Die Verwandtenmorde Konstantins des Grossen," *Zeitschrift für Wiss. Theologie,* XXXIII (1890), 63–77.

Seston, W., "La Conversion de Constantin et l'opinion paienne," *Rev. Hist. Phil. Rel.,* XVI (1936), 250–264.

————, *Dioclétien et la Tétrarchie,* I (Paris, 1946).

————, "Diokletian," *Reallexikon für Antike und Christentum,* III (1957), col. 1036–1053.

Setton, K. M., *Christian Attitude Towards the Emperor in the Fourth Century* (New York, 1941).

Spranger, P., "Der Große. Untersuchungen zur Entstehung des historischen Beinamens in der Antike," *Saeculum,* IX (1958), 22–58.

Straub, J., "Vom Herrscherideal in der Spätantike," *Forschungen zur Kirchen und Geistesgeschichte,* XVIII (1939).

————, "Konstantins Verzicht auf den Gang zum Kapitol," *Historia,* IV (1955), 297–313.

————, "Kaiser Konstantin als EPISKOPOS TŌN EKTOS," *Studia Patristica* I (*Texte und Untersuchungen,* LXIII, 1957), 678–695.

————, "Constantine as KOINOS EPISKOPOS," *Dumbarton Oaks Papers,* XXI (1967), 37–55.

Taeger, F., *Charisma,* II (Stuttgart, 1960).

Teall, J. L., "The Age of Constantine: Change and Continuity in Administration and Economy," *Dumbarton Oaks Papers,* XXI (1967), 11–36.

Telfer, W., "The Author's Purpose in the Vita Constantini" *Studia Patristica,* I (*Texte und Untersuchungen,* LXIII 1957), 157–167.

Tengström, E., *Donatisten und Katholiken. Soziale, wirtschaftliche und politische Aspekte einer nordafrikanischen Kirchenspaltung* (Göteborg 1964).

Treitinger, O., *Die oströmische Kaiser- und Reichsidee nach ihrer Gestaltung im höfischen Zeremoniell* (Jena, 1938; reprinted Darmstadt 1956).

Vittinghoff, R., "Konstantin der Große und das konstantinische Zeitalter der Kirche," in *Staat und Kirche im Wandel der Jahrhunderte* (1966), pp. 21–33.

Voelkl, L., "Die konstantinischen Kirchenbauten nach Eusebius," *Rivista di Archeologia della Libia*, XXIX (1953), 49–66.

————, *Der Kaiser Konstantin. Annalen einer Zeitenwende* (Munich, 1957).

Vogt, Joseph, "Zur Frage des christlichen Einflusses auf die Gesetzgebung Konstantins des Grossen," *Festschrift L. Wenger*, II (1945), 118–148.

————, "Die Bedeutung des Jahres 312 für die Religionspolitik Konstantins des Grossen," *Zeitschrift für Kirchengeschichte*, LXI (1942), 171–190.

————, "Kaiser Julian über seinen Oheim Konstantin den Grossen," *Historia*, IV (1955), 339–352.

————, "Zur Religiosität der Christenverfolger im Römischen Reich," *Sitzungsber. d. Heidelberger Akad. d. Wiss. Phil.-hist. Kl.* (1962) vol. I.

————, *Sklaverei und Humanität. Studien zur antiken Sklaverei und ihrer Erforschung* (Wiesbaden 1965).

————, and H. Last, "Christenverfolgung," in *Reallexikon für Antike und Christentum*, II (1954), col. 1159ff.

————, and Seston, W., "Die konstantinische Frage," in: *Relazioni del X Congresso Internazionale di Scienze Storiche*, vol. VI (Florence, 1955), 733ff.

Wallace-Hadrill, D. S., *Eusebius of Caesarea* (London, 1960).

Wallon, H., *Histoire de l'esclavage dans l'antiquité*, 3 vols. (Paris, 1879²).

Warmington, B. H., *The North African Provinces from Diolectian to the Vandal Conquest* (Cambridge, 1954).

Weinreich, O. *Triskaidekadische Studien* II: Konstantin der Große als Dreizehnter Apostel und die religionspolitische Tendenz seiner Grabeskirche (1916).

Wieacker, F., "Vulgarismus und Klassizismus im Recht der Spätantike," *Sitzungsber. d. Heidelberger Akad. d. Wiss. Phil.-hist. Kl.* (1955) vol. III.

Winkelmann, F., "Die Textbezeugung der vita Constantini des Eusebius von Casearea," *Texte und Untersuchungen*, LXXXIV (1962).

————, "Zur Geschichte des Authentizitätsproblems der Vita Constantini," *Klio*, XL (1962), 187–243.

Index

Revised January, 1970

harper ☙ torchbooks

The New American Nation Series, edited by Henry Steele Commager and Richard B. Morris.
American Perspectives series, edited by Bernard Wishy and William E. Leuchtenburg.
History of Europe series, edited by J. H. Plumb.
The Library of Religion and Culture, edited by Benjamin Nelson.
Researches in the Social, Cultural, and Behavioral Sciences, edited by Benjamin Nelson.
Harper Modern Science Series, edited by James A. Newman.
Not for sale in Canada.
Documentary History of the United States series, edited by Richard B. Morris.
Documentary History of Western Civilization series, edited by Eugene C. Black and Leonard W. Levy.
The Economic History of the United States series, edited by Henry David et al.
European Perspectives series, edited by Eugene C. Black.
* Contemporary Essays series, edited by Leonard W. Levy.
The Stratum Series, edited by John Hale.

2